Doing Practical Ethics

A Skills-Based Approach to Moral Reasoning

IAN STONER AND JASON SWARTWOOD
Department of Philosophy
Saint Paul College
Saint Paul, MN

New York   Oxford
OXFORD UNIVERSITY PRESS

Oxford University Press is a department of the University of Oxford.
It furthers the University's objective of excellence in research,
scholarship, and education by publishing worldwide.
Oxford is a registered trademark of Oxford University Press
in the UK and certain other countries.

Published in the United States of America by Oxford University Press
198 Madison Avenue, New York, NY 10016, United States of America.

© 2022 by Oxford University Press

Library of Congress Cataloging-in-Publication Data

Names: Stoner, Ian, author. | Swartwood, Jason, author.
Title: Doing practical ethics : a skills-based approach to moral reasoning
  / Ian Stoner and Jason Swartwood, Department of Philosophy Saint Paul
  College, Saint Paul, MN.
Description: New York : Oxford University Press, 2021. | Includes
  bibliographical references. | Summary: "Stoner and Swartwood's Doing
  Practical Ethics if the first book to offer a framework for acquiring
  the component skills required to philosophize about applied ethics. The
  book accomplishes this by providing clear explanations and models of
  basic argument and critical thinking skills. Demonstration Exercises
  with solutions that provide clear and immediate feedback, and further
  Practice Exercises for honing skills"—Provided by publisher.
Identifiers: LCCN 2021015732 (print) | LCCN 2021015733 (ebook) | ISBN
  9780190078447 (paperback) | ISBN 9780190078492 (epub) | ISBN
  9780197605103
Subjects: LCSH: Applied ethics—Textbooks.
Classification: LCC BJ1012 .S844 2021 (print) | LCC BJ1012 (ebook) | DDC
  170—dc23
LC record available at https://lccn.loc.gov/2021015732
LC ebook record available at https://lccn.loc.gov/2021015733

9 8 7 6 5 4 3 2

Printed by Sheridan Books, Inc., United States of America

CONTENTS

SECTION III ARGUMENT FROM ANALOGY

SECTION IV MORAL INFERENCE TO THE BEST EXPLANATION

PREFACE

None of us has only true beliefs. No matter where we were born, how we were raised, or what we have learned, none of us is infallible. We all *know* that some of our beliefs—about chemistry, astronomy, psychology, history, politics, religion, ethics, etc.—must be false; the challenge is that we don't know which beliefs are true and which are beliefs we should revise or abandon.

We wrote this book to help you meet this challenge when it comes to your beliefs about questions of practical ethics. Our goal is neither to advocate for a particular ethical view nor to describe common professional or legal standards for behavior. Instead, we hope to help you develop several of the critical thinking skills and techniques philosophers use to refine their own moral beliefs and to productively discuss moral controversies with others.

You'll practice these skills using many arguments on a variety of topics. Some of these practice arguments are good and some are not. Some argue for conclusions you endorse and others for conclusions you reject. The goal, throughout, is to use this material to practice techniques for understanding, evaluating, and articulating ethical arguments in a clear and careful way.

We know from experience that some students enjoy debating ethical controversies and others dread it. We are excited to share these techniques with all of you. Those of you who dread ethical debate will find these philosophical techniques can make moral disagreement more illuminating and less painful. Those of you who thrive on disagreement will find these techniques improve the quality of your debates. We believe you will find the experience of doing practical ethics rewarding, even empowering; we hope you will find it fun.

PREFACE FOR TEACHERS

*D*oing *Practical Ethics* offers scaffolded practice to support the development of
the component skills that philosophers integrate in arguments about practical ethics. We have found that the approach that structures this book—explicit
instruction on component skills, plus repeated exercise with practice problems—
significantly improves our students' ability to participate in the activity of philosophy. We have used this approach in skills-focused and content-focused versions of
practical ethics courses, such as contemporary moral problems, bioethics, and
environmental ethics, and we have designed the book for use in both skills-first
and content-first modes.

Practical ethics courses focused centrally on teaching critical thinking skills
can use the book as a primary text. In that case, the early weeks of the course
should focus on practice with the exercises from the book. We recommend assigning chapters with selected practice exercises as homework due in class. In
class, students can work together in groups to discuss their homework answers
with each other, thus providing them with valuable skill-building feedback.

Once students have developed the component skills of representing arguments in standard form, offering counterexamples, testing disanalogies, and so
on, the challenge for instructors becomes one of designing learning activities that
require students to integrate these skills into coherent philosophical discussions.
Structured debates on controversial topics, role-playing activities that require
structured dialogue, and critical analysis of arguments in the news are reliably
effective classroom activities that require students to participate in philosophizing about questions of practical ethics.

In more traditional practical ethics courses that foreground important philosophical papers, supplementing them with this book can enhance student
learning. If you teach a large lecture course, discussion sections are an excellent
opportunity for students to practice argument skills. If students enter your lecture hall with a firm grasp of argument forms and evaluation techniques, they
will be much better equipped to understand your modeling of that process in
your lecture. If you teach a smaller course without breakout sections, assigning a

chapter from this book alongside a paper that centrally features that chapter's skill will often generate insightful questions and vigorous full-group discussion. Most of the papers traditionally assigned in practical ethics courses use the argument forms and evaluation techniques we cover here, and practice with the book helps students build the skills they'll need to engage deeply with them.

In most of our courses, we aim for a hybrid of skills-focused and content-focused approaches. Since the techniques the book teaches are ubiquitous in published practical philosophy, it is easy to select traditional topics and famous papers that require practice of any particular chapter's skills. A small sampling of the pairings that have worked well for us:

- The chapter on counterexamples supports active student engagement in ground-clearing weeks on ethical egoism and moral relativism.
- The chapters on illustrative examples and counterexamples help students discover for themselves the appeal, and the significant limitations, of the "four principles" approach common in bioethics.
- The chapters on analyzing and evaluating Arguments from Principle pair well with Iris Young's "Five Faces of Oppression," simultaneously introducing an influential account of an important concept and inviting practice of the skills required to apply and evaluate it.
- The chapters on analyzing and evaluating Arguments from Analogy pair well with Judith Jarvis Thomson's "A Defense of Abortion."
- The chapters on moral Inference to the Best Explanation pair well with many environmental ethics papers that seek to defend and apply theories of intrinsic value.

In the later portion of the semester, after they have practiced argument skills with a variety of important philosophical texts, we shift in the direction of assignments and activities that ask students to develop their own arguments and to evaluate each other's.

The book is arranged in a semi-modular fashion that allows for some flexibility in adapting it for different course goals and calendars. The section on Argument from Analogy, for example, does not depend on previous chapters and can be taught before the section on Argument from Principle, after Inference to the Best Explanation, or omitted. For courses that require students to evaluate arguments but not to write their own, the chapters on developing arguments may be omitted without interrupting the flow of the book. The chapters in Section I provide an introduction to some basic skills that later chapters will deepen and further develop, but Sections II–IV can stand alone.

This modularity is limited. We recommend assigning the Introduction first; it explains how to use the book, especially its Demonstration Exercises, effectively. For the three argument forms covered in Sections II–IV, complete the chapters in each section in order, because the skills of understanding, evaluating, and developing arguments build upon one another.

Demonstration and practice exercises are core components of this book. In order to facilitate practice on arguments expressed in different voices from a variety of perspectives, we have drawn materials from a range of sources, including news reports, classroom debates, blogs, and published papers. We have excerpted quotations from original sources when possible, although more often we have needed to paraphrase, simplify, or otherwise adapt arguments to fit our pedagogical needs. We have used the citation "Adapted from . . . " to cover the entire range of sources we have modified for pedagogical purposes, from arguments we have closely paraphrased to rewrites that bear only a resemblance to the passages that inspired them.

Whether quoted or adapted, please keep in mind that practice exercises by their very nature are short, substantially shorn of context, and unlikely to fully convey the ideas of their original authors. If any quoted or adapted passage strikes you or your students as provocative, interesting, or outrageous, please seek out the primary source for a complete understanding of the cited author's views.

ACKNOWLEDGMENTS

Doing Practical Ethics was born and raised in classrooms around the Twin Cities. We thank countless students at the University of Minnesota, Anoka-Ramsey Community College, Normandale Community College, University of Saint Catherine, Metropolitan State University, and Saint Paul College for working with drafts of varying degrees of maturity.

Tyler Carroll, Mollie Lynch-Packard, and Jack Skagen offered thoughtful comments that improved Chapters 11–13.

Crystal Bergstrom and Ruth Swartwood read many early drafts and helped us fuse our writing styles.

Thanks to Robert Miller and Andy Blitzer, our editors at Oxford University Press, for their excitement about this book and their work to bring it to publication.

We are especially grateful to Valerie Tiberius, whose mentorship and repeated encouragement gave us the courage to take on a project of this size. Without her support, *Doing Practical Ethics* may never have made it out of our classrooms.

Ian would like to thank Crystal, who kept madness and hunger at bay. And to Jason, already looking forward to future joint projects.

Jason would like to thank his colleagues (especially those in room 3450) and his students at Saint Paul College for helping to make the College a fruitful place to teach and learn. He would especially like to thank Ian for the philosophical friendship that led to this book, and Ruth and Adelaide for their love, patience, and support throughout this process (and any corresponding book-related fugues).

We also wish to thank the following reviewers for their valuable feedback on the project:

Devora Shapiro, Southern Oregon University
Rich McGowan, Boston College

David Burris, Arizona Western College
Michael Cholbi, California State Polytechnic University, Pomona
Susanne Sreedhar, Boston University
John Martin, Southern Nazarene University
Tony Manela, Sienna College

How and Why to Use
Doing Practical Ethics

*If people want to raise a mahogany tree from a sapling that could
fit in your hands, they know how to care for it. But when it comes
to their own selves, they do not know how to care for them. Could
it be that they do not love their own selves as much as they love a
mahogany tree? It is simply because they do not reflect upon it.*

—MENGZI, *MENGZI* 6A13

Philosophers typically divide ethical questions into three areas of study.

Meta-ethics concerns the meanings of moral terms and judgements. For example: what are we doing when we say, "What he did was morally wrong"? Are we expressing disapproval of his action? Are we making a factual claim about it? Are we commanding others not to do that type of thing?

Normative ethics (sometimes called ethical theory) concerns the general justification of our moral judgements. For example: what feature do all right actions share that makes them right actions? Is it that they promote the best consequences? Or that they are characteristic of virtuous people? Or that they treat people with respect?

Practical ethics (sometimes called applied ethics) concerns specific real-world ethical controversies. For example: is euthanasia morally permissible? Do corporations have moral obligations to people other than their shareholders? Is it wrong to farm animals for meat? What are our obligations to people living in extreme poverty? Under what circumstances is civil disobedience morally permissible?

This book is intended to help you participate in philosophical debates about real-world ethical controversies; it is designed to help you learn to *do* practical ethics.

HOW THE BOOK CAN HELP

When you pick up your first assigned article on a topic in practical ethics, you can be confident of two things. First, it is an article your instructor judges to be an important contribution to an ongoing conversation about an ethical controversy. Second, it will contain an argument written by a philosopher who has a great deal of experience arguing with other philosophers.

Your first glimpses of these philosophical conversations are likely to be . . . confusing. Part of the challenge is that philosophers use techniques and argument forms they've mastered after years of practice. When you listen in on a philosophical conversation as a newcomer, not yet familiar with their methods, the conversation can be difficult to follow.

This book will introduce you to several of the techniques and argument forms used in the articles you will read in your practical ethics class. Developing these skills will allow you to respond more effectively to those articles: to better understand them, to critically evaluate them, to decide if you should be persuaded by them.

The methods philosophers use will be helpful to you outside the classroom, too. At some point, we all face ethical decisions in our personal lives, in our communities, and in our places of work. As citizens of democracies, we are all called on to participate in crafting public policies that have moral ramifications. It is never easy to reflect deeply about the ethical questions that matter most to us, but the methods introduced here will make it a little bit easier.

HOW TO USE THE BOOK

Martial arts such as Tae Kwon Do are complex skills made up of many integrated component skills. Students of Tae Kwon Do do not begin their studies by fighting. They begin, instead, by practicing component skills: balancing, breathing, specific kicks and strikes, and so on. Only after they have mastered basic component skills can students begin to integrate them into the complex skill of Tae Kwon Do.

Philosophizing about practical ethics is also a complex skill made up of many integrated component skills. Each chapter of this book identifies, explains, and invites practice of a particular component skill. As you read the articles and complete the tasks your instructors assign, you will begin to integrate these component skills into the complex skill of philosophizing well about practical ethics.

Each chapter is divided into three main sections.

Introductory Explanation. Chapters begin with our explanation of the component skill, illustrated with examples of that skill in action. These sections are relatively short, and you might need to read portions of them more than once. When you are confident that you understand the examples, move on to the next section.

Demonstration Exercises. Explanations alone are never sufficient for skill-building; you must attempt to *use* a skill in order to develop it. Imagine trying to learn to ride a bicycle by reading an explanation of how to ride. No matter how clear the explanation, you do not begin to develop bike-riding skill until you climb on a bike and attempt it.

Demonstration exercises are practice problems that come with solutions. They are the beating heart of each chapter, for this is where you begin to develop skill through practice attempts. Demonstration exercises are most effective as learning tools if you approach them in several steps.

1. Write up your attempt at answers for *all* the demonstration exercises in the chapter.
2. Once you think you've got all of them right, then check your answer to the *first* demonstration exercise. Resist the urge to peek ahead. If you got the first one right, then check your answer to the second. If you got the second one right, check your answer to the third, and so on.
3. When you find an answer you got wrong, review the relevant Introductory Explanation portions of the chapter. Re-read the examples and work until you understand *why* you got the answer wrong. When you've figured it out, review and if necessary revise your answers to the remaining demonstration exercises. *Return to step two.*
4. When you consistently and confidently complete the demonstration exercises correctly, you are ready to take on Practice Exercises.

Practice Exercises: Practice exercises are your opportunity to further hone your skill. Your instructors may assign these as in-class activities or homework and might give you feedback on your performance. If not, practice exercises can be used effectively by study groups. If you and a few classmates work problems and compare answers, you will almost always be able to check your own work.

Our final recommendation to get the most not just from this book, but from every aspect of your practical ethics class: every step of the way, work with your peers. Take every opportunity to talk through examples, to offer and critique arguments, to ask for help when you need it and offer help when you can. Practical ethics is a serious subject that can improve the way you approach difficult decisions in your own life. It can also be fun. Collaboration promotes both good outcomes.

CHAPTER 1

Recognizing Moral Arguments

CHAPTER GOALS

By reading this chapter and completing the exercises, you will learn how to:

- Distinguish moral claims from descriptive claims.
- Explain what an argument is.
- Determine if an argument is a moral argument.
- Identify at least one reason the distinction between moral claims and descriptive claims is important.

MORAL REASONING AND MORAL ARGUMENTS

In public debates, in discussions with friends and colleagues, and in quiet moments of personal reflection, we all face questions about how we ought to live. We all face questions about what is right or wrong, good or bad. These are *moral* questions.

Although we all face moral questions, there is no guarantee that we will answer them well. Reasoning about moral questions is a critical thinking skill. As with any other skill, it can be done poorly. And as with any other skill, it can be improved through practice. The goal of this book is to help you improve your moral reasoning skills through practice.

This chapter begins by characterizing the difference between moral claims and other kinds of claims. It also introduces the central tool that philosophers and others use to clarify and communicate their moral reasoning: moral arguments. Later chapters introduce specific skills and strategies for understanding, evaluating, and developing moral arguments.

MORAL CLAIMS AND DESCRIPTIVE CLAIMS

Claims are the basic building blocks of arguments. *Claims* (or, equivalently, *statements*), are simply declarative sentences—sentences that must be either true or false, or correct or incorrect.

Consider the following sentences:

A. Don't steal things!
B. Is stealing always wrong?
C. Stealing is morally wrong.
D. Stealing is illegal.
E. Dogs are mammals.

Sentences C, D, and E are claims because they are either true or false, or correct or incorrect. Sentences A and B are not claims, because they are not the kinds of sentences that could be true or false. (It would make no sense for someone to say "False!" or "True!" in response to the question posed in sentence B. Nor would it make sense to say "True!" in response to the command delivered in sentence A.)

Claims may be either *moral* or *descriptive*. Consider a selection of claims people have made about abortion:

F. Abortion terminates the life of a developing human organism.
G. Abortion causes breast cancer.
H. There will be fewer abortions in 2050 than there were in 2020.
I. Abortion is morally permissible.
J. Having a first-trimester abortion usually does not harm the well-being of the person who has it.
K. Assassinating abortion doctors should be legal.
L. You ought not get an abortion.

Moral claims are claims that evaluate something as *right, wrong, good* or *bad,* or prescribe something as a thing we *should* or *may* do.[1] I and J are moral claims because they assert evaluations; K and L are moral claims because they assert prescriptions. *Descriptive claims*, in contrast, assert something about how the world actually is or tends to be. Claims F, G, and H are descriptive claims, because they assert something about how the world actually *is* (or *was*, or *will be*) without saying anything about what's right, wrong, good, bad or what we should or shouldn't do.

Note two aspects of this distinction between descriptive and moral claims. First, our definition of a moral claim is broad; claims that prescribe or evaluate the morality of individual conduct (such as I and L), claims that evaluate individual well-being (such as J), and claims about what laws we ought to have (such as K) all count as *moral* claims in our sense.

---

[1]Philosophers generally call these *normative* claims; other disciplines (such as psychology) use the term "normative" to mean something else, which can be a source of terminological confusion.

Second, note that establishing whether a claim is true or false, justified or unjustified, plausible or implausible, has nothing at all to do with classifying it as a moral or descriptive claim. Claim F is true, claim G is false, claim H is unknowable until sometime after 2050, but they are all descriptive claims. Claims I and L are controversial, claim J is plausible, and claim K is implausible, but they are all moral claims. We classify claims as moral or descriptive based on the kind of assertion they make, not whether we have good reason to believe them.

ARGUMENTS

An *argument* is a chain of reasoning in which a set of claims—the premises—are intended to give us reason to accept a further claim—the conclusion.

For instance, drivers in the United States have probably seen a billboard that makes this claim:

M. Abortion takes human life.

Sentence M is a claim, because it can be true or false, or correct or incorrect. More specifically, Sentence M is a descriptive claim, not a moral claim, because it aims to describe how the world is; it attempts to characterize the outcome of abortion, but it does not evaluate or prescribe that outcome.

Still, if you're familiar with public discussions of abortion in the United States, you'll be well aware that the person who wrote the billboard assumes that you already believe an unstated moral claim: that taking human life is wrong. Furthermore, the author of the billboard thinks that these two claims, taken together, imply that you should accept an additional claim: that abortion is wrong. The billboard implicitly offers an *argument*:

1. Abortion takes human life.
2. Taking human life is wrong.

Therefore, abortion is wrong.

Claims (1) and (2) are the *premises* of the argument. Taken together, they constitute a chain of reasoning in support of the *conclusion* that abortion is wrong.

Here's another example. At protests of abortion restrictions, protesters sometimes carry signs that say "my uterus, my rules." These signs implicitly offer an argument. The text of the sign is a pithy expression of something like the following claim:

N. A person should be allowed to do what they want with their own body.

This is a moral claim because it asserts something about what people *should* be allowed to do. As it is written, the protest sign does not mention abortion. But if you're familiar with abortion debates, you'll be well aware that the protestor who wrote the sign assumes that you already believe an unstated descriptive claim: abortion is a procedure performed on a pregnant person's body. These two claims, taken together, imply that people should be allowed to choose abortion. The protest sign implicitly offers this argument:

1. A person should be allowed to do what they want with their own body.
2. Abortion is an action that concerns a pregnant person's own body.

Therefore, a pregnant person should be allowed to choose an abortion.

Claims (1) and (2) are the *premises* of the argument. Taken together, they constitute a chain of reasoning in support of the *conclusion* that people should be allowed to choose an abortion.

In later chapters you'll learn how to evaluate arguments such as these. For now, our goal is simply to recognize the relationship between claims and arguments. An argument is a chain of reasoning in which a set of claims—the premises—is offered as evidence or justification in support of a further claim—the conclusion.

MORAL ARGUMENTS

This book is especially concerned with *moral arguments*, and not all arguments are moral arguments. You can determine whether an argument is a moral argument by classifying its conclusion. An argument is a moral argument when its conclusion makes a moral claim.

The following arguments are *not* moral arguments:

O:

1. Geological examination of the rocks from the moon have concluded that they are made of the same minerals as rocks on Earth.
2. The Earth is not made of green cheese.

So, the moon is not made of green cheese.

P:

1. People tend to be more likely to help others when they're not in a hurry.
2. Ayan is not in a hurry but Erin is.

Therefore, Ayan is probably more likely to help than Erin is.

Neither O nor P is a moral argument, because their conclusions describe the world without prescribing or evaluating any aspect of their subject matter. The descriptive nature of the conclusion in example O is obvious. But example P is about helping behaviors, and people associate helping with morality. Nevertheless, P's conclusion merely describes Ayan and Erin's likely behaviors. It says nothing about whose behavior is morally better, or what Ayan and Erin ought to do. P's conclusion is descriptive, so P is not a moral argument.

In contrast, the following examples are moral arguments:

Q:

1. Keeping animals in zoos greatly reduces those animals' well-being merely for human enjoyment.
2. It's wrong to treat animals in ways that greatly reduce their well-being merely for human enjoyment.

Thus, it's wrong to keep animals in zoos.

R:

1. White lies—that is, lies intended to save someone unhappiness, discomfort, or awkwardness—treat a person like a mere thing to be manipulated.
2. It's wrong to treat someone like a mere thing to be manipulated.

So, white lies are wrong.

The conclusions of Q and R are claims about how things ought to be or what's right, wrong, good or bad. Because their conclusions are moral claims, they are moral arguments.

THE PROCESS OF THINKING ABOUT MORAL ARGUMENTS

Identifying moral arguments, and distinguishing them from arguments with descriptive conclusions, is the first step in moral reasoning. In later chapters, you'll learn additional skills:

Analyzing a moral argument involves understanding an argument's component parts and how they fit together.

Evaluating a moral argument involves determining whether or not an argument actually gives us good reason to accept its conclusion.

Developing a moral argument involves generating, structuring, and explaining your own moral argument.

When we read or hear an argument offered by someone else, our first step must always be to take care that we have charitably and accurately understood the author's reasoning. Only then can we proceed to evaluating the argument. This order—understand first, then evaluate—is especially important when we examine an argument whose conclusion we would like to reject. In our rush to find problems with an argument we disagree with, it can be tempting to skip a charitable and complete analysis. But it wastes everyone's time to present criticisms—even devastating, blistering criticisms—of an argument that is not actually the argument the author intended to offer. Yielding to the temptation to rush straight to evaluation sacrifices truth and understanding in exchange for unearned self-satisfaction.

THE VALUE AND LIMITATIONS OF SCIENTIFIC EVIDENCE

We've seen that one reason the distinction between moral and descriptive claims is important is that it helps us *identify* when we're looking at a moral argument and when we're not. [2] Distinguishing descriptive claims from moral claims is also important for *evaluating* arguments, because descriptive claims require a different kind of evidence than moral claims. While empirical scientific evidence is often useful or necessary for evaluating descriptive claims, scientific evidence cannot by itself give us any verdict on moral claims.

Consider, for example, this moral claim: you ought not drive while intoxicated. Is this claim true? You might feel the urge to support this claim by appeal to empirical evidence: driving while intoxicated undoubtedly puts you and others at increased risk of injury or death. This would give us the following simple argument:

1. Driving while intoxicated puts you and others at increased risk of injury or death.

   Therefore, you should not drive while intoxicated.

This argument is incomplete. The claim that driving while intoxicated risks injury or death is a descriptive claim, but the conclusion of the argument is a moral claim. The argument needs an additional premise to connect the well-documented effects of intoxicated driving to a moral claim about how we ought to behave. A moral claim about the kinds of effects that *should* be avoided can bridge that gap:

1. Driving while intoxicated puts others and oneself at increased risk of injury or death.
2. *You should not put yourself and others at increased risk of injury or death.*

   Therefore, you should not drive while intoxicated.

This argument now expresses a complete chain of reasoning: if the premises are true, then they give us good reason to believe the conclusion is true, too. Note that, in the complete argument, its moral conclusion is no longer supported by purely descriptive premises. The argument now relies on one descriptive claim (premise 1) and one moral claim (premise 2). For a complete argument for a moral claim, we need at least one moral claim as a premise. The conclusion does not follow from a descriptive claim (premise 1) alone.

Arguments for other moral claims work similarly. Consider, for example, an argument in support of moral claim I: having a first-trimester abortion usually does not harm the well-being of the person who has it. There is empirical evidence that supports this claim. According to the American Psychological Association, "the

---

[2] This section is adapted from Jason D. Swartwood and Valerie Tiberius, "Philosophical Foundations of Wisdom," in *The Cambridge Handbook of Wisdom*, ed. Robert J. Sternberg and Judith Glück (Cambridge, UK: Cambridge University Press, 2019), 10–39.

prevalence of mental health problems observed among women in the United States who had a single, legal, first-trimester abortion for non-therapeutic reasons was consistent with normative rates of comparable mental health problems in the general population of women in the United States."[3] In other words, women who have a single, legal, first-trimester abortion tend not to be more prone to mental illnesses like depression and anxiety than the general population of women. Suppose it is also true that most women who have abortions of this type don't suffer any significant physical health problems. Someone might suggest that these descriptive facts by themselves imply a conclusion about the prudential goodness or badness of abortions:

1. Usually, having a legal, first-trimester abortion doesn't make a person more prone to mental illness or significant physical injury.

So, usually, having a legal, first-trimester abortion is not bad for the person who has it.

This argument, like the first version of the intoxicated driving argument, is incomplete. The claim that first-trimester abortions do not usually cause physical injury or mental illness is a descriptive claim, but the conclusion of the argument is a moral claim. The argument needs an additional premise to connect these well-documented effects of first-trimester abortions to a moral claim about the well-being of people who have had an abortion. A moral claim about the kinds of effects that promote or harm a person's well-being (what sorts of things are good or bad for them) can bridge that gap:

1. Usually, having a legal, first-trimester abortion doesn't make a person more prone to mental illness or significant physical injury.
2. *A thing does not harm the well-being of a person if it doesn't make the person more prone to mental illness or significant injury.*

So, usually, having a legal, first-trimester abortion does not harm the well-being of the person who has it.

The addition of premise 2 makes the argument complete: if the premises are true, then that gives us good reason to think the conclusion is true, too. But the completed argument does not rely exclusively on descriptive premises; fixing the argument required adding a *moral* claim that connects its descriptive first premise to its moral conclusion.

The point of the last two examples (about drunk driving and the effects of abortion) is that the descriptive premises of these arguments are not by themselves enough to establish their moral conclusions. Most moral philosophers believe this point generalizes: empirical research alone cannot ever establish a moral conclusion. If empirical research shows that donating 10% of your income to effective

_____

[3]See the APA statement on "Mental Health and Abortion." http://www.apa.org/pi/women/programs/abortion/

charities saves the lives of strangers, this does not by itself establish that you *ought* to donate 10 percent of your income; it could only establish that it were also true that saving these strangers' lives is the sort of thing we *ought* to do. If empirical research shows that zoo animals suffer terribly from confinement, this does not itself establish that you *ought* to stop visiting zoos; it could only establish that if it were also true that contributing to institutions that cause animal suffering is the sort of thing we *ought not* do. If empirical research shows that marriages survive longer when spouses hide their infidelities from each other, this does not itself establish that you *ought* to hide your own infidelity; it could only establish that if it were also true that extending the length of these marriages is the sort of thing we *ought* to do.

Empirical research can tell us many important things about the features and consequences of our choices. But empirical research alone cannot tell us which features or consequences are good or bad, or which consequences ought to be pursued and which ought to be avoided.

The lesson to draw from this brief discussion: scientific evidence will often be relevant to assessing the truth of descriptive claims included in moral arguments, *but scientific evidence alone cannot help us assess the truth of moral claims.* To evaluate a moral claim requires figuring out not only how things *are* but also figuring out what *matters*. Science helps us describe the world as it actually is, but it cannot by itself tell us what we should value or what we should do.

REVIEW

Claims may be descriptive or moral.

> **Claim:** a declarative sentence that must be true or false, correct or incorrect.
> **Descriptive claim:** a claim about the way the world *is* (or *was* or *will be*).
> **Moral claim:** a claim that either *prescribes* (by saying what *ought* or *ought not* be) or *evaluates* (by saying what's *good* or *bad*, or *right* or *wrong*).

It is important to distinguish descriptive claims and moral claims because they require different kinds of evidence to evaluate. Scientific or other empirical evidence can often establish whether a descriptive claim is true or false, but scientific evidence alone cannot ever establish whether a moral claim is true or false.

When we disagree with each other about a moral claim, we should do our best to explain the reasons why we believe the claim we do. Philosophers typically explain their reason for believing a moral claim by offering a moral argument in support of it.

> **Argument:** a chain of reasoning in which a set of claims (the **premises**) is offered in support of a further claim (the **conclusion**).
> **Moral argument:** an argument with a conclusion that is a moral claim.

Practicing the philosophical skills of understanding, evaluating, and developing moral arguments can help us all improve our ability to think carefully about moral questions. The goal of this book is to help you develop those skills.

Demonstration Exercises

Demonstration Exercises are designed to give you immediate feedback on your grasp of the skills introduced in this chapter. To use them effectively, you should attempt answers to all of them, then check your work against our suggested answers, which follow. For a detailed explanation of how best to use Demonstration Exercises, read the book's Introduction.

Demonstration Exercises 1A: Distinguishing Moral and Descriptive Claims

Exercise Instructions: For each of the following claims, determine whether it is a moral claim or a descriptive claim.

1. Spanking children is less effective for producing compliant children than other methods. D
2. Physician-assisted suicide ought to be illegal. M
3. Keeping gorillas in small urban zoos is cruel. M
4. Lying is fairly common. D

Demonstration Exercises 1B: Identifying Moral Arguments

Exercise Instructions: For each of the following arguments, determine whether or not it is a moral argument, and concisely explain your answer.

1. Not
   1. A person has an addiction when they repeatedly engage in risky behavior in ways that significantly impede their own life goals.
   2. Many people repeatedly use social media (such as Twitter) in ways that are risky and significantly impede their life goals.

   Therefore, many people have a social media addiction.[4]

2. Moral
   1. In a study of 1,170 children from six countries, children from religious families were less likely than children from non-religious families to share and were more likely to judge and punish others for bad behavior.[5]
   2. The best explanation of the study results is that a religious upbringing tends to cause people to be less prosocial (that is, less concerned with others' well-being and less concerned with sustaining social relationships).

   So, probably, a religious upbringing tends to cause people to be less prosocial.

---

[4]Adapted from Steve Albrecht, "Hi, I'm Steve and I'm a Twitterholic," *Psychology Today*, July 31, 2018. https://www.psychologytoday.com/us/blog/the-act-violence/201807/hi-i-m-steve-and-i-m-twitteraholic
[5]For an overview of this research, see https://www.sciencedaily.com/releases/2015/11/151105121916.htm.

3.

  1. Drunk driving is wrong.

  2. Refusing (without good medical reason) to vaccinate your children is similar in the ways that matter to drunk driving: both put other innocent people at significant risk of harm for no good reason.

  Thus, refusing (without good medical reason) to vaccinate your children is wrong.[6]

4.

  1. Trigger warnings (warnings professors give to students about potentially upsetting content in readings or class materials) undermine some students' emotional resilience.[7]

  2. Professors should not do things that undermine students' emotional resilience.

  Therefore, professors should not give trigger warnings.

---

[6]Adapted from an argument in Sanjeev K. Sriram, "Anti-Vaxxers, Like Drunk Drivers, Are a Danger to Us All," *The Huffington Post*, April 4, 2015. https://www.huffingtonpost.com/sanjeev-k-sriram/dr-america-antivaxxers-ar_b_6587538.html
[7]Adapted from a claim in Katherine Timpf, "Trigger Warnings Might Be Harmful, a Study Concludes," *The National Review*, July 31, 2018. https://www.nationalreview.com/2018/07/study-says-trigger-warnings-might-harm-readers/

===

Solutions to the Demonstration Exercises

Demonstration Exercises are most useful if you make your best attempt to complete them before you look at the answers. If you haven't yet attempted answers to all the Demonstration Exercises, go back and do that now.

Demonstration Exercises 1A: Distinguishing Moral and Descriptive Claims

  1. Spanking children is less effective for producing compliant children than other methods.

This is a descriptive claim and not a moral claim. It is a descriptive claim because it says something about how the world *is* or tends to work (specifically, it focuses on the effects of particular disciplinary strategies on children). It is not a moral claim, because it does not prescribe or evaluate spanking: it does not make any claims about whether we ought to do it or whether it is right or wrong.

  2. Physician-assisted suicide ought to be illegal.

This is a moral claim, because it is prescribing rather than just describing. If it had said that physician-assisted suicide *is* illegal, then it would have been a descriptive claim. But, it says that physician-assisted suicide *ought* to be illegal, which means it is prescribing. This makes it a moral claim in our broad sense of the term, though we should distinguish it from the distinct moral claim that "physician-assisted suicide is morally wrong for individuals to perform or take part in."

(continued)

3. Keeping gorillas in small urban zoos is cruel.

This is a moral claim, because it evaluates an action rather than merely describing it. To say something is cruel both describes and evaluates it: it says it is wrongfully or viciously showing disregard for someone's well-being. (Philosophers call concepts that both describe and evaluate "thick" concepts.) Because this claim evaluates an action, it is a moral claim.

4. Lying is fairly common.

This is a descriptive claim and not a moral claim, because it describes how the world is without prescribing or evaluating. Specifically, this claim describes how often a particular type of behavior (lying) actually occurs but doesn't say anything about whether we ought to engage in that behavior or whether doing so is right or wrong.

Demonstration Exercises 1B: Identifying Moral Arguments

1. This is not a moral argument. The conclusion of the argument makes the purely descriptive claim that many social media behaviors match the definition of addictive behavior.

2. This is not a moral argument. The conclusion of the argument makes a purely descriptive, statistical claim about the social behaviors of people with religious upbringings.

3. This is a moral argument. The conclusion *evaluates* vaccine refusals as wrong.

4. This is a moral argument. The conclusion *proscribes* the use of trigger warnings in college classes; that is, it asserts that professors *should not* use them.

To test your understanding of the material introduced in this chapter, complete the Demonstration Exercises and then check your answers against the solutions that follow.

CHAPTER 1 PRACTICE EXERCISES

RECOGNIZING MORAL ARGUMENTS

Exercises 1A: Distinguishing Moral and Descriptive Claims

Exercise Instructions: *For each of the following claims, determine whether it is a moral claim or a descriptive claim.*

1. People tend to do what's in their own best interest. M
2. Abortion in the first and second trimesters is legal. D
3. Physician-assisted suicide is morally wrong. Moral
4. A nurse has a moral obligation to treat all patients with respect. Moral
5. Genetically modified wheat is an artificial crop. descriptive

6. Legalizing recreational drug use produces more total pleasure in society than criminalizing those drugs. *descriptive*

7. People often make sacrifices for their friends and family. *descriptive*

8. Policies that systematically make it harder for racial minorities to vote are unjust. *Moral*

9. You're morally required to save another person's life if you can do so without risking your own. *Moral*

10. Students should never cheat on an exam. *Moral*

11. Physicians who withhold potential risks from patients undermine their community's trust in medical institutions. *descriptive*

Exercises 1B: Identifying Moral Arguments

Exercise Instructions: *For each of the following arguments, determine whether or not it is a moral argument, and concisely explain your answer.*

1.   *No*
   1. Voter intimidation (intimidating someone to get them to vote for a particular candidate or to prevent them from voting) is illegal. *Not*
   2. Impersonating an election official to falsely convince someone they don't have the right kind of ID to vote is voter intimidation.

   So, impersonating an election official to falsely convince someone they don't have the right kind of ID to vote is illegal.

2. *Moral*   *Yes*
   1. It is good for teachers to have policies that improve student engagement in the classroom and that improve student comprehension and performance.
   2. Banning laptop and phone use in the classroom improves student engagement, comprehension, and performance.

   Therefore, it is good for teachers to ban laptop and phone use in the classroom.

3. *Moral*   *Yes*
   1. It is wrong to put your pets at unnecessary risk.
   2. Keeping lilies in a place where they are accessible to your cat is an unnecessary risk to your pet.

   Thus, it is wrong to keep lilies in a place where they are accessible to your cat.

4. *Not Moral   Yes*
   1. Any practice that exploits vulnerable people ought to be illegal.
   2. Commercial surrogacy exploits vulnerable people.

   So, commercial surrogacy ought to be illegal.

5. *Moral   Not   No*
   1. Gene editing technology (like CRISPR) could one day allow us to eliminate genes for serious diseases (such as Huntington's disease, etc.).

2. Eliminating genes for serious diseases would promote longer, healthier lives.

Therefore, gene editing technology could one day promote longer, healthier lives.

6. Not

1. People have a moral right to be able to obtain effective means of self-defense.
2. Owning handguns is an effective means of self-defense.

Thus, people have a moral right to own handguns.

CHAPTER 2

Generating Illustrative Examples

CHAPTER GOALS

By reading this chapter and completing the exercises, you will learn
how to:

- Identify the features of a good illustrative example.
- Generate a realistic or fanciful example that illustrates a general claim.

ILLUSTRATING WITH EXAMPLES

People think and talk in abstractions and generalizations. Navigating the world
would be more or less impossible if we *couldn't* abstract our specific experiences
into general beliefs that can in turn be applied to novel circumstances. For example, you have probably formed the general belief that "fruits and vegetables are
nutritious." This is a useful generalization to have come lunchtime. You do not
have to wonder, about every new piece of fruit you see, "Is this piece of fruit I see
before me nutritious?" Instead, you apply your general belief to this novel cir-
cumstance and assume that this banana, being a fruit, is nutritious.

Generalizations, like any other variety of claim, can either be *descriptive* or
moral. The generalization "fruits and vegetables are nutritious" is a descriptive
generalization, because it makes a claim about how the world *actually is* or tends
to be. Other generalizations, such as "you *ought to* eat vegetables" or "stealing
fruit is *wrong*" are moral generalizations, because they express prescriptive or
evaluative claims.

There is nothing wrong with thinking and talking in generalizations, either
in philosophical debate or in everyday life. We couldn't avoid using generalizations even if we wanted to. But using generalizations comes with some risks: generalizations can cause miscommunication, and they sometimes masquerade as
true even when they are false. This chapter introduces a technique that mitigates
these risks: the technique of illustrative example.

THE RISKS OF GENERALIZATIONS

One risk of generalizations is that if we learn them from other people, or absorb them from our community, instead of abstracting them for ourselves, it can be easy to accept them as true without ever checking to confirm that they are. For example: many people in the United States accept the generalization that pit bulls are typically aggressive, dangerous dogs. One of the authors of this book, Jason, assumed this was true until he started working as a veterinary technician. After meeting many pit bulls—even ones rescued from dog-fighting operations—he never met a single one that was aggressive and dangerous. That experience made it impossible to accept the generalization that pit bulls are typically dangerous; he now recognizes pit bulls as tending to be sweet and friendly dogs. When a generalization cannot be illustrated with an example after looking carefully in all the right places, that is evidence that the generalization is not true, no matter how many people believe it.

The same weakness can appear in generalizations we've made for ourselves. If we allow our own generalizations to become too abstract, too disconnected from the kinds of concrete examples that lead us to form them in the first place, they can drift away from the truth. For example: when the other author of this book, Ian, was younger he watched and enjoyed many slasher movies, and so he formed the generalization "I like slasher movies." For most of his adult life he has believed that generalization to be true. But when a friend asked him recently what slasher movies he'd recommend from the last ten years, he couldn't offer a single recommendation because it has been longer than ten years since he saw a slasher movie he enjoyed. Apparently, Ian no longer likes slasher movies. When a generalization cannot be illustrated with an example, that is evidence that the generalization is not true, even if it's a generalization we've made for ourselves.

A different risk of generalizations is that they can introduce miscommunication when two people understand the same generalization differently. In these cases, people think they are talking about the same thing when they aren't. For example, in one of our classrooms, a student made the comment that "men could be pregnant." He intended this generalization to highlight a familiar point about the conceptual difference between sex and gender. He meant that someone who is biologically female, and potentially able to be pregnant, might identify as a man. But several other students misunderstood his intent, and assumed he was making a point about future scientific possibilities. They thought he was claiming that, someday, science will probably allow biologically male people to carry fetuses in artificial wombs. When a generalization isn't illustrated with an example, it risks introducing confusion, rather than clarity, to a conversation.

WHEN TO USE ILLUSTRATIVE EXAMPLES

Illustrating generalizations with concrete examples keeps generalizations tied to the sorts of concrete cases that are supposed to ground them. This makes generalizations less risky and more useful in almost every case. Developing the habit of illustrating generalizations with examples will improve your writing, reading, and thinking.

Philosophers often use illustrative examples when they introduce new generalizations. In a famous article about global poverty relief, Peter Singer suggests we should all accept the following moral principle: "If it is in our power to prevent something very bad from happening, without thereby sacrificing anything morally significant, we ought, morally, to do it." At first glimpse, this abstract moral principle may not be entirely clear. What, for example, does Singer mean by "sacrificing anything morally significant?" To help make clear what the principle means, Singer immediately offers an illustrative example: "If I am walking past a shallow pond and see a child drowning in it, I ought to wade in and pull the child out. This will mean getting my clothes muddy, but this is insignificant, while the death of the child would presumably be a very bad thing."[1] In this case, an illustrative example helps to clarify what might, initially, be unclear.

Illustrative examples are useful in all modes of writing. In the previous section of this chapter, we identified three risks of generalizations:

- Generalizations we absorb from our community are sometimes false.
- Generalizations we abstract from our own experiences are sometimes false.
- Generalizations can introduce miscommunication when different people understand the same generalization in different ways.

After introducing each of these general claims, we immediately offered an illustrative example of it. Even if you understood right away what we were getting at in all three cases, you almost certainly felt more confident in your understanding of what we meant after reading the illustrative examples. Developing the habit of offering illustrative examples will improve the effectiveness of your written and spoken communication.

Generating your own illustrative examples will also improve your reading. Whether or not authors provide illustrative examples of the general claims they make, you should, as an active reader, generate your own illustrative examples as you read. When an author fails to offer illustrative examples, generating at least one for yourself is a necessary part of critically evaluating the author's general claim. But even when authors illustrate their claims, you should generate at least one illustrative example of your own. Is the author's example somehow tricky or unrepresentative? Or is the general claim genuinely plausible? Generating your own examples is the best way to start thinking about those questions.

FEATURES OF A GOOD ILLUSTRATIVE EXAMPLE

Effective illustrative examples have two key features:

1. For (almost) everyone in the intended audience, a good illustrative example is immediately recognizable as a concrete instance of the general claim; it is *broadly accessible*.

---

[1]Peter Singer, "Famine, Affluence, and Morality," *Philosophy and Public Affairs*, 1, no. 1 Spring 1972): 229–243. Available online: http://www.utilitarian.net/singer/by/1972----.htm

2. For (almost) everyone in the intended audience, a good illustrative example will strike them as a case in which the general claim is *uncontroversially true.*

Consider four possible illustrations of the generalization: "Some people do not take proper care of their pets."

Bad illustrative example #1: This generalization is true, because lots of people don't take proper care of their pets.

This is not an illustrative example at all, but rather an endorsement of the generalization. An example that *illustrates* this generalization should identify a specific person who doesn't take proper care of their pets.

Bad illustrative example #2: Anne is a person who doesn't take proper care of her pets.

This is a bad example, because none of you knows who Anne is, and so cannot know whether she is a concrete instance of the claim. Even if it is true that Anne doesn't take proper care of her pets, this cannot function as an effective illustrative example because it is not *broadly accessible.*

Bad illustrative example #3: One of my friends sometimes feeds his dog scraps from the dinner table. He shouldn't do that. It encourages bad habits and risks hurting the dog with food it shouldn't eat. It isn't proper care.

The author of this example clearly believes that feeding dogs from the dinner table constitutes improper pet care. But many people will disagree with that judgment. For most of us, even if we think feeding from the table isn't ideal behavior, it doesn't rise to the level of improper care. This is a bad illustrative example because it fails to offer a concrete case in which the generalization is *uncontroversially true.*

Better illustrative example: In 2013 police took custody of nine dogs from a home in Meeker County, MN. The dogs' owner was financially unable to feed them all, but instead of adopting them out to other people who could feed them, she kept them and fed them a small fraction of what they needed to survive. When the police took custody of the dogs, they were all starved to the brink of death, with associated undernourishment problems including big patches of missing fur. She didn't appear to have any malign intent—she claimed to love the dogs—but she definitely didn't take proper care of them.

This example satisfies both criteria of effective illustrative examples. It fills in enough detail that readers unfamiliar with the case can form a judgment about it for themselves, and nearly everyone who hears the example will form the judgment that it is a case of improper care. This illustrative example, like all good illustrative examples, is *broadly accessible* and *uncontroversial.*

REALISTIC EXAMPLES AND FANCIFUL EXAMPLES

Some illustrative examples are *realistic examples*—they are drawn from real-world events or common situations we've all experienced. Many philosophers also use *fanciful examples*—short, wholly invented scenarios that range from unlikely to wildly imaginative.[2] Each kind of example has its place.

Consider the claim: "In some situations, suicide could be morally required."

Either a fanciful example or a realistic example could illustrate this general claim, and each kind of example has advantages and disadvantages.

Fanciful illustrative example: imagine a flying saucer enters orbit of Earth and beams you up onto it. On the ship, the aliens explain that they want to test the limits of the human instinct for self-preservation. They have set up a gallows in a cargo bay, and they tell you that if you hang yourself on the gallows, that will give them the information they need, and they will leave, never to return. If you refuse to hang yourself, they will randomly select one million people on Earth to kill with a death-ray, then they will beam up a different person and run the experiment again. If you found yourself in such a situation, suicide would be morally required.

The advantage of this fanciful example is that it clearly satisfies our two criteria of effective examples: it includes enough detail that everyone can form a judgment about it, and most people who hear it will form the judgment that you *should* kill yourself in order to save a million (or more) other people. The disadvantage of this example is that it so wild that it might not actually tell us much about suicide in the real world. It establishes the conceptual point that it's *possible* for suicide to be morally required, but that conceptual point could still be true even if no circumstances morally requiring suicide have ever happened in the real world. Depending on the context of the debate and the views of people participating in it, this example might shed little light on the question of the permissibility of suicide.

Realistic illustrative example: imagine a group of people undertaking a dangerous mountain climb. They have tied themselves together, which is a standard safety precaution. Imagine that the last person on the line falls over a cliff and, instead of being securely held by the others, his weight is pulling all the others toward the edge of the cliff. If he is able, the right thing to do is to kill himself by cutting himself free of the safety rope. If he doesn't kill himself, then everyone, including him, will die. This is an example of a morally required suicide.

The advantage of this example is that it is drawn from the real world—people who do dangerous climbs have to contemplate possibilities like this when they set off up a mountain. The disadvantage of the example is that it doesn't as clearly

---

[2]We defend the use of fanciful examples in Ian Stoner and Jason D. Swartwood, "Fanciful Examples," *Metaphilosophy* 48, no. 3 (2017): 325–344.

satisfy the requirements it is supposed to meet. The trouble: is this definitely an example of *suicide*? A climber in this situation probably does not think: "I should commit suicide, in order that my friends may live." Rather, he presumably thinks, "I must cut this rope to save my friends, even if that is almost certain to result in my own death." There might be people in some potential audiences who think this choice is not the same thing as choosing suicide.

These examples of morally required suicide illustrate a common tension between realistic and fanciful examples. Fanciful examples tend to be clearer in establishing conceptual points, but sometimes those conceptual points aren't obviously applicable to the real world. The clarity of fanciful examples sometimes comes at the cost of applicability. Realistic examples, because they are drawn from the real world, are obviously applicable to the real world. But sometimes realistic examples, like the real world itself, can be harder to make sense of, and harder to achieve consensus about. The applicability of real-world examples sometimes comes at the cost of clarity.

Both kinds of examples have their place in practical ethics, and philosophers use both fanciful and realistic examples in their writing. Philosophers typically choose the kind of illustrative example that best serves their argumentative goals. As you develop the skill of reading and writing with illustrative examples, an easy way to avoid trade-offs between realistic and fanciful examples is always to generate one of each.

REVIEW

We often rely on generalizations in thought and communication. Illustrating generalizations with examples allows us to read, think, and communicate more effectively.

Generalization: a claim that is not about an individual case but rather about a range of cases.

Illustrative example: a specific, concrete case of the type identified by a generalization.

A good illustrative example is one that is both broadly accessible and relatively uncontroversial.

Broadly accessible example: an example that nearly everyone in the target audience is able to understand and evaluate.

Uncontroversial example: an example that nearly everyone in the target audience evaluates in the same way.

Depending on the context and the goal of the discussion, you may have reason to prefer either a realistic or a fanciful illustrative example.

Realistic example: an example drawn from real-world events, or from areas of broadly shared experience.

Fanciful example: a short, wholly fictional scenario, invented for the purpose of illustration, which may be unrealistic or even wildly imaginative.

To test your understanding of the material introduced in this chapter, complete the Demonstration Exercises and then check your answers against the solutions that follow.

Demonstration Exercises

Demonstration Exercises are designed to give you immediate feedback on your grasp of the skills introduced in this chapter. To use them effectively, you should attempt answers to all of them, then check your work against our suggested answers, which follow. For a detailed explanation of how best to use Demonstration Exercises, read the book's Introduction.

Demonstration Exercises 2A: Illustrating Simple Descriptive Claims

Exercise Instructions: Offer an illustrative example for each of the following descriptive generalizations.

1. Often, a nation's capital city is not its most populous city.
2. Most varieties of wood are flammable.
3. Four-year colleges and universities typically consider the high-school GPA of applicants when making admissions decisions.

Demonstration Exercises 2B: Illustrating Moral Claims

Exercise Instructions: Offer one fanciful and one realistic example that illustrate each of the following moral claims.

1. Helping out a frustrated child is sometimes the wrong thing to do.
2. In most cases, doctors should accept the clear medical directives given to them by their patient, even when they disagree with or disapprove of their patient's directives.
3. Defying the orders of a qualified authority figure is sometimes morally required.
4. In some cases, taking someone else's property without their permission is the right thing to do.

Solutions to the Demonstration Exercises

Demonstration Exercises are most useful if you make your best attempt to complete them before you look at the answers. If you haven't yet attempted answers to all the Demonstration Exercises, go back and do that now.

Note: The range of possible good illustrative examples is effectively unlimited. Thus, the illustrative examples we offer here are merely samples. You will have to ask yourself if your own illustrative examples function in the same way as ours. If they do, you're probably in good shape. If our sample answers appear to be doing something different from your own answers, that's evidence that you

(continued)

need to take another pass at the explanation of the skill before attempting the Practice Exercises.

Demonstration Exercises 2A: Illustrating Simple Factual Generalizations

1. Often, a nation's capital city is not its most populous city.

Example: Washington, D.C. is not the most populous city in the United States. (It doesn't even make the top 10.)

2. Most varieties of wood are flammable.

Example: Untreated oak, cedar, apple, and pine are all examples of woods that burn.

3. Four-year colleges and universities typically consider the high-school GPA of applicants when making admissions decisions.

Example: Nearly all famous four-year colleges and universities consider GPA in their admissions decisions, including Harvard, Stanford, the Ohio State University, and UC Berkeley.

Demonstration Exercises 2B: Illustrating Moral Claims

1. Helping out a frustrated child is sometimes the wrong thing to do.

Realistic example: Some degree of frustration is a necessary part of learning. Imagine a math teacher who gave students the answer the moment they started to get frustrated. Those students would never learn how to do it for themselves. That math teacher would do the wrong thing by helping out frustrated students.

Fanciful example: Imagine a child who has grown frustrated with her inability to figure out how to detonate a bomb. Lending a hand would be the wrong thing to do, even though it would ease her frustration.

2. In most cases, doctors should accept the clear medical directives given to them by their patient, even when they disagree with or disapprove of their patient's directives.

Realistic example: Some patients are excessively suspicious of pain-management drugs and refuse to take them even when they're in considerable pain. When a patient has made their refusal clear, doctors should respect that decision, even if they believe it is ill-informed. It would quite obviously be wrong for them to add drugs to the patient's IV in secret, for example.

Fanciful example: Suppose a patient subscribed to an obscure religion that, on its long list of rules for human conduct, requires that any blood drawn *must*, on threat of eternal damnation, be drawn from the right arm. Doctors should respect this request, even if it would be easier to draw blood from the left arm.

3. Defying the orders of a qualified authority figure is sometimes morally required.

Realistic example: Imagine a fourteen-year-old who has taken a job babysitting his neighbors' toddler. He's been given clear and firm instructions that the toddler should be put to bed before 8 p.m. As the evening wears on, the sitter becomes increasingly worried that the child is very sick. At 7:30, he calls his parents for help in taking the toddler to the doctor. In this case, caring for the welfare of the child is morally more important than obeying the order to put the child to bed by 8 p.m., and so defying those orders is morally required.

Fanciful example: Imagine a dystopian future in which a cruel ruler has seized absolute power in your town. He enjoys pitting children against each other in deadly battles for food. If he were to order you to round up a dozen of your town's children, you should refuse. Even though that order came from an authority figure, it is an immoral order, and defying it is morally required.

4. In some cases, taking someone else's property without their permission is the right thing to do.

Realistic example: Suppose you're at a picnic with friends and family, when someone allergic to bee stings gets stung. You know there's an emergency epinephrine injection in your friend's purse, but you have no idea where she has gone, and so you can't ask her permission to use it. The right thing to do is to take your friend's emergency epinephrine injection and save the currently endangered person, even though you don't have your friend's permission to do that.

Fanciful example: The villains in James Bond movies typically have complicated devices intended to foster global destruction. If you have the chance to steal some key component of their doomsday device, thereby thwarting their plans, you should do that.

CHAPTER 2 PRACTICE EXERCISES
GENERATING ILLUSTRATIVE EXAMPLES

Exercises 2A: Illustrating Simple Descriptive Claims
Exercise Instructions: *Offer an illustrative example for each of the following descriptive generalizations.*

1. Dogs usually have tails. broadly
2. Many people cannot or will not eat bacon. broadly
3. Large planets sometimes have more than one moon. #controversial
4. Some popular hobbies require expensive equipment. uncontroversial
5. It is easy to be misunderstood when communicating through writing. broadly
6. Sometimes, new public policies have unexpected consequences. broadly

Exercises 2B: Illustrating Moral Claims
Exercise Instructions: *Offer one fanciful and one realistic example that illustrates each of the following moral claims.*

1. It is morally wrong to claim credit for work you didn't do. –
2. Morally good intentions sometimes result in terrible outcomes.
3. Malicious intentions sometimes result in good outcomes.
4. It is morally permissible to cause someone temporary pain if that is the only way to save them from significant harm.
5. In some cases, it is morally wrong to hold a person responsible for a crime he or she has committed.
6. Death is sometimes a benefit to the person who has died.

7. Telling the truth is sometimes morally required, even if the truth hurts the feelings of the person you're telling it to.
8. There are some situations in which answering a question truthfully is the morally wrong thing to do.
9. In most cases, parents should allow their teenage children to act on the decisions they've made, even when the parents believe the teen's decision was a bad one.
10. In some cases, when parents are sure their teenage children have made a bad decision, they have an obligation to step in and stop their children from acting on that decision.
11. A health care provider ought not unnecessarily harm a patient.
12. A health care provider ought to promote a patient's capacity to freely guide their life according to their own values.
13. A health care provider ought to promote a patient's well-being.
14. We should work to maintain the trust of people who are dependent upon us.
15. Destroying natural resources simply for fun is disrespectful and wrong.
16. Sometimes, when the interests of a person and a non-human animal come into conflict, the interests of the animal should be prioritized.
17. There are situations in which it would be morally wrong to kill a plant.
18. Breaking the law is sometimes the right thing to do.
19. Some disgusting acts are not morally wrong.
20. There are cases in which nurses should refuse to do what doctors order them to do.
21. Sometimes people become convinced they should prefer a social arrangement, even if that arrangement is oppressive for them.
22. Policies that unfairly exclude a social group from work and social life are oppressive.

CHAPTER 3

Generating Counterexamples

CHAPTER GOALS

By reading this chapter and completing the exercises, you will learn how to:

- Identify the features of a good counterexample.
- Generate a counterexample to a universal claim.

THE TECHNIQUE OF COUNTEREXAMPLE

A universal claim is a generalization that purports to hold true of every possible case. "Cats are mammals" and "any practice that puts people at risk of serious harm should be illegal" are examples of universal claims. Philosophers test the plausibility of universal claims using the technique of *counterexample*. A counterexample is a special form of illustrative example intended to show that a universal claim is *not* true. This technique has many philosophical applications, and it will play a central role in Chapters 6 and 12, where we will use counterexamples to evaluate arguments that appeal to moral principles.

COUNTEREXAMPLES TO UNIVERSAL CLAIMS

Universal claims all take some (possibly elaborate) version of the form "All Xs have feature Y." Some universal claims are true:

- All objects that have mass exert a gravitational force.
- Cats are mammals.
- Every US President in the nineteenth and twentieth centuries was a man.
- Genocide is morally wrong.

Other universal claims are false. Sometimes universal claims (such as "cats are reptiles") are *obviously* false. But some universal claims *often* hold true, even though they don't *always* hold true. Because they *often* hold true, they can be mistaken for true-in-general when, in fact, they are not. A counterexample is a special form of illustrative example that can be used to prove that a universal claim is false.

In order to generate an effective counterexample to a false universal claim, you must pay attention to its "All Xs have feature Y" structure. All good counter-examples will be concrete examples of things that everyone agrees *are* instances of X that *lack* feature Y.

Example universal claim: All human beings have two feet

To show this claim isn't always true, we need an example of a creature every-one agrees *is* a human being but who *lacks* the feature of having two feet.

Oscar Pistorious, the South African sprinter, is a human being who has no feet.

Example Universal Claim: Mammals Don't Lay Eggs

To show this claim isn't always true, we need an example of an animal that everyone agrees *is* a mammal but *lacks* the feature 'doesn't lay eggs.' In other words, we need an example of a mammal that lays eggs.

The duck-billed platypus and the spiny anteater are both mammals that *do* lay eggs.

Many moral principles take the form of universal claims that purport to hold true in all circumstances. The method of counterexample is useful for revealing the limited nature of some principles that appear, at first blush, to be general principles.

Example Universal Claim: It Is Morally Wrong to Trespass on Someone's Property If They Have Posted Signs Saying "No Trespassing"

To show this claim isn't always true, we need an example of a case that every-one agrees *is* an example of trespassing but that *lacks* the feature of being morally wrong.

Suppose it were like this. You're out in the countryside for a walk and notice that one of the property owners has covered the perimeter of his land with "no trespassing" signs. While looking at this man's house from the public street, you see him fall off his roof and land face-down in a puddle, apparently un-conscious. If you do nothing, he will drown. If you run to pull him out of the puddle, you will be trespassing on his property. In this case, it would be mor-ally wrong to let him drown. You morally ought to cross his property line, despite his posted signs, in order to save him.

FEATURES OF A GOOD COUNTEREXAMPLE

The features of a good counterexample are identical to the features of a good il-lustrative example: a good counterexample is broadly accessible and uncontro-versial. As with illustrative examples, you must keep in mind what your audience probably knows and believes; only then can you attempt to describe a case that nearly everyone in your target audience will agree is an example of an X that lacks feature Y.

Example Universal Claim: You Are under No Obligation to Correct Anyone Else's False Beliefs

To show this claim isn't always true, we need an example that everyone agrees is a case in which a person *does* have an obligation to correct someone else's false belief.

Bad counterexample #1: This claim isn't always true—sometimes you should correct someone else's false beliefs.

This is not a counterexample, but rather a denial of the universal claim. A counterexample would identify a specific case in which someone has an obligation to correct someone else's false belief.

Bad counterexample #2: Lando should have told Han that he was walking into a trap.

This is a bad counterexample, because even if the author of the example is correct about what Lando should have done, most audiences don't know who Lando and Han are, and so the example means nothing to them. This counterexample is ineffective because (except when offered to an audience of *Star Wars* fans) it is *not broadly accessible.*

Bad counterexample #3: Jenny McCarthy understands just how dangerous vaccines are. But most people have accepted the medical establishment's profit-driven propaganda that vaccines are safe and effective. Jenny McCarthy has a moral obligation to use her knowledge and her platform to help correct the false beliefs most people have about the safety of vaccines.

This is a bad counterexample because many (one hopes nearly all) people disagree with the author's judgment about Jenny McCarthy's medical wisdom, as well as her obligations in this case. This counterexample is ineffective because it is *controversial.*

Better realistic counterexample: Last month I was waiting for a train I use routinely. While standing on the platform, I overheard a family standing next to me talking about their travel plans for the day. It was immediately obvious to me that they were from out of town and were confused about how the train platforms are set up. The train they were about to board would have taken them in the wrong direction. In that case, I had a (very easily accomplished) obligation to tell them that they were about to board the wrong train.

Better fanciful counterexample: Suppose you have stored some gasoline in an apple juice bottle in your refrigerator. A friend comes over on a hot day and pours herself a glass from that bottle. You have an obligation to tell her that it isn't actually apple juice in her glass before she drinks it.

Both better counterexamples include enough information to ensure that anyone can form a judgment about them, and most people in most audiences will form the judgment that the people in these examples do indeed have a moral obligation to correct someone else's false belief.

Like illustrative examples, counterexamples may be either realistic or fanciful, and we find similar tradeoffs between them. Fanciful counterexamples are often useful for clearly and decisively establishing conceptual points, but they are sometimes not applicable to the real world. Realistic counterexamples are obviously applicable to the real world, but they are sometimes more controversial than their fanciful cousins. As with illustrative examples, it is good philosophical practice to develop the habit, when in need of a counterexample, of offering both kinds.

REVIEW

Philosophers often test universal claims by looking for counterexamples.

Universal claim: a generalization that purports to hold true of every possible case.

Counterexample: a description of a specific case that shows a universal claim is false.

Effective counterexamples, like effective illustrative examples, must be broadly accessible and uncontroversial.

To test your understanding of the material introduced in this chapter, complete the Demonstration Exercises and then check your answers against the solutions that follow.

Demonstration Exercises

Demonstration Exercises are designed to give you immediate feedback on your grasp of the skills introduced in this chapter. To use them effectively, you should attempt answers to all of them, then check your work against our suggested answers, which follow. For a detailed explanation of how best to use Demonstration Exercises, read the book's Introduction.

Demonstration Exercises 3A: Counterexamples to Descriptive Generalizations

Exercise Instructions: Offer a counterexample for each of the following universal generalizations.

1. Birds can fly.
2. Human beings are capable of rational thought.
3. The target audience for animated TV shows is children.

Demonstration Exercises 3B: Counterexamples to Moral Generalizations

Exercise Instructions: Offer a counterexample for each of the following moral claims. For additional practice and fun, try offering one fanciful and one realistic counterexample in each case.

1. Death is the worst thing that could befall the person who has died.
2. You must, morally speaking, return things that have been loaned to you when the person who loaned it asks for it back.
3. No doctor should ever touch a patient without first securing that patient's explicit, voluntary, and informed consent.
4. One must always help one's family first, strangers second.

Solutions to the Demonstration Exercises

Demonstration Exercises are most useful if you make your best attempt to complete them before you look at the answers. If you haven't yet attempted answers to all the Demonstration Exercises, go back and do that now.

Note: the range of possible good counterexamples is effectively unlimited. The solutions we offer here are samples. You will have to ask yourself if your own counterexamples function in the same way as ours. If they do, you're probably in good shape. If our sample answers appear to be doing something different than your own answers, that's evidence that you need to take another pass at the explanation of the skill.

Demonstration Exercises 3A: Counterexamples to Factual Generalizations

1. Birds can fly.

To show this claim isn't always true, we need an example of an animal that *is* a bird, but which lacks the ability to fly.

Penguins and ostriches are two examples of birds that can't fly.

2. Human beings are capable of rational thought.

To show this claim isn't always true, we need an example of a human being who is not capable of rational thought.

Babies are human beings, but are not capable of rational thought. Elderly people deep in the grip of dementia are human beings who are not capable of rational thought.

3. The target audience for animated TV shows is children.

To show this claim isn't always true, we need an example of an animated TV show whose target audience is not children.

The Simpsons, Rick and Morty, and *Archer* are all animated TV shows intended for adults.

Demonstration Exercises 3B: Counterexamples to Moral Generalizations

1. Death is the worst thing that could befall the person who has died.

To show this claim isn't always true, we need an example of a person who has died, and dying was *not* the worst thing that could have happened to them.

(continued)

Fanciful counterexample: Imagine a soldier in World War II who is wounded on the battlefield and dies just before he is found by the Nazis. If he'd survived any longer, the Nazis would have captured him, run gruesome and painful medical experiments on him, and then killed him when he was no longer useful. In this case, it was better for him to die before capture than to survive to be captured. Death, in this case, was *not* the worst thing that could befall him.

Realistic counterexample: Imagine an elderly woman dying of terminal cancer. She has, at most, a few months to live and is in such terrible pain that she cannot enjoy time with her family or do any of the activities that used to bring her joy. She hopes she will die sooner rather than later. Now imagine two stories branching from this point. In one, she has a heart attack during the night and dies peacefully in her sleep. In the other, she has a heart attack, but her doctors notice soon enough that they resuscitate her, and she lives for another three months of painful loneliness before her cancer kills her. The first version of the story shows that a peaceful death in her sleep was not the worst thing that could befall her.

2. You must, morally speaking, return things that have been loaned to you when the person who loaned it asks for it back.

To show this claim isn't always true, we need an example of a case in which returning borrowed property would be the *wrong* thing to do.

Fanciful counterexample: Imagine that you have borrowed a chainsaw from your neighbor to trim an overgrown tree in your backyard. The next morning he knocks on your door with a manic look in his eyes, wearing a leather butcher's apron. He says he spotted some teens in a van down the street and needs his chainsaw so he can go carve them to pieces. In this case, you should not return his property to him when he asks for it.[1]

Realistic counterexample: Suppose your best friend is a recovering alcoholic, sober for nearly two years. You recently borrowed $20 from her and have every intention of paying her back. One afternoon she calls, and you sense she's upset. She asks to stop by and pick up the $20 you owe her. She tells you she has just been fired, and plans to buy and drink a bottle of gin. In this case you should provide whatever support you can to your friend in this time of crisis, but you should not enable her return to drinking by repaying the money you owe her.

3. No doctor should ever touch a patient without first securing that patient's explicit, voluntary, and informed consent.

To show this claim isn't always true, we need an example that *is* a case of a doctor touching a patient without that patient's consent, but is *not* morally wrong.

Realistic counterexample: Emergency room doctors do this all the time. When a patient comes in injured and unconscious, doctors must begin treating the injuries while the patient is still unconscious. Providing that emergency treatment is morally required even though informed consent is impossible.

Fanciful counterexample: Suppose a prankster spikes the Senior Prom punchbowl with a powerful hallucinogen. While in the grip of hallucinations, one of the attendees cuts herself badly enough to need medical attention. Suppose she is calm and perfectly happy for the doctor to clean and bandage her wound, but because she is hallucinating she cannot understand her situation well enough to give her informed consent. In this case, it is morally permissible for the doctor to

---

[1]Adapted from Plato's *Republic*, Book I (331c).

clean and bandage her wound even though she is temporarily incapable of consenting to treatment.

4. One must always help one's family first, strangers second.

To show this claim isn't always true, we need an example of a case in which helping family first, strangers second, is the morally wrong thing to do.

Realistic counterexample: In situations in which a family member might like a little help and a stranger desperately needs help, the needs of the stranger can uncontroversially outweigh the needs of your family member. Suppose, for example, that your brother has asked for your help in moving an old sofa to the alley for trash pickup, and on your way over to his house you see a person collapse on the sidewalk. In that situation, you should help the seriously needy stranger before you help your mildly needy brother.

Fanciful counterexample: If your family were very, very bad, they might not deserve any of your help at all. Suppose, for example, that you come from a family of bank robbers who has asked for your help driving a getaway car. You shouldn't help them. If there are less awful strangers around who need your help, you should help them instead.

CHAPTER 3 PRACTICE EXERCISES
GENERATING COUNTEREXAMPLES

Exercises 3A: Counterexamples to Descriptive Generalizations
Exercise Instructions: *Offer a counterexample for each of the following universal generalizations.*

1. Cats are domesticated animals.
2. Everyone likes to eat peanuts.
3. Every planet has at least one moon.
4. Television shows are half an hour long.
5. Everyone pays income taxes.
6. Everyone likes to be hugged.
7. No one has ever offered to help someone without expecting something in return.

Exercises 3B: Counterexamples to Moral Generalizations
Exercise Instructions: *Offer a counterexample for each of the following moral claims. For additional practice and fun, try offering one fanciful and one realistic counterexample in each case.*

1. Physically hurting a child is always morally wrong.
2. If it's a non-human animal, there's nothing morally wrong with eating it.
3. People should be held morally responsible for all of the consequences of their voluntary choices.
4. It's never OK to call the police on your neighbors.
5. You should stand by your spouse through thick and thin.

6. You should always do what your parents tell you to do.
7. You should choose the career path that will bring you the most joy.
8. Parents should never lie to their children.
9. One ought never loan money to a friend.
10. A health care provider ought never upset a patient.
11. A health care provider ought always do the procedure or treatment a patient has freely and voluntarily decided to do.
12. A health care provider ought always do the treatment that would most benefit a patient's health or well-being.
13. You should always treat people the way they want to be treated.
14. The right thing to do in a situation is always to treat another person in the way you would want to be treated in that situation.
15. You should always keep your promises.
16. Intentionally doing something that you know could result in harm to your partner or spouse is wrong.
17. Teachers should never do anything that offends their students.
18. The duty of a psychologist to maintain client confidentiality is without exception..
19. Within the limits of the law, the morally obligatory choice for a CEO of a big business is whatever choice will maximize the business's profits.
20. Because they are not sentient, there could never be a *moral* reason not to eat a plant.
21. Using someone's property without their permission is always morally wrong.
22. It's always wrong to destroy natural resources.
23. Any policy that excludes a whole group from work or social life is oppressive.
24. If women are in charge of performing an activity and view it as important, then that activity is not gender oppressive.

CHAPTER 4

Representing Arguments in Standard Form

CHAPTER GOALS

By reading this chapter and completing the exercises, you will learn how to:

- Represent in standard form a simple argument from a passage.
- Represent in standard form complex arguments with implicit content or supplementary information.

STANDARD FORM: A TOOL FOR ANALYZING ARGUMENTS

Arguments are at the heart of nearly all philosophical writing. When philosophers offer arguments, they make clear the chain of reasoning that has led them to accept a conclusion. That conclusion might be challenging, controversial, or surprising, but if the argument in favor of it is a good one, it gives us all reason to believe the conclusion is true.

Before we, as readers, can evaluate whether or not an argument is a good one—the kind of argument that gives us reason to believe the conclusion is true—we must first *understand* it. Philosophers commonly check their understanding of arguments by representing them in standard form. Using this presentation technique allows us to confirm that we have identified all the component parts of an argument and understood how they fit together.

This chapter introduces the technique of representing arguments in standard form. Careful practice of this technique will pay dividends, as every chapter in the remainder of the book makes use of standard form.

REPRESENTING ARGUMENTS IN STANDARD FORM: THREE STEPS

An argument is a chain of reasoning in which a set of claims (the premises) is offered in support of a further claim (the conclusion). Written and spoken arguments typically include supplemental material intended to make them clearer or more convincing to the audience. Such material might include digressions, asides, or rhetorical flair. A *standard form* representation of an argument is a minimalist representation of the argument in which each crucial premise is placed on its own numbered line and any supplemental, supporting, extraneous, or stylistic material is stripped away. An argument's standard form representation is, in effect, the argument's skeleton.

Example: Singer's give-to-charities argument

A number of global poverty relief agencies have programs that are proven to prevent suffering and death at very low cost.[1] De-worming treatments for schoolchildren, for example, cost less than $1/child/year. Programs that support the distribution and effective use of mosquito nets cost as little as $50 per net. If you were to donate 1 percent of your total income to programs like these, you would undoubtedly save lives and prevent serious suffering at very little cost to yourself.

It is true that donating 1 percent of your income to effective relief agencies would require you to make *some* sacrifices—you might have to eat at restaurants less often or wait to upgrade your phone. But compared to suffering and death, these sacrifices are incredibly small. We all acknowledge that, in general, we have a moral obligation to prevent suffering and death when we can do so at little cost to ourselves. Since charitable giving does that, it follows that we all have an obligation to donate 1 percent of our total income to effective relief organizations.

A standard-form representation of the argument in this passage looks like this:

1. We could prevent serious suffering at little cost to ourselves by donating 1 percent of our total income to effective relief agencies. (PREMISE)
2. We have a moral obligation to prevent serious suffering when we could do so at little cost to ourselves. (PREMISE)

Therefore, we have a moral obligation to donate 1 percent of our total income to effective relief agencies. (CONCLUSION)

This minimalist representation of the argument clearly states the conclusion and numbers the premises the author offers in support of that conclusion. These are the premises we must evaluate in order to determine whether we should accept the argument's conclusion.

How do we get from the original passage to its standard-form representation? There is no mechanical method. We have to read carefully to sort examples, evidence, and commentary from the essential bones of the argument. We have to

---

[1]Adapted from an argument in Peter Singer, *The Life You Can Save: How to Do Your Part to End World Poverty* (Random House Incorporated, 2010).

understand the passage well enough to recognize the premises essential to the argument the passage makes.

Even though there is no mechanical method for properly representing an argument in standard form, the process always involves three phases.

FIRST: Identify the conclusion of the argument.

Ask yourself: what is the claim the author is trying to persuade me to accept? That point is the conclusion, the claim that all other claims support. If you are ever in doubt about which claim is the conclusion, ask: does the author make this claim in support of a different claim? Or is this the claim that all the other claims support? In the example above, the claims about the effectiveness of relief organizations and about our moral obligation to prevent suffering are both intended to support the claim that we *should* give 1 percent of our income to charity. That is this argument's conclusion.

SECOND: Articulate the premises that are essential to the author's case for that conclusion.

Ask yourself: what are the key claims the author offers in support of the conclusion? For the passage above, that means asking what claims would have to be true to show that we have a moral obligation to donate 1 percent of our total income to effective aid agencies. One reason offered in the passage is that by donating 1 percent of our total income we could prevent serious suffering at little cost to ourselves. This is the point of the first paragraph, and we represent that claim as our first premise:

1. We could prevent serious suffering at little cost to ourselves by donating 1 percent of our total income to effective aid agencies.

But this premise, alone, does not establish the conclusion that we ought to donate 1 percent of our income. To connect the author's first premise to the conclusion, we must pay attention to the second paragraph. There, the author makes a claim about our moral obligations to prevent serious suffering when we can. That is the second premise of the argument:

2. We have a moral obligation to prevent serious suffering when we could do so at little cost to ourselves.

These two premises, taken together, entail the conclusion that we ought to donate 1 percent of our income.

THIRD: Check that your standard form representation is clear, accurate, and charitable.

Reread the original passage and your standard-form representation of it. Ask yourself: Would the author accept my standard-form representation of this argument? A standard-form representation that an author would not embrace as a fair and accurate representation of the argument's skeleton is probably not a good representation. In this case, after reviewing the original passage and our standard form representation of it, we think the author would approve of our work.

Example: Phillips's restrict-access-to-guns argument

[The point of gun legislation should be to reduce the number of gun deaths. The case for laws restricting access to guns thus emerges from the answer to a simple question:] "Would more guns prevent gun deaths? The data would seem to suggest it would not. The United States already has the highest gun-ownership rate in the world—an average 88.8 guns owned per 100 people . . . (The No. 2 gun-owning-country is Yemen, at 54.8.) We don't have the highest crime rate among developed nations . . . but we do have the highest firearm-homicide rate . . . In other words: Lots of guns don't seem to have prevented us from becoming top in the world in gun deaths. So why do we believe more guns would change that?"[2] [We ought to change course and pass laws that restrict access to guns.]

We use the same three-step process to analyze the argument in this passage. Ask first: what is the conclusion? Then: what are the premises that are supposed to justify that conclusion? Finally: would the author approve of our representation?

Here is our representation of the Phillips's argument:

1. We ought to pass laws concerning access to guns that reduce the number of gun deaths.
2. Laws *restricting* access to guns would reduce the number of gun deaths.

Therefore, we ought to pass laws that restrict access to guns.

Is this a fair, accurate, and charitable representation of the original passage? You might be concerned that the author was careful to include statistics about global gun-ownership rates and gun-homicide rates, and those statistics do not appear in our standard-form representation. That is how it should be. She included those statistics as empirical evidence in support of her belief, expressed in premise 2, that laws restricting access to guns reduce the number of gun deaths. It is only the premise itself that should appear in a standard-form representation, and that is what we have done here.

This argument illustrates one reason philosophers are careful to clearly distinguish the premises intended to support the conclusion. Public debates about gun control often fail to do this, which can lead to frustrating and unproductive disagreement. The author of this passage endorses *two* premises: one about what laws ought to do, and one about the expected effects of gun restrictions. It is certainly possible that someone who disagrees with her *conclusion* about gun control might agree with *one* of these premises. Someone might, for example, accept the proffered evidence that gun restrictions reduce the number of gun deaths, but disagree that reducing the number of gun deaths should be the goal of gun

---

[2]Quoted from Amber Phillips's column "The Gun Control Debate, Explained in 5 Questions" for *The Fix*, Dec. 3, 2015. Online: https://www.washingtonpost.com/news/the-fix/wp/2015/10/08/how-to-argue-about-gun-control/

policy. Putting the argument in standard form allows us to pinpoint the location of our disagreements, which helps participants in the discussion avoid talking past each other or arguing in circles.

Learning to represent even straightforward arguments, such as the previous two examples, takes practice. But many arguments include complicating factors that make them even more challenging to analyze. Two especially common complicating factors are *implicit content* and *supplementary information*.

ANALYZING ARGUMENTS WITH IMPLICIT CONTENT

Implicit premises and conclusions are claims, critical to an argument's structure, that an author leaves unstated. Authors sometimes leave the conclusion of an argument unstated, trusting readers to gather from context what the conclusion of the passage is supposed to be. More commonly, an author will leave a premise implicit: they will assume but not explicitly state a claim essential to their argument.

In some cases, an author believes a claim is so obvious that it isn't worth stating explicitly. In some cases, an author simply hasn't noticed that the argument depends on an unstated claim. Whatever the reason, when representing an argument in standard form, you should explicitly state all claims, including any the author has left implicit.

Example: Davis's vegetarians-are-hypocrites argument

Many vegetarians argue that god's creatures shouldn't be sacrificed simply to appease our craving for a thick, juicy rib eye. While there may be some merit to their arguments, their rationale also reeks of hypocrisy. Although vegetarians openly decry the slaughter of animals, they think nothing of tearing carrots and spuds out of the earth or of sticking a zucchini into a high-speed blender. Like it or not, plants are also living organisms that respond to stimuli like light, gravity, and touch.[3] [This argument will convince even the most self-righteous vegetarians that they are hypocrites.]

What is the conclusion? The author's ultimate point seems to be that vegetarians are hypocrites.

What premises does the author appeal to in order to convince us to accept that conclusion? The author clearly asserts that vegetarians eat living things: plants. That appears to be a premise of the argument. But what claim is supposed to connect the fact that vegetarians eat living plants to the conclusion that vegetarians are hypocrites? The author has left that premise implicit, so we have, essentially, this:

1. Vegetarians eat plants, which are living things.
2. ????

Therefore, vegetarians are hypocrites.

---

[3]Quoted from Lyle Davis's column "How To: Argue Against Vegetarians," for askmen.com, publication date unclear: http://www.askmen.com/money/how_to_400/477_how-to-argue-against-vegetarians.html

Implicit in the original passage is the claim that non-hypocritical vegetarianism requires vegetarians to refuse to eat any living thing. When we make the implicit premise explicit, we get the following standard form representation:

1. Vegetarians eat plants, which are living things.
2. If vegetarians eat any living things, then they are hypocrites.

Therefore, vegetarians are hypocrites.

Would the author accept this representation of his argument? We see no grounds for complaint.

Representing arguments in standard form lays the groundwork for a careful discussion of their strengths and weaknesses. But sometimes a standard form representation can, all on its own, expose a weak argument. In this case, premise 2, once stated explicitly, is obviously implausible. Most ethical vegetarians believe it is wrong to cause *unnecessary suffering*. Plants cannot suffer, which is why most ethical vegetarians believe there's no moral problem with eating them. The implausibility of premise 2 might have been obscured by the pugilistic tone of the original passage; once we have the argument properly represented in standard form, its weakness is obvious.

ANALYZING ARGUMENTS WITH SUPPLEMENTARY INFORMATION

In addition to implicit premises, many real-world arguments include *supplementary information*, which is information intended to support or clarify an argument's premises or conclusion. Learning to recognize supplementary information makes it easier to represent arguments in standard form.

Example: No-platforming is morally wrong
Consider this excessively minimalist passage about controversial speech on college campuses:

It has happened several times now that student groups have no-platformed controversial speakers. It is morally wrong for students to do this. No-platforming undermines productive democratic discourse, and that is something we ought not do.

This passage contains a complete argument. Even without understanding what the author means by any single sentence here, you could still recognize the premises and conclusion and represent them in standard form, like so:

1. It's morally wrong to undermine productive democratic discourse.
2. No-platforming undermines productive democratic discourse.

Therefore, no-platforming is morally wrong.

Both the original passage and its standard form representation are so succinct that, to many readers, they will not make sense. To effectively convey the argument, the author of the passage should include additional information to help readers understand the context of the debate and the meanings of important terms. Given that this is an area of significant controversy and high personal stakes, the author should make some effort to show why the premises are plausible, and they should take special care not to be misunderstood. This expanded passage takes a step in that direction:

> A recent student movement on college campuses advocates the 'no-platforming' (also known as 'de-platforming') of certain speakers. To no-platform a speaker means to prevent them from speaking on campus, either by physically blocking their access to the stage or by shouting them down once they're there. Although no-platforming is often motivated by the noble goal of protecting vulnerable students, it is wrong because it undermines productive democratic discourse.
>
> Democratic societies depend on the free discussion of diverse viewpoints on issues affecting the community. Taking diverse viewpoints seriously is the best way to overturn old, misguided dogmas. Remember: lots of people used to believe racial slavery was morally permissible. No one believes that now. It was the free and open exchange of ideas—productive democratic discourse— that changed people's minds.
>
> To no-platform speakers—even bigoted and offensive ones—undermines productive democratic discourse. Even when a speaker is completely, offensively wrong—even if they are anti-Muslim bigots, racists, or homophobes— it promotes productive democratic discourse to allow them to speak. There are at least two reasons that this is so. First, if someone has mistaken views, there is no chance of them ever changing their mind if they don't talk about them. Second, it is important for all of us to maintain our ability to respond to mistaken views. If we shout them down instead of explaining our objections, we risk losing the ability to explain why they're wrong.
>
> My argument is that no-platforming speakers is wrong because it undermines productive democratic discourse. This argument does not imply that there is something valuable or true in the *content* of the speech of people with stupid or offensive views. The benefit to society is in maintaining our ability to *refute* those views. And further, allowing speakers with offensive views to speak is compatible with doing everything we can to support the people who are the targets of their speech. For example, if an anti-Muslim bigot is scheduled to speak on campus, student groups could band together to celebrate the Muslim students and publicly refute the views of the speaker. That would be much more effective than no-platforming the speaker.[4]

---

[4]Adapted from an argument in John Stuart Mill, *On Liberty* (Electric Book Company London, 2001).

The argument contained in this longer passage is fundamentally the same as the minimalist original; we would represent both passages in standard form the same way. But the second, extended presentation of the argument adds supplementary information that makes the argument easier to understand. Some of the information is *background information*: it defines unfamiliar terms and provides context for understanding the topic. For instance, the first paragraph explains what the word "no-platforming" means, and the second explains what "productive democratic discourse" means. Some of the information is aimed at *illustration or justification* of premises. For instance, the second paragraph supports premise 1, and the third paragraph supports premise 2. Finally, the passage includes *clarifying explanation* that aims to avoid misunderstanding. For instance, the last paragraph clarifies the conclusion by explaining what it is *not* saying. Effective presentations of arguments typically include some or all of these types of supplementary information.

The lesson: supplementary information makes arguments more accessible by supporting, clarifying, and contextualizing the premises and conclusion. When you work to represent an argument in standard form, be sensitive to the distinction between premises and the supplementary information that supports them. At the outset, it can be helpful to be on the lookout for common types of supplementary information, such as background information, illustrative examples, justifications of premises, and clarifying explanations.

Example: Shambley's unfair trauma argument

The following passage contains an argument. As you read it, pay special attention to sorting supplementary information from the argument:

> During an undergraduate honors course titled "Scholar Citizen" at Augsburg University in Minneapolis, Minnesota, students were asked to read James Baldwin's book *The Fire Next Time* (1963). In the book, Baldwin explores themes related to race in America. During class, professor Phillip Adamo asked students to take turns reading passages. The class was shocked when a student read a particular quotation: "You can really only be destroyed by believing that you really are what the white world calls a n-----." In response, Adamo tried to open a discussion of how the class should use the slur word when reading the text, but in the process he said the word himself.

> This led to a serious discussion on campus: Should a professor (or students) say words that are used as racial epithets, even if the words are part of legitimate course texts? A number of students were outraged that a White teacher would speak that word in class, and they began to mount a campaign for various campus reforms, including having Adamo removed or sanctioned. In his defense, Adamo stated that he was only mentioning the word as it was stated in the course text, not using the word as a slur.

> Many students were not convinced by this defense. One, Terrence Shambley, Jr., argued: "If you have to evoke trauma in your students to teach them

something, it seems counterproductive to me . . . It's not a fair situation, especially because other students in class don't have to feel that trauma. That trauma is only evoked for the black students in the room.[5] [So, professor Adamo should not have said the N-word in class.]"

The first two paragraphs of the passage describe a controversy in some detail. Those paragraphs don't make an argument; instead, they offer the context we need to understand the argument.

The last paragraph contains an argument about the controversy. Once we recognize that we are reading an argument, we can use the same three-step process to represent it in standard form.

First, what is the conclusion? The student intends to persuade us that "the professor should not have said the N-word in class." That is the claim all the other claims support; it is the conclusion of the argument.

Second, what are the premises? What claims would have to be true to show that the professor should not have used the N-word in class? In this case, there are two. The argument makes the descriptive claim that the N-word evoked trauma in some students but not others. It also makes the moral claim that evoking trauma in some students but not others is unfair, and (this is implied) professors should not do that. Together, these claims are necessary to establish the conclusion that professor Adamo should not have said the N-word in class. We thus get this representation of the argument in standard form:

Trauma Argument:

1. When the professor said the N-word in class it evoked trauma in some students but not others.
2. Professors shouldn't do things that evoke trauma in some students but not others.

So, the professor should not have said the N-word in class.

Third, is our representation of the argument clear, accurate, and charitable? Would the author accept our representation of their argument?

We have emphasized that representing arguments in standard form is not a mechanical process—there is an element of art to it. In some cases, there are multiple defensible ways to represent a single passage. Comparably good representations can even have different numbers of premises. That is true of this example. Note that the student making the argument explicitly appeals to the value of fairness, and we have not mentioned fairness in our standard-form representation. An alternative approach would include the student's claim about fairness.

Trauma Argument (Fairness Version):

1. Using the N-word in class evoked trauma for black students that it did not evoke for other students.

---

[5]This quotation is from Osei, Zipporah, "Do Racial Epithets Have Any Place in the Classroom? A Professor's Suspension Fuels that Debate," *The Chronicle of Higher Education*, Feb. 8, 2019. https://www.chronicle.com/article/Do-Racial-Epithets-Have-Any/245662

2. It is unfair to treat students in a way that evokes trauma for some but not others.
3. It's morally wrong for professors to treat their students unfairly.

Therefore, using the N-word in class was morally wrong.

The main difference between these representations is that the three-premise version treats the claim about fairness as a distinct step in the argument, while the original two-premise version treats the discussion of fairness as supplemental information in support of the moral claim about how professors should behave. You should proceed with the version of the argument that you believe most clearly and charitably represents the author's reasoning. That is a judgment call.

THE VALUE OF REPRESENTING ARGUMENTS IN STANDARD FORM

If arguments typically require supplementary information to be clear and persuasive, then why do we strip all that out when we put the argument into standard form? What is the point of representing an argument in a form that is so skeletal that it isn't, on its own, clear and persuasive?

The primary reason to represent arguments in standard form is that doing so successfully requires us to identify all the essential components of the argument and to understand how those components fit together. Representing an argument in standard form is thus an effective way of confirming that we have charitably and accurately *understood* it. Before we can ask if an argument is a *good* argument, we must understand it, and the technique of standard form helps ensure that we get this order right: understand first, then evaluate.

In addition to the foundational benefit of requiring understanding before evaluation, representing arguments in standard form improves philosophical discussion in the following ways:

- Clearly identifying the essential components of the argument can, itself, highlight weaknesses of an argument. (We saw this in the vegetarians-are-hypocrites argument.)
- Standard form facilitates focused discussion by clearly separating the conclusion from the reasoning that supports it. (When we disagree with each other, we should focus our attention not on each other's conclusions, but rather on each other's reasons for accepting those conclusions.)
- Clearly identifying and labeling the essential components of the argument is a convenience that makes discussion easier. (As we saw in the restrict-access-to-guns argument, a single argument can have multiple controversial premises. Having the premises clearly distinguished and numbered allows us to focus on areas of potential disagreement more precisely: "I think premise 2 is false because . . . ")

You will probably find that working with arguments in standard form improves your work in other classes. Many students report that drafting in standard form improves the clarity and organization of their writing in all their courses. Beyond the classroom, skill in representing arguments in standard form will help you understand quickly and deeply the arguments you find in the wild.

REVIEW

An argument is a chain of reasoning in which a set of claims (the premises) supports a further claim (the conclusion). Philosophers commonly represent arguments in standard form.

> **Standard form:** a style of argument presentation in which each essential premise is placed on its own numbered line, followed by the conclusion.

Arguments in real-world discussions, articles, books, and newspapers often include implicit content and supplementary information. One key reason to use standard form is that presenting arguments in that format forces us to state explicitly every component piece of the argument and to sort its premises from the material intended to support them. Representing an argument in standard form thus helps ensure that we have *understood* it; only after we have understood an argument can we evaluate it.

> **Implicit content:** a premise or conclusion that is essential to an argument but not explicitly stated by the argument's author.
> **Supplementary information:** information beyond the main premises and conclusion that is intended to help audiences better understand the argument.

To test your understanding of the material introduced in this chapter, complete the Demonstration Exercises and then check your answers against the solutions that follow.

Demonstration Exercises

Demonstration Exercises are designed to give you immediate feedback on your grasp of the skills introduced in this chapter. To use them effectively, you should attempt answers to all of them, then check your work against our suggested answers, which follow. For a detailed explanation of how best to use Demonstration Exercises, read the book's Introduction.

Demonstration Exercises 4A: Representing Simpler Arguments in Standard Form

Exercise Instructions: The following passages contain simple arguments, some of which are moral arguments and some of which are non-moral arguments. Represent each argument in standard form.

    1. Spanking your children is wrong if there are other less painful and humiliating forms of discipline that are at least as effective at shaping children's behavior. Since there are indeed more effective methods—such as using positive reinforcement, holding to clear expectations, and encouraging collaborative communication—it is therefore wrong to spank your children.

(continued)

2. A person would be a good US president if they're a successful business person. Therefore, Ms. Chambley would be a good president, because she runs a very successful business.

3. Being a good business person is not enough to make you a good US president, because being a good business person is enough to make you a good president only if presidents don't need to focus on anything but economic success. But, clearly, presidents do need to focus on additional things, such as justice and people's well-being.

4. Some people claim that we should never judge the morality of practices from other cultures. This is plainly false. If it were so, then it would be wrong to condemn genocide when it is practiced by another culture. Condemning genocide, however, is not only morally permissible but morally required. It follows that it is not always wrong to condemn the practices of other cultures.

Demonstration Exercises 4B: Representing Arguments with Implicit Content

Exercise Instructions: The following passages contain arguments with implicit premises and/or conclusions. Represent each argument in standard form, and be sure to make explicit any content the author of the passage has left implicit.

1. Routinely playing video games by yourself all day prevents you from developing your social and intellectual capacities, so it's clearly bad for you.

2. David is great at magic tricks, and people who are great at magic tricks are the life of the party. So, . . .

3. People who are fair, thoughtful, socially skilled, and courageous would be good candidates for the CEO position. That's why Fardosa would clearly be a good candidate.

4. Since war is morally unjustified when most of the casualties are civilians, most wars are morally unjustified.

Demonstration Exercises 4C: Representing More Complex Arguments in Standard Form

Exercise Instructions: The following passages make arguments that are somewhat more challenging to analyze, either because they make complicated claims or because they contain a lot of supplementary information. Represent each argument in standard form.

1. The mystery is solved

Only three people had keys to the vault with the jewels: Alice, Bob, and Charlie. It must have been one of those three who stole them. But on the night of the theft, Alice was overseas, more than 1,000 miles away from the room. She couldn't possibly have stolen them. That same night, Bob was locked up in a county jail for an unrelated crime. So it couldn't have been Bob, either. Therefore, it must have been Charlie who stole the jewels.

Hint: arguments can have one, two, three, or more premises. The most straightforward way to represent "The mystery is solved" is with three premises.

2. In favor of fifteen-minute passing periods

Saint Paul College should switch to fifteen-minute passing periods. The reason is simple: the school ought to choose policies that best support student learning, and longer passing periods would support student learning better than the current five-minute policy. There are at least three reasons that longer passing periods are better. First, studies show that reflecting on new information and new skills immediately after being introduced to them significantly improves learning. When students only have five minutes to get to class, they have no time to pause and think about what they've just learned. Second, the time immediately after class is an ideal time for students to talk to their professors about that day's new material. Or rather, it *would* be an ideal time if students and professors had more than five minutes before they had to be at their next class. Third, for students who have to cross the building, or stop at the restroom between classes, the rush to arrive on time at the next class introduces needless stress to what should be a routine process. Students who arrive at class flustered, having had to run through the halls, or skip going to the bathroom, arrive in no condition to start learning right away.

3. Star Trek versus Star Wars

There are many ways to evaluate the quality of television shows and movies. Some shows have excellent actors, or excellent writing, or excellent directors of photography, or excellent sound design. Some shows have all these things. But at the end of the day, what really matters, when evaluating the quality of shows that meet a certain threshold of competence with respect to craft, is the effect they have on the world. The best TV shows and movies make the world a better place; they teach their audiences something important or invite them to think hard about what changes would make the world better. Judged by this standard, *Star Trek* is clearly superior to *Star Wars*. *Star Trek* is a story told in a world much like our own, in which tolerance and diplomacy are almost always the right tools to deal with the conflicts that inevitably arise between basically good people with different understandings of the good life. *Star Wars*, with its cartoonishly good and evil characters, teaches a comic-book version of morality, and actually makes the world a worse place by reinforcing the idea that some groups of people are rotten to the core and must be exterminated. Give me *Star Trek* any day of the week.

4. The problem of evil[6]

God (at least god understood as an all-powerful, all-knowing, benevolent entity in the sky) definitely doesn't exist. If such a god did exist, then there would be no pointless suffering on Earth, because god would foresee it and, out of kindness, act to prevent it. (Just as you would act to prevent a toddler from wandering accidentally into traffic, god would prevent the rest of us from accidentally being hurt in terrible and pointless ways.) But the world is jam-packed with pointless suffering. People are trapped in war zones through no fault of their own. Kids are born into families with abusive parents. Entire cities are devastated by hurricanes, earthquakes, and tidal waves. Since no benevolent supernatural being steps in to stop this pointless suffering, we can confidently conclude that no benevolent supernatural being exists.

5. A cosmological argument[7]

Here's an easy argument that something (or someone) caused the universe to exist. Think of every object you have interacted with today. Think of the books you've touched, the chairs, cars, walls, roads, air, dirt, water, and so on. Not a

---

[6]Adapted from David Hume, *Dialogues Concerning Natural Religion* (William Blackwood, 1907), pt. X.

[7]Adapted from arguments advanced by Medieval Islamic theologians Al-Ghazali and Ibn Rushd. Today it is sometimes called the Kalām Cosmological Argument, and it is typically used as the first half of an argument for the existence of god.

(continued)

single one of those things has existed forever—they all began to exist at some point. Some artifacts, like books and cars, began to exist because they were caused to exist by workers in factories. Others, like buildings and roads, began to exist because they were caused to exist by construction workers. Living parts of the natural world, like plants and animals, began to exist because they were caused to exist by natural processes of reproduction and growth. Non-living parts of the world, like rocks and air, began to exist because they were caused to exist by inorganic natural causes, including geologic processes and stellar evolution. These are all individual illustrations of a general point that is obviously true: if something *began* to exist, then it was *caused* to exist.

But science tells us that the universe itself has not always existed. At some point, the universe itself *began* to exist. Therefore, the universe was *caused* to exist.

6. Bodily resurrection[8]

Many religions teach that at some point in the future, everyone who has previously died will be bodily resurrected and restored to the healthiest form of their original bodies. But when we think through some of the puzzles that this teaching presents, it becomes clear that such bodily resurrection is conceptually incoherent, which is to say it is impossible.

When a person dies, their body eventually dissolves into a multitude of particles that are scattered to the soil, air, and water. Could those particles be gathered and re-formed to restore the person's body at some later date? Perhaps an omnipotent god could do that.

Some of those scattered particles are absorbed by the roots of plants, and eventually eaten by beasts or fish. In this case, the component parts of the dead person's body have been entirely transformed and transmuted by the processes of growth and digestion. Could those particles be gathered, un-transmuted, and re-formed to restore the body at some later date? Perhaps an omnipotent god could do that.

Here is where things get especially tricky. Some of a dead person's scattered particles are absorbed by plants that are eaten by *people*. Or those scattered parts are eaten by animals that are eaten by *people*. Or in the case of cannibals, the parts of the dead person's body are directly devoured by *people*. In short: over time, the same material particles can be component parts of the bodies of *many different people*.

If it were possible for everyone to be bodily resurrected, then it must be possible for everyone to have all their own particles restored to them. But if it were possible for everyone to have all their own particles restored to them, then it must be possible for a single particle to be part of many different bodies at the same time. This cannot be. Even an omnipotent god could not place a single particle in many places at a single time. Bodily resurrection of *everyone*, as promised by many religions, is therefore impossible.

---

[8]Adapted from Robert Boyle, *Some Physico-Theological Considerations about the Possibility of the Resurrection* (Herringman, 1961). Boyle's project in this essay is to critically engage the argument paraphrased here.

===== **Solutions to Demonstration Exercises** =====

Demonstration Exercises are most useful if you make your best attempt to complete them before you look at the answers. If you haven't yet attempted answers to all the Demonstration Exercises, go back and do that now.

Note: your standard-form representations should identify the same premises and conclusions as we have, but variation in wording or expression is perfectly fine.

Solutions to Demonstration Exercises 4A

1.

> 1. Spanking children is wrong if there are less painful and humiliating forms of discipline that are at least as effective at shaping children's behavior.
>
> 2. There are forms of discipline that are less painful and humiliating than spanking but just as effective at shaping children's behavior.
>
> Therefore, spanking children is wrong.

2.

> 1. A person would be a good US president if they're a good business person.
>
> 2. Ms. Chambley is a good business person.
>
> Thus, Ms. Chambley would be a good US president.

3.

> 1. Being a good business person is enough to make you a good US president only if presidents only need to focus on economic success.
>
> 2. Presidents don't need to focus only on economic success.
>
> So, being a good business person is not enough to make you a good US president.

4.

> 1. If people should never judge the morality of practices in other cultures, then it's wrong to condemn genocide committed by another culture.
>
> 2. It's not wrong to condemn genocide committed by another culture.
>
> Thus, it's not true that people should never judge the morality of practices in other cultures.

Solutions to Demonstration Exercises 4B

1.

> 1. Something is bad for you if it prevents you from developing your social and intellectual capacities. [IMPLICIT PREMISE]
>
> 2. Routinely playing video games by yourself all day prevents you from developing your social and intellectual capacities.
>
> Therefore, routinely playing video games by yourself all day is bad for you.

(*continued*)

2.

   1. People who are good at magic tricks are the life of the party.

   2. David is good at magic tricks.

   Thus, David is the life of the party. [IMPLICIT CONCLUSION]

3.

   1. People who are fair, thoughtful, socially skilled, and courageous would be good candidates for the CEO position.

   2. Fardosa is fair, thoughtful, socially skilled, and courageous. [IMPLICIT PREMISE]

   So, Fardosa would be a good candidate for the CEO position.

4.

   1. War is morally unjustified when most of the casualties are civilians.

   2. In most wars, most of the casualties are civilians. [IMPLICIT PREMISE]

   Thus, most wars are morally unjustified.

Solutions to Demonstration Exercises 4C

1. The mystery is solved

   1. Only Alice, Bob, or Charlie could have stolen the jewels.

   2. Alice didn't steal them.

   3. Bob didn't steal them.

   Therefore, Charlie stole the jewels.

2. In favor of fifteen-minute passing periods

   1. Saint Paul College should choose school policies that best promote student learning.

   2. Fifteen-minute passing periods would better support student learning than five-minute passing periods.

   Thus, Saint Paul College should switch to fifteen-minute passing periods

3. Star Trek versus Star Wars

   1. Good TV shows and movies make the world a better place, while bad TV shows and movies make the world worse.

   2. *Star Trek* makes the world a better place, while *Star Wars* makes it worse.

   So, *Star Trek* is better than *Star Wars*.

4. The problem of evil

   1. If God exists, then there would be no pointless suffering in the world.

   2. There is pointless suffering in the world.

   Therefore, God doesn't exist.

5. A cosmological argument

   1. Everything that begins to exist was caused to exist.

2. The universe began to exist.

Thus, the universe was caused to exist.

6. Bodily resurrection

1. If bodily resurrection of everyone is possible, then it's possible for everyone to have all their original particles restored to them.

2. If it's possible for everyone to have all their original particles restored to them, then it's possible for a particle to be in many places at the same time.

3. It is impossible for one particle to be in many places at the same time.

So, bodily resurrection of everyone is impossible.

CHAPTER 4 PRACTICE EXERCISES

REPRESENTING ARGUMENTS IN STANDARD FORM

Exercises 4A: Representing Simpler Arguments in Standard Form

Exercise Instructions: *The following passages contain simple arguments, some of which are moral arguments and some of which are non-moral arguments. Represent each argument in standard form.*

1. Is death bad for the one who dies? No. After all, something is bad for you only if you exist when it happens. But you do not exist when you are dead.[9]
2. A being has moral rights only if it makes sense to hold it accountable for its choices and praise or blame it, in moral terms, for those choices. Thus, non-human animals do not have moral rights, since it makes no sense to hold them morally accountable for the things they do.
3. Parkinson's Disease, like every other disease, must be caused either by inherited genetic factors or by environmental factors. Examples of inherited diseases are sickle cell anemia, cystic fibrosis, and Huntington's disease. Examples of environmentally caused diseases are skin cancer and lead poisoning. The evidence is strong that there is, in most cases, no inherited cause of Parkinson's. (One especially strong piece of evidence: it appears to be the case that the children of parents with Parkinson's are no more at risk of developing the disease than are people in the general population.) Given this evidence, we can conclude that Parkinson's is caused by environmental factors.
4. If something doesn't care about its own interests, then there is no reason for the rest of us to extend it moral consideration. So non-conscious organisms (such as plants, mushrooms, microbes, and oysters) don't deserve our moral consideration, since they don't care about their own interests.
5. If something exhibits goal-directed behaviors, then it is possible to benefit or harm it. And if it is possible to benefit or harm something, then its interests

_____

[9]Adapted from Epicurus, "Letter to Menoeceus."

deserve moral consideration. Furthermore, all living things exhibit goal-directed behavior. (Every living thing strives, grows, procreates, and so on. All these behaviors count as goal-directed behaviors.) That's why all living things deserve moral consideration.[10]

6. It's possible to care about the well-being of something for its own sake only if that thing has interests. And something has interests only if it exhibits goal-directed behavior. Ecosystems do not exhibit goal-directed behavior. Therefore, an ecosystem is not the kind of thing whose well-being we can possibly care about for its own sake.[11]

7. It is incredible to me that people continue to tolerate such an obviously rights-violating institution as the modern system of taxation. No clear-thinking person could deny that taxation violates our rights. After all, taxation is a form of slavery. Lest you think I'm speaking metaphorically, allow me to disabuse you of that confusion. Slavery is forcing someone to work for no pay; taxation confiscates the pay people would have received if there were no taxation. It's literally the same thing. Slavery, obviously, is a rights violation. So, too, is taxation.

8. Some people claim that the institution of taxation is the same thing as the institution of slavery. These people are wrong. Slavery is, fundamentally, the claim of one person or group to own another person or group of people as property. A system of taxation does not involve anyone claiming another person or group as property—it claims that people should contribute some portion of their income to the common good. Institutions that are based on fundamentally different claims cannot be the same institution.

Exercises 4B: Representing Arguments with Implicit Content

Exercise Instructions: *The following passages contain arguments with implicit premises and/or conclusions. Represent each argument in standard form, and be sure to make explicit any content the author of the passage has left implicit.*

1. Women aren't oppressed in America today, since men are subject to serious burdens that are often more significant than those women face: for instance, many more men are in prison, are killed by street or combat violence, and are hurt or killed doing dangerous jobs.[12]

2. You should always eat locally grown food, because eating locally grown food uses resources in a less environmentally damaging way than imported food.

3. All actors are self-involved narcissists. Will Ferrell is an actor. Need I say more?

4. Creatures with central nervous systems are sentient, and therefore dogs are sentient.

---

[10]Adapted from an argument in Paul W. Taylor, *Respect for Nature: A Theory of Environmental Ethics* (Princeton University Press, 2011).

[11]Adapted from an argument in Harley Cahen, "Against the Moral Considerability of Ecosystems," *Environmental Ethics* 10, no. 3 (1988): 195–216.

[12]Adapted from an argument in http://www.foxnews.com/opinion/2013/02/05/to-be-happy-must-admit-women-and-men-arent-equal.html.

5. God has commanded us not to steal, and therefore stealing is morally wrong.

6. There are objective moral values only if God exists. Therefore, God exists.

7. God's commanding something is not what makes it right or wrong. If it were, then it would be right to torture a baby for fun if God had commanded us to do that.

8. People act like it's obvious that there are objective moral facts: that there are at least some things that are right or wrong independently of what anyone happens to think or feel about the matter.

   Some simple reflection, however, shows that this belief is false. If there's substantial disagreement about a topic even after it has been extensively discussed for millennia, then that's evidence that there are no objective facts about that topic. Given what we know about people's views of morality, it follows that there are no objective moral facts.

9. Some people believe that the rightness or wrongness of a person's actions depends on that person's culture. On this view, whether arranged child marriages (for instance) are actually right or wrong for a person just depends on whether their culture endorses or frowns upon the practice. But the idea that what's right or wrong depends on cultural attitudes is highly implausible. If what's actually right for you depends on what your culture says, then committing rape would be right for you if your culture endorsed rape as a wholesome practice.

10. [The idea that there are objective values is unlikely to be true.] If there were objective values, then they would be entities or qualities or relations of a very strange sort, utterly different from anything else in the universe. Correspondingly, if we were aware of them, it would have to be by some special faculty of moral perception or intuition, utterly different from our ordinary ways of knowing everything else.[13]

Exercises 4C: Representing More Complex Arguments in Standard Form

Exercise Instructions: *The following passages make arguments that are somewhat more challenging to analyze, either because they make complicated claims or because they contain a lot of supplementary information. Represent each argument in standard form.*

1. There is no afterlife. To see why, consider the following: if the soul does not consist of something physical, then it cannot interact with the body. But, the soul *does* interact with the body. And, if the soul consists of something physical, then it decays with the body after death. Furthermore, if the soul decays with the body after death, then there is no afterlife.

2. If we look at the historical record, we can find *many* cases of non-resistant disbelief in a personal, loving God—that is, we can find many examples of people who despite genuine openness to the possibility, lacked any good reason

---

[13]Quoted from J. L. Mackie (2015), "The Subjectivity of Values," in *The Ethical Life*, 2nd Edition, ed. Russ Shafer-Landau (Oxford University Press), 177.

to think a personal, loving God exists. But, if there really was a personal, loving God, then there would not be any non-resistant disbelief. A relationship with a loving, personal God would be very important and beneficial, and a loving and personal God would have the power and motivation to ensure that we would have no reason to doubt we could have such a relationship. Thus, there is not a personal, loving God.[14]

3. The choices I make and the things I do might, some of the time, be noticed by the people who live around me right now. That gives some of those choices the illusory feel of meaningfulness. But with very few exceptions, the choices I make and the things I do right now will soon be forgotten by me and everyone else. This fact remains true whether I am kind or callous, generous or self-absorbed, hard-working or lazy. No matter what I do with my life, the choices I make, the things I do, all will be quickly forgotten.

   It is almost certainly true that in 100 years, I will be completely forgotten. And it is undoubtedly true that I will be completely forgotten in a million years. Why should I invest time and effort in choices and activities that will, ultimately, be completely forgotten? To invest such time and effort would be absurd. To invest such time and effort would be to behave as if my life is meaningful when the perspective of a million years into the future reveals this inescapable conclusion: life is meaningless.

4. Elementary schools across the nation have ceased instruction in cursive penmanship. This is a bad choice that should be reversed. Here's why. Surely we can all agree to this general principle of curriculum design: useful skills that benefit students in a variety of ways throughout their lives ought to have a place in the elementary school curriculum. The skill of writing in cursive benefits students in so many ways that it's hard to count them all. Here is but a small sampling. For children, writing in cursive develops fine motor skills faster than typing, and gives them an achievable challenge they can enjoy meeting. For adults, the ability to read cursive gives them access to letters, journals, and other historical documents written by people in previous generations. For adults, the ability to write in cursive allows them to write more meaningful personal letters—handwritten letters that don't look like they were written by a child. These are a few of the many ways that cursive is a useful skill that benefits students throughout their lives. Cursive should be restored to the elementary school curriculum.

5. In the past, a common definition used to determine whether someone was dead was this: a person is dead if, but only if, they were not respirating and their blood was not circulating. Call this *the cardiopulmonary definition* of death. It turns out that this definition of death is implausible. This becomes clear when we contemplate cases where a person's brain is irreversibly damaged so that it no longer functions at all. A patient in this condition could be put on an artificial respirator and thus would be respirating. The cardiopulmonary definition classifies a person whose brain is entirely non-functional as *not*

---

[14]Adapted from an argument in John L. Schellenberg, *The Hiddenness Argument: Philosophy's New Challenge to Belief in God* (New York: Oxford University Press, 2015).

dead. The cardiopulmonary definition is therefore implausible, since a person with no brain function clearly should be classified as dead.[15]

6. When we think about living things in general (from microbes and plants to humans and other animals), we can see that an organism is alive if, and only if, it is functioning as an integrated whole. Certain parts of an organism can stop working and it will still count as being alive because it is still a distinct individual that maintains its own structure and functioning: a plant can still be alive even if one of its leaves dies, and a person can still be alive even if they have poor liver function. Furthermore, because a human organism functions as an integrated whole if, but only if, its brain has not entirely and irreversibly ceased to function, we can conclude that a human is dead if, and only if, their entire brain has irreversibly ceased to function.

7. Eben Alexander, a neurosurgeon, has described his own near-death experience. During an acute bout of meningitis, Alexander fell into a coma. When he eventually emerged from the coma he described some vivid experiences he had had: he traveled through a meadow with a beautiful woman who telepathically revealed spiritual truths, such as the existence of heaven and God, that Alexander had abandoned earlier in his life. Years later, Alexander discovered a photo of a sister he never knew he had—a sister who had died many years before. The woman Alexander had seen in his coma strongly resembled the photograph of his long-dead sister.

   Doctors insisted that Alexander's neocortex was not functioning during his coma. If we are purely physical beings, then how could Alexander have such vivid experiences when his brain was supposedly shut down? And how could he have had such a profound conversation with a woman whom he later found out so strongly resembled his dead sister if he wasn't actually experiencing something real and true? Either we are purely physical beings, or we have an immaterial soul. Alexander's experiences, being incompatible with the former, show that the latter must be true.[16]

8. Philosopher René Descartes argues that human persons are made up of two things: an immaterial (non-physical) mind and a material (physical) body. He also believed that the mind and the body causally interact, meaning that they each cause changes in the other. For instance, my mind (by thinking and desiring) causes my hand to reach out and pick up a book. Or my hand, burned by fire, causes my mind to have the conscious experience of pain.

   However, it is unclear how the mind and body could causally interact if one is immaterial and the other is material. Physical things cause changes in other things only through physical contact: a car is stopped through contact with another car's bumper, an arm is burned through contact with fire, and so on. But, if the mind is immaterial, then it cannot physically contact anything,

---

[15]Adapted from an argument discussed in David DeGrazia, "The Definition of Death," *The Stanford Encyclopedia of Philosophy* (Spring 2017 Edition), ed. Edward N. Zalta, <https://plato.stanford.edu/archives/spr2017/entries/death-definition/>

[16]Adapted from the argument in Eben Alexander, *Proof of Heaven: A Neurosurgeon's Journey in the Afterlife* (New York: Simon and Schuster, 2012).

including the body. So, if the mind is immaterial and the body material, then the mind and body cannot causally interact.[17]

9. Without God, life [would have no] purpose. For man and the universe would then be simple accidents of chance, thrust into existence for no reason. Without God, the universe is the result of a cosmic accident, a chance explosion. There is no reason for which it exists. As for man, he is a freak of nature—a blind product of matter plus time plus chance. Man is just a lump of slime that evolved rationality. As one philosopher has put it: "Human life is mounted upon a subhuman pedestal and must shift for itself alone in the heart of a silent and mindless universe."

What is true of the universe and of the human race is also true of us as individuals. If God does not exist, then you are just a miscarriage of nature, thrust into a purposeless universe to live a purposeless life.[18]

10. . . . God, if we are to believe an orthodox story, has prescribed eternal torment [in Hell] as a punishment for insubordination . . . The orthodox story is explicit about the temporal scale of the punishment: it is to go on forever. Many of those who tell the orthodox story are also concerned to emphasize the quality of the punishment. The agonies to be endured by the damned intensify, in unimaginable ways, the sufferings we undergo in our earthly lives . . . Although those who elaborate the orthodox account are sometimes concerned with the fit between crime and punishment, there is no possibility of a genuine balance. For the punishment of the damned is infinitely disproportionate to their crimes. [Therefore, God could never be justified in condemning anyone to Hell.][19]

11. According to the Medical Model of disability, a disability is an impairment that inherently causes a person to face significant personal and social limitations. The Medical Model doesn't imply that disabled people matter less or that people with disabilities don't have lives worth living. The Medical Model does, however, imply that their disabilities make their lives worse, no matter where they live. For example, the Medical Model says that, regardless of the society in which they live, a Deaf person's hearing impairment causes communication challenges, which in turn cause significant personal and social limitations.

A thought experiment can show that the Medical Model doesn't stand up to scrutiny. Suppose you wake up one morning having been magically transported to another planet, where there are humans who have evolved the ability to communicate telepathically. You lack this ability. Relative to them, you are

---

[17]Adapted from an argument by Elisabeth of Bohemia, offered in personal correspondence with Descartes. See *The Philosophical Writings of Descartes: The Correspondence*, vol, 3, ed. John Cottingham, Dugald Murdoch, Robert Stoothoff, and Anthony Kenny (Cambridge, UK: Cambridge University Press, 1991).

[18]Quoted from William Lane Craig, "The Absurdity of Life without God." Available online: http://www.reasonablefaith.org/the-absurdity-of-life-without-god

[19]Quoted from David Lewis (2007), "Divine Evil," in *Philosophers Without Gods*, ed. Louise Antony (Oxford University Press), 232.

telepathically impaired. But is your lack of telepathy a disability? Will your lack of telepathy cause you to face significant limitations?

Importantly, this depends on the details of the society you find yourself in. If much of their business, communication, and entertainment relies on their ability to communicate telepathically, then lacking this ability would make you worse off. And if they stigmatize people who don't have telepathy—if they treat you with pity or scorn—then you would be worse off. In these kinds of conditions, a lack of telepathy is disabling. But suppose this mostly telepathic society was set up to accommodate those who lack telepathy. Suppose that everyone is able and willing to use verbal communication instead of telepathy so no one is excluded from social interaction. Suppose that a lack of telepathy is valued as a form of diversity and is thus not stigmatized. In that society, you wouldn't be disabled by lacking telepathy, even if it was an ability others tended to have.

The point of this hypothetical example is that social arrangements play a key role in determining whether or not this impairment makes you worse off. The same point can be made about real-world impairments. Just as with telepathic impairment, the effects of hearing impairment, vision impairment, mobility impairment, and so on all depend on social arrangements. If deafness, for example, were accommodated and not stigmatized, then the social limitations most Deaf people currently face would be eliminated. This shows the Medical Model is implausible because it totally ignores society's role in turning an impairment into a disability.[20]

12. In Chapter 1 of this book, in the section entitled "The Value and Limitations of Scientific Evidence," we argue that empirical research alone cannot provide answers to moral questions. Put the argument for that conclusion into standard form.

---

[20]Adapted from arguments in Amundson, R., "Disability, Handicap, and the Environment," *Journal of Social Philosophy*, 23, no. (1992): 105–119. See also William Vicars, http://www.lifeprint.com/asl101/topics/disability-deafness.htm

CHAPTER 5

Analyzing Arguments from Principle

CHAPTER GOALS

By reading this chapter and completing the exercises, you will learn how to:

- Represent an Argument from Principle in standard form using the General Form of Argument from Principle.

- Recognize and articulate implicit premises in an Argument from Principle.

- Distinguish premises from the supplementary information that supports them.

ANALYZING ARGUMENTS FROM PRINCIPLE

Arguments that appeal to general moral principles pervade public debates about moral and political controversies, and philosophers writing about practical ethics often use this argument form. This chapter demonstrates how to understand Arguments from Principle by representing them in standard form. Only after you have *understood* an Argument from Principle can you undertake to *evaluate* it, which is the subject of the next chapter.

MORAL JUDGMENTS AND MORAL PRINCIPLES

We sometimes make moral judgments about specific cases, such as: "It was wrong of Dan to lie to Ryoka," or "the Federal mandatory minimum sentence for crack possession is unjust." Moral principles, by contrast, are claims about a *range of cases*. Instead of making a claim merely about the rightness or wrongness of a single case, a moral principle is a claim about what *kinds* of things are right or wrong, good or bad.

You have probably heard people endorse at least a few of the principles from this list of examples:

a. Lying is always wrong.
b. Lying is only permissible in cases where it clearly does more good than harm.

    c. There is nothing morally wrong with lying—though it's best not to get caught.

    d. It is never morally permissible to force an adult to do something against their will.

    e. Helping other people achieve their goals is morally good.

    f. Torture is always morally wrong.

    g. Torture is morally permissible if it is necessary to protect the homeland.

    h. Torture is morally permissible if it is necessary to achieve some important end.

    i. Legal punishment is only morally justified when it will deter future crimes.

    j. Legal punishment is only morally justified when it is deserved.

    k. Gratitude is the morally appropriate response to a sincerely given gift.

    l. Children should obey the explicit commands of their parents.

    m. Children should obey the explicit commands of their parents unless they have good reason to think their parents are wrong.

    n. Character traits that help you get along with others are morally good.

    o. Aesthetic preferences for degrading art are morally bad.

    p. A law is only morally defensible if it promotes the well-being of the people it covers.

    q. A law is only morally defensible if it increases the liberty of the people it covers.

Although these are all examples of moral principles that real people endorse, not all of them can be true. Principles (a) and (b) can't both be true. Principles (f) and (h) can't both be true. What makes these things moral principles is not their truth, but rather that they are general claims about what *types* of choices, behaviors, traits, policies, and laws are forbidden, required, or permissible.

THE GENERAL FORM OF ARGUMENTS FROM PRINCIPLE

An Argument from Principle is an argument that applies a moral principle to a particular case in order to generate a conclusion about that case. In their most basic form, Arguments from Principle are two-premise arguments: they assert a moral principle, and they assert that the case under discussion is of the type governed by the principle.

General Form of Arguments from Principle

    1. Cases of type A have moral status S.

    2. Case x is of type A.

    Therefore, case x has moral status S.

We've already seen an example of an Argument from Principle in Chapter 4: Peter Singer's give-to-charities argument. We represented the argument in standard form this way:

    1. If you are able to prevent terrible suffering at very little cost to yourself, then you ought, morally, to do that. (PRINCIPLE)

    2. Donating 1 percent of your total income to effective charities would prevent terrible suffering at very little cost to yourself. (CASE)

    Therefore, you ought to donate 1 percent of your income to effective charities. (CONCLUSION)

The first premise asserts a moral principle: it says that actions of a certain *type* (those that prevent terrible suffering at little cost to you) have a particular moral status (they are morally required or ought to be done). The second premise asserts that modest charitable giving is an action of the type that prevents terrible suffering at little cost to you. If these two premises are true, then Singer's conclusion has to be true as well: you are morally required to donate to effective charities.

REPRESENTING ARGUMENTS FROM PRINCIPLE IN STANDARD FORM

The process of faithfully representing any argument in standard form involves three phases. First, identify the *conclusion* the author is arguing for. Second, articulate the key claims the author appeals to in order to justify that conclusion; that is, articulate the argument's *premises*. Third, reread both your standard-form representation and the author's original passage to confirm that you have accurately and charitably represented the author's argument. (For a more detailed discussion of standard form, see Chapter 4.)

If you have recognized that you are working with an Argument from Principle, phase two of this process becomes easier, because you know exactly what key claims you need to find. First, you must articulate the principle the argument relies on. Second, you must articulate the author's claim about the relationship between the principle and the case at hand.

Example: The no-immoral-laws argument for voluntary active euthanasia

"Voluntary active euthanasia" is a term describing situations in which a doctor, at the request of a terminally ill patient, directly causes a patient's death by, for example, administering an overdose of pain medication. Most states in the United States ban doctors from administering life-ending drugs to patients who have requested help in dying. The following argument makes the case that laws and policies banning voluntary active euthanasia ought to be changed.

    Laws and policies should be arranged in such a way that they do not regularly require people to act immorally. The Fugitive Slave Act in America required people to turn escaped slaves over to slave hunters. Laws in Nazi Germany required neighbors to notify authorities of the presence of suspected Jews. These are two of the many possible illustrations of shameful, despicable laws. They were shameful and despicable laws *because* they required their subjects to act immorally.

But think, now, about what laws banning voluntary active euthanasia require of doctors. In cases of terminal illness, it is sometimes the case that patients choose to die, and so request the cessation of treatment. In some of those cases, patients will suffer for weeks or months before they finally die. In those cases, voluntary active euthanasia (VAE) would support and promote patient self-determination by allowing them to choose their time and circumstances of their own death. VAE would also improve patient well-being by saving the patient from pointless and unwanted suffering. VAE, in other words, promotes the very values doctors have a moral obligation to promote. Laws and policies *banning* voluntary active euthanasia thus prevent doctors from promoting patient autonomy and well-being; which is to say, laws banning VAE require doctors to act immorally. That's why laws and policies banning VAE should be scrapped in favor of policies that permit it under certain carefully regulated circumstances.

First, what is the conclusion the author argues for? In this case, it's clearly flagged, right at the end of the passage: "laws and policies banning VAE should be scrapped in favor of policies that permit it under certain carefully regulated circumstances."

Second, what premises are essential to make the case for this conclusion? Because this is an Argument from Principle, you can be confident that there will be two key premises. The moral principle, explained in the first paragraph, asserts that laws that require people to act immorally should be changed. This should stand out to you as a moral principle. It isn't a claim about any specific law—rather, it is a general claim about what *types* of laws morally ought to be changed. The second premise, defended in some detail in the second paragraph, asserts that laws banning voluntary active euthanasia require doctors to act immorally.

In standard form for Argument from Principle:

1. Laws that require people to act immorally should be changed. (PRINCIPLE)
2. Laws banning voluntary active euthanasia require doctors to act immorally. (CASE)

So, laws banning voluntary active euthanasia should be changed. (CONCLUSION)

Would the author of the original passage approve of this standard-form representation of the argument? We think so.

Example: The protect-vulnerable-people argument against voluntary active euthanasia

Proponents of voluntary active euthanasia too often have a skewed view of the fundamental purpose of laws and policies. What laws and policies ought to do is to protect vulnerable people from harm. That's the fundamental reason why voluntary active euthanasia should be illegal: making it illegal would protect the vulnerable from harm.

Consider the issue from the perspective of someone with a terminal diagnosis who wants—as many, many patients in the real world actually do—to fight on until the end. And consider the additional pressures that would be piled on them were voluntary active euthanasia an available option. They would have to justify to their loved ones why they are continuing to live, even though their suffering puts serious emotional strain on the family. They would have to justify to their community why they are continuing to spend financial resources when there is no hope of recovery. They would have to justify to the doctors why they are taking up a bed in a hospital that could instead be occupied by a patient with a more hopeful prognosis. In such situations, it is likely that many patients would choose euthanasia when that isn't what they themselves actually want. They would, in short, be pressured by their communities into choosing death. There is no more profound harm than that. Laws banning voluntary active euthanasia effectively protect terminal patients—people in one of the most vulnerable positions imaginable—from exactly this harm.

First, what is the conclusion the author argues for? In this case, it's embedded in the first paragraph, but relatively clearly flagged: "voluntary active euthanasia should be illegal."

Second, what premises are essential to make the case for this conclusion? Because this is an Argument from Principle, you can be confident that there will be two key premises. In this passage, the principle and the case claim are both quickly summarized in the first paragraph. The second paragraph then provides support for the argument's case claim.

Here's how we would represent this argument in standard form for Argument from Principle:

1. We ought to have laws that protect vulnerable people from harm. (PRINCIPLE)
2. Laws banning VAE protect vulnerable people (the terminally ill) from harm. (CASE)

   Therefore, VAE ought to be illegal. (CONCLUSION)

Your own standard-form representation of this passage is probably not *exactly* the same as ours. That might be OK. For instance, this is also a perfectly good representation of the passage:

1. If a law would protect vulnerable people, then we ought to pass the law. (PRINCIPLE)
2. Laws banning VAE would protect vulnerable people. (CASE)

   So, we ought to pass laws banning VAE. (CONCLUSION)

Alternatively, if you tried to stay as close as possible to the General Form of Argument from Principle, you might have ended up with this:

1. Laws that protect vulnerable people from harm are laws we ought to have. (PRINCIPLE)
2. Laws banning VAE are laws that protect vulnerable people. (CASE)

Therefore, laws banning VAE are laws we ought to have. (CONCLUSION)

All three of these standard-form representations of the passage clearly express the argument; they say the same thing in three different ways. English grammar allows for a wide variety of expressions of the same thought, and the particular approach you choose is, in part, a matter of personal style. Your goal is to represent the argument in a way that would secure the approval of its author, and differences in phrasing and expression are perfectly compatible with that goal as long as they clearly, accurately, and charitably represent the author's thoughts.

ANALYZING ARGUMENTS WITH IMPLICIT PREMISES

Arguments published in essays or offered in public debates often include *implicit premises* that are crucial to the argument but not explicitly stated by the author and *supplementary information* that supports or clarifies the premises and conclusion. (See Chapter 4 for a more detailed discussion of implicit premises and supplementary information.) When analyzing arguments, you should identify implicit premises and state them explicitly in your standard-form representation. Understanding the General Form for Arguments from Principle makes this task easier.

Example: Genetic modification is unnatural

Genetically modified organisms (GMOs) include crops, like corn and soybeans, that are genetically engineered to have desirable traits, such as resistance to certain pests. Although GMOs might have some practical benefits, we should not use them. Genetically modifying crops is morally wrong because it is unnatural.

The first sentence of this passage provides a definition of the term "GMO"; this sentence is not a premise or conclusion but rather an explanation of a term used in a premise and the conclusion. The third sentence contains the entire argument, the explicitly stated parts of which we could represent as follows:

1. . . .
2. Genetically modifying crops is unnatural. (CASE)

So, genetically modifying crops is morally wrong. (CONCLUSION)

If we recognize that what we have here is two-thirds of an Argument from Principle, then identifying the implicit premise is easy.

The Argument	General Form of Argument from Principle
1. . . .	**1.** Cases of type *A* have moral status *S*.
2. Genetically modifying crops is unnatural.	**2.** Case *x* is of type *A*.
So, genetically modifying crops is wrong.	So, case *x* has moral status *S*.

To complete this Argument from Principle we need to supply premise 1: the moral principle that attributes a certain moral status to a range of cases. In this argument, the implicit premise must assert that actions of the type *unnatural* have the moral status *wrong*. Thus, the completed argument goes like this:

1. Unnatural actions are morally wrong. (PRINCIPLE)
2. Genetically modifying crops is unnatural. (CASE)

So, genetically modifying crops is wrong. (CONCLUSION)

It is important to make explicit the implicit premise because it is an essential component of the argument. We have not *understood* the argument until we recognize that it is grounded in the moral principle that unnatural actions are morally wrong. And because this principle is an essential component of the argument, *evaluating* the argument will require evaluating the principle. (The method of counterexample discussed in Chapters 3 and 6 reveals that this implicit principle has serious flaws.) These lessons generalize: identifying and articulating implicit premises is *always* an important part of understanding and evaluating arguments.

Example: A death-bed lie

On his deathbed in 2017, Michael Elliott asked his wife, Teresa, if President Donald Trump had been impeached.[1] In response, Teresa lied. She told Michael that Trump had indeed been impeached, because she thought this would make Michael's last moments happier. Teresa's action was wrong, because lying is only permissible when it is the only way to save lives.

The moral argument is contained in the last sentence, where the moral principle and the conclusion are both explicitly stated. We can represent them this way:

1. Lying is only permissible when it is the only way to save lives. (PRINCIPLE)
2. . . .

Therefore, Teresa's lie was not permissible. (CONCLUSION)

Premise 2 is left implicit in the original passage and should be stated explicitly in our standard form representation. Once we've recognized that the missing

---

[1]This is a hypothetical argument based upon a real life case. https://www.washingtonpost.com/news/the-fix/wp/2017/04/18/she-wanted-her-ex-husband-to-die-with-a-happy-memory-she-told-him-trump-has-been-impeached/?utm_term=.a9b16f979563

piece is a statement of the relationship between the case and the principle, it is easy to articulate the implicit premise. The author believes that the case in question (Teresa's lie) is of the type the principle says is wrong (it's not necessary for saving lives). Thus, we have the complete representation of the argument:

1. Lying is only permissible when it is the only way to save lives. (PRINCIPLE)
2. Teresa's lie was not necessary to save lives. (CASE)

    Therefore, Teresa's lie was not permissible. (CONCLUSION)

If you tried to stay as close as possible to the General Form for Arguments from Principle, you might have ended up with this:

1. Lies that are not necessary to save lives are not morally permissible. (PRINCIPLE)
2. Teresa's lie was a lie that was not necessary to save lives. (CASE)

    Therefore, Teresa's lie was not morally permissible. (CONCLUSION)

Both standard-form representations of the passage clearly express the argument; they say the same thing in different ways.

The lesson: understanding the General Form of Arguments from Principle makes it easy to recognize and articulate premises authors have left unstated.

ANALYZING PASSAGES WITH SUPPLEMENTARY INFORMATION

Arguments in the real world typically include supplementary information. This information is usually important to the author's case—it provides support for premises, and it provides context, illustration, or information intended to help the audience understand the argument. A standard-form representation of an argument should sort the premises from the material that supports them, and present only the premises themselves.

When you are first learning to represent arguments in standard form, sorting premises from supplementary information can sometimes feel like digging for fossils in an expansive field. In Chapter 4 we identified several common types of supplementary information; being on the lookout for those types can make it a little bit easier to sift the fossils from the soil. But if you have recognized that the passage you are analyzing contains an Argument from Principle, using the General Form of Argument from Principle as your guide makes it *much* easier to sort premises from the supplementary information that supports them.

Example: The necessary protest argument

On July 6, 2016, Philando Castile was pulled over for a broken taillight by police officer Jeronimo Yanez in Falcon Heights, Minnesota. Within forty seconds, Yanez had shot Castile seven times and the incident had been captured and shortly thereafter broadcast on social media by Castile's fiancé. Many members of the community and the public were outraged by what they saw as another example of the oppression and violence African Americans face at the hands of the police. When Yanez was later found not guilty of criminal charges in the shooting, people were understandably frustrated and angry. In protest of the verdict, a group of people marched onto Interstate 94, shutting it down for several hours.

This form of protest is unjustifiable. A disruptive method of protest is justified only if it is a necessary means to rectifying injustice. It would not be justifiable, for instance, for sanitation workers upset about their wages to go around throwing garbage in the road to illustrate the importance of their work. This kind of protest would not be justifiable because it isn't necessary for making changes toward fairer wages. The same principle holds here. It was unjustifiable for protesters to shut down I-94 in response to the Yanez verdict, because doing so was not necessary to achieve racial justice in policing.

This passage explicitly states the premises and the conclusion, but it also includes supplementary information. The sentences in the first paragraph provide *background information* to help us understand the context of the moral controversy. The sentence beginning "It would not be justifiable, for instance, for sanitation workers. . ." is an *illustrative example*. None of these sentences is a premise; all are intended to clarify and support the component premises of this Argument from Principle.

The principle the author defends concerns the permissibility of disruptive protests. The specific case in question is the protest that shut down I-94. Represented in standard form, using the General Form as our guide, the argument looks like this:

1. A protest is justified only if it is a necessary means to rectifying injustice. (PRINCIPLE)
2. Shutting down I-94 after the Yanez verdict was not a necessary means to rectifying injustice. (CASE)

So, shutting down I-94 after the Yanez verdict was not justified. (CONCLUSION)

The lesson: understanding the General Form of Arguments from Principle makes it easy to sift premises from the supplementary information that supports them.

WHY USE ARGUMENTS FROM PRINCIPLE?

Nearly everyone has had to make decisions they recognize as morally difficult. And most of us, when faced with those decisions, have found ourselves searching for principles that might help. When we recognize that a moral principle we accept applies to a situation we're in, it is easier to see what that situation requires of us. But figuring out which moral principles are principles we ought to accept is not easy. Nor is it always clear which moral principles apply in real-life situations. Imagine you find yourself in a situation in which telling the truth will seriously hurt another person's feelings. Are principles related to truth-telling the relevant ones in that situation? Or are principles related to kindness the relevant ones? It can be difficult to tell.

Arguments from Principle formalize the everyday process of reasoning with moral principles. Articulating a candidate moral principle and the relationship that principle bears to the controversial case clarifies the argument and makes it easier to understand. Keeping those two components distinct makes it easier to evaluate the strength of each claim individually. Analyzing principle-based arguments by representing them in standard form can thus improve discussions, debates, and personal reflection about practical moral controversies.

REVIEW

Arguments from Principle support a moral conclusion about a specific case by applying a moral principle to that case. Arguments with this structure are common in philosophical writing and in public discourse. Familiarity with the General Form of Arguments from Principle will make it easier to represent these arguments in standard form.

Moral principle: a claim about the moral status of a range of cases, such as types of actions, types of traits, types of policies, etc.

General Form of Arguments from Principle:

1. Cases of type *A* have moral status *S*. (PRINCIPLE)
2. Case *x* is of type *A*. (CASE)

Therefore, case *x* has moral status *S*. (CONCLUSION)

To test your understanding of the material introduced in this chapter, complete the Demonstration Exercises and then check your answers against the solutions that follow.

Demonstration Exercises

Demonstration Exercises are designed to give you immediate feedback on your grasp of the skills introduced in this chapter. To use them effectively, you should attempt answers to all of them, then check your work against our suggested answers, which follow. For a detailed explanation of how best to use Demonstration Exercises, read the book's Introduction.

Demonstration Exercises 5A: Identifying Premises and Conclusions

Exercise Instructions: Supply the missing premise or conclusion to make a properly structured Argument from Principle.

1.

   1. It is wrong for doctors to enter into agreements that pressure them to make decisions that are not in the best interest of their patients.

(continued)

2. . . .

So, it's wrong for doctors to become paid spokespeople for pharmaceutical companies.

2.

1. . . .

2. Illegally downloading movies uses the fruits of someone's labor without their permission.

Therefore, illegally downloading movies is wrong.

Demonstration Exercises 5B: Representing Arguments from Principle in Standard Form

Exercise Instructions: Represent the following arguments in standard form using the General Form of Argument from Principle.

1. In favor of affirmative action

There's nothing wrong with colleges using affirmative action policies to give admission preference to members of disadvantaged minorities over equally qualified white students. Policies that promote a diverse range of perspectives in the incoming group of students are morally permissible. Affirmative action policies do that.

2. Against affirmative action

Any policy that treats people differently based upon their gender is oppressive. So, using affirmative action policies that favor a woman over an equally qualified male candidate is oppressive.

3. Against the permissibility of suicide[2]

Life is God's gift to us. And it is wrong to destroy or discard a gift you have been so lovingly given. That's why it is wrong to commit suicide.

4. For the permissibility of suicide

As long as you are not seriously harming anyone else, you are not doing anything wrong. Thus, it is not wrong to commit suicide as long as you are not seriously harming anyone else.

5. Coretta Scott King on Jefferson Sessions

This is the first paragraph of the 1986 letter Coretta Scott King (who was married to Martin Luther King, Jr.) sent to Strom Thurmond (who was Chairman of the Senate Judiciary Committee) opposing the nomination of Jefferson Sessions to a judgeship in the Federal Court.

I write to express my sincere opposition to the confirmation of Jefferson B. Sessions as a federal district court judge for the Southern District of Alabama. My professional and personal roots in Alabama are deep and lasting. Anyone who has used the power of his office as United States Attorney to intimidate and chill the free exercise of the ballot by citizens should *not* be elevated to our

---

[2]Adapted from an argument made by Saint Thomas, Aquinas in *Summa Theologiae* Q64, 5.

courts. Mr. Sessions has used the awesome powers of his office in a shabby attempt to intimidate and frighten elderly black voters. For this reprehensible conduct, he should not be rewarded with a federal judgeship.[3]

6. The best consequences protest argument

On July 6, 2016, Philando Castile was pulled over for a broken taillight by police officer Jeronimo Yanez in Falcon Heights, Minnesota. Within forty seconds, Yanez had shot Castile seven times and the incident had been captured and shortly thereafter broadcast on social media by Castile's fiancé. Many members of the community and the public were outraged by what they saw as another example of the oppression and violence African Americans face at the hands of the police.

When Jeronimo Yanez was acquitted of the shooting of Philando Castile, those members of the community committed to racial justice had several options. They could channel their anger by filing for a permit to engage in a public protest march,, they could focus their energies solely on using the typical legal channels to support changes to problematic laws or police training procedures, or they do all of that but also engage in direct, disruptive protest. Many protesters undertook the latter: they engaged in a predominantly peaceful march to shut down I-94 in order to force people to pay attention to the problem of racial injustice. This surely disrupted people's lives, but that's the point: no other method of protest would be as likely to result in progress towards eliminating racial injustice in policing. For that reason, the protest was morally justified.

7. The medical necessity argument against SRS

Background for demonstration arguments #7 and #8. What follows are paraphrases of two arguments that were common in the early days of the availability of sex reassignment surgery (SRS) for transgender people. "Sex reassignment surgery" (also sometimes known as "gender confirmation surgery") is an umbrella term for a variety of surgeries intended to bring a transgender person's physical sex characteristics more closely in line with their gender identity.[4] When modern techniques became available in the 1980s, these surgeries were controversial in the medical community. So imagine that it's 1984, you work at a hospital, and you're listening in on arguments about whether or not your hospital should begin offering SRS to patients who want it.

Patients who request SRS are requesting a surgical alteration of their bodies for reasons that have nothing to do with promoting the physical health of their body. The tissues the surgeon is asked to remove or modify are not damaged or diseased. In SRS, it is *healthy* tissues that go under the knife. But any surgery that fits that description is almost certainly morally wrong; surgery should *only* be used when it is necessary to promote the physical health of the body.

Imagine that a patient walked into a hospital and requested to have his ring fingers surgically removed, not because there was anything wrong with them, but because he really didn't want to have ring fingers. Any surgeon who

---

[3]https://www.documentcloud.org/documents/3259988-Scott-King-1986-Letter-and-Testimony-Signed.html

[4]For an overview of terminology, and a bit more information on SRS, start here: http://www.transequality.org/issues/resources/transgender-terminology

(continued)

performed that surgery would be doing something morally wrong, because they would be violating the principle that surgery should only be used to promote the health of the patient's body. Sex reassignment surgery violates the same principle, and so is always morally wrong.

8. The well-being argument in favor of SRS

There is more to human well-being than just the health of bodily tissues, and surgical techniques can promote human well-being even in cases where the patient's body is not damaged or diseased. Consider a few examples. Surgical correction of a cleft lip does not promote the physical health of a child's body; the surgery is entirely cosmetic. But such surgeries make it easier for a child to navigate the horrible, superficial, and judgmental world of other children, and so surgeons ought to do them. The same is true of surgeries to correct crossed eyes. It's a surgery that has no effect on the physical health of a person's tissues, but it makes social integration easier, and so promotes well-being. Women who have undergone successful mastectomies to treat breast cancer often choose to have their breasts surgically reconstructed. Breast reconstruction doesn't promote the physical health of their bodies—it was the mastectomy that did that. But it does promote their well-being by restoring their physical body to something similar to what they have lived with their entire life.

All of these examples make the point that surgery is a good, morally justifiable choice not only in cases in which it promotes the physical health of a patient's body, but also in cases in which it promotes the general well-being of the patient. Does SRS promote the well-being of the people who choose it? The data on that is clear: in the overwhelming majority of cases, transgender people who seek SRS are happier after they receive it. SRS is thus morally permissible because it promotes the well-being of the patients who receive it.

Solutions to Demonstration Exercises 5

Demonstration Exercises are most useful if you make your best attempt to complete them before you look at the answers. If you haven't yet attempted answers to all the Demonstration Exercises, go back and do that now.

Demonstration Exercises 5A: Identifying Premises and Conclusions

1.
    1. It is wrong for doctors to enter into agreements that pressure them to make decisions that are not in the best interest of their patients.
    2. *Working as paid spokespeople for pharmaceutical companies puts pressure on doctors to make decisions that are not in the best interest of their patients.*

       So, it's wrong for doctors to become paid spokespeople for pharmaceutical companies.

2.

1. *It is morally wrong to use the fruits of someone's labor without their permission.*

2. Illegally downloading movies uses the fruits of someone's labor without their permission.

Therefore, illegally downloading movies is wrong.

Demonstration Exercises 5B: Representing Arguments from Principle in Standard Form

Note: your standard-form representations should identify the same principle, case claim, and conclusion as we have, but variation in wording or expression is perfectly fine.

1. **In favor of affirmative action**
   1. Policies that promote a diverse range of perspectives are morally permissible. (PRINCIPLE)
   2. Affirmative action policies promote a diverse range of perspectives. (CASE)

   Therefore, affirmative action policies are morally permissible. (CONCLUSION)

2. **Against affirmative action**
   1. Policies that treat people differently based on their gender are oppressive. (PRINCIPLE)
   2. Affirmative action policies treat people differently based on their gender. (CASE)

   Thus, affirmative action policies are oppressive. (CONCLUSION)

3. **Against the permissibility of suicide**
   1. It is wrong to destroy a gift you have been lovingly given. (PRINCIPLE)
   2. Suicide destroys a gift (life) you've been lovingly given (by God). (CASE)

   So, suicide is wrong. (CONCLUSION)

4. **For the permissibility of suicide**
   1. Actions that don't seriously harm anyone else are morally permissible. (PRINCIPLE)
   2. Some instances of suicide don't seriously harm anyone else. (CASE)

   Therefore, some instances of suicide are morally permissible. (CONCLUSION)

5. **Coretta Scott King on Jefferson Sessions**
   1. No one who has used their political powers to intimidate voters should be allowed to serve as a federal judge. (PRINCIPLE)
   2. Jeff Sessions used his political powers to intimidate voters. (CASE)

   Thus, Jeff Sessions should not be allowed to serve as a federal judge. (CONCLUSION)

(continued)

6. The best consequences protest argument

  1. A method of protest is justified if it is the method most likely to result in progress towards eliminating an injustice. (PRINCIPLE)

  2. Shutting down I-94 was the method of protest most likely to result in progress towards racial injustice in policing. (CASE)

  So, shutting down I-94 was justified. (CONCLUSION)

7. The medical necessity argument against SRS

  1. Surgery is only morally permissible when it is necessary to promote the physical health of the body. (PRINCIPLE)

  2. SRS is *not* necessary to promote the physical health of the body. (CASE)

  Therefore, SRS is *not* morally permissible. (CONCLUSION)

8. The well-being argument in favor of SRS

  1. Surgery is morally permissible when it promotes the well-being of the patient. (PRINCIPLE)

  2. SRS promotes the well-being of transgender people who request it. (CASE)

  Thus, SRS is morally permissible. (CONCLUSION)

CHAPTER 5 PRACTICE EXERCISES

ANALYZING ARGUMENTS FROM PRINCIPLE

Exercises 5A: Identifying Premises and Conclusions

Exercise Instructions: *supply the missing premise or conclusion to make a properly structured Argument from Principle.*

1.

  1. You ought to minimize the amount of pollution you generate.
  2. . . . .

  So, you ought to recycle your bottles and cans.

2.

  1. Lying is always wrong.
  2. . . . .

  So, intentionally misrepresenting your finances on your tax forms is wrong.

3.

  1. A person's personal preferences are morally objectionable if those preferences place a disproportionate psychological burden on a subgroup of people.[5]

---

[5]Adapted from an argument in Robin Zheng, "Why Yellow Fever Isn't Flattering: A Case Against Racial Fetishes," *Journal of the American Philosophical Association*, 2, no, 3 (2016): 400–419.

   2. The personal preference of some white men to date or marry Asian women places a disproportionate psychological burden on Asian and Asian-American women.

   Therefore, . . .

4.
   1. An action is racist only if it is based upon harmful and false stereotypes about people of a particular race.[6]
   2. At least some white men who prefer to date Asian women are not acting based upon harmful and false stereotypes about people of a particular race.

   Therefore, . . .

5.
   1. . . .
   2. Cheating on an exam gives a student an unfair advantage over others in the job market.

   Thus, it's wrong for a student to cheat on an exam.

6.
   1. A practice should be illegal if it encourages desperate people to do potentially harmful or degrading things.
   2. . . .

   So, prostitution should be illegal.

7.
   1. It's wrong to do things that make serious problems worse.[7]
   2. . . .

   Therefore, driving a gas-guzzling car is wrong.

8.
   1. . . .
   2. Illegally downloading movies doesn't take anything physical from anyone else.

   Thus, illegally downloading movies is not wrong.

---

[6]Adapted from an argument discussed in Raja Halwani, "Racial Sexual Desires," in *The Philosophy of Sex*, 7th Ed (London: Rowman & Littlefield, 2017).

[7]Adapted from an argument discussed in Walter Sinnott-Armstrong, "It's Not *My* Fault: Global Warming and Individual Moral Obligations," *Perspectives on Climate Change: Science, Economics, Politics, Ethics*, (Bingley: Emerald, 2005): 293–315.

Exercises 5B: Representing Arguments from Principle in Standard Form

Exercise Instructions: *Represent the following arguments in standard form using the General Form of Argument from Principle.*

1. It's always wrong to end a human life. Abortion ends a human life. So, abortion is always wrong.
2. Abortion should clearly be legal. It is, after all, health care.
3. Suicide is always wrong, because it is always wrong to kill an innocent human being, and suicide does that.
4. Killing is only wrong when the thing killed wants not to be killed. (Bacteria, for example, have no desire to live, which is why it's perfectly fine to kill them.) First-trimester fetuses have no desires at all, so they do not have the desire not to be killed. That is why abortion is not morally wrong.
5. There's nothing wrong with using other people's property as long as your use doesn't cause them any unhappiness. Since using your neighbor's Wi-Fi internet without their permission doesn't cause them any unhappiness, it isn't wrong.
6. A person is morally required to aid others only if doing so doesn't require using their own hard-earned money. So, we're not obligated to donate 1 percent of our income to effective poverty relief agencies, because doing so would require using our own hard-earned money.
7. It's always wrong to do things that cause harm, however indirect, to other people. Driving a gas-guzzling car (a car that gets far lower gas mileage than the average car) harms other people by contributing to global warming. So, it's wrong to drive a gas-guzzling car.[8]
8. There's nothing wrong with driving a gas-guzzling car just for fun—tons of people do it.
9. Obviously, no one deserves blame for doing something that's perfectly legal. It therefore follows that we're totally misguided if we blame people for driving gas-guzzling cars.
10. Why do some people believe it is wrong to eat animals? It isn't! Non-human animals eat each other all the time!
11. There's nothing wrong with eating animals. Do you really think that, if given half a chance, those animals wouldn't eat you?
12. I can't believe you tattled on Heather for cheating on the chemistry midterm. That was so wrong of you to do that to her. It's not like she killed someone.
13. It was completely wrong of your chemistry professor to fail you just because you didn't turn in any of the work. She *knows* you need that class to graduate.
14. Does the pornography industry wrongfully exploit women, or is a job in porn just another job like any other? I think it is clear that the pornography industry

---

[8]Adapted from an argument discussed in Walter Sinnott-Armstrong, "It's Not *My* Fault: Global Warming and Individual Moral Obligations," *Perspectives on Climate Change: Science, Economics, Politics, Ethics*, (Bingley: Emerald, 2005): 293–315.

wrongfully exploits women. Many of the women who work in the industry would leave it if they had good alternatives for well-paid work. That means the pornography industry makes money off of people doing things they wouldn't otherwise do if they had other options. Any industry that does that is a wrongfully exploitative industry.

15. The Black Lives Matter (BLM) movement is a response to racial disparities in policing. BLM protesters hope to raise awareness about, among other things, the inordinate violence African Americans and other people of color suffer in the United States at the hands of the police. BLM uses various actions to try to achieve their goals, including organized marches and protests. Sometimes, however, they're met with counter-protesters. In some encounters, these (mostly White) counter-protesters have shouted "All lives matter!" in response to BLM's chant of "Black lives matter." The counter-protestors' aim seems to be to counter what they see as an unfair focus on one group's needs.

    The "All lives matter!" chant has itself become controversial, with some people claiming that it is racist for white people to shout "All lives matter!" at a BLM demonstration. Regardless of the merits of the counter-protesters' views, chanting "All lives matter" is not racist. After all, an action is racist only if it is based upon feelings of hatred for a racial group, and chanting "All lives matter" doesn't express hatred for anyone.

16. It's always wrong to deprive an animal of the ability to do things that are natural for its species. For that reason, keeping animals in zoos is wrong. I mean, look at how animals live in zoos. Polar bears pace back and forth around concrete pools and get no chance to hunt on the ice as they would in the wild. Penguins wait by the door for zookeepers to bring in buckets of fish instead of exercising their natural skill at catching prey in the water. Clearly, zoo animals' lives are a pale imitation of those their wild counterparts live.

17. Many medical treatments and procedures are tested out on non-human animals. For instance, cancer drugs and pacemaker implants are tested out on dogs, monkeys, or mice to see if they are safe. Sometimes, the animals end up being harmed or killed by the procedures. Some people claim this is morally wrong, because those animals have rights. But that's nonsense. A being has the right not to have potentially unsafe medical experiments performed on them only if it is capable of the sort of complex thought that you and I can do. But dogs, monkeys, and mice are not capable of that—they can't read novels, do algebra, or discuss the merits of different political policies. Thus, dogs, monkeys, and mice don't have a right not to have potentially unsafe medical experiments performed on them.

18. The Makah Tribe is a culture indigenous to the Pacific Northwest. Among many practices special to the Makah is an annual whale hunt, in which men of the tribe set out in cedar canoes to hunt, and hopefully kill, a gray whale. The returning hunters are met with ceremonies and songs, and precise rules govern how the whale is divided up between the families who make up the tribe.

    Many American and European environmentalists are especially protective of whales. This has led some environmentalists to criticize the Makah culture for its annual whale hunt. In criticizing Makah whale hunts, environmentalists go too far.

Makah culture views whale hunts as spiritually important and good, and when Makah people head out on a whale hunt, they are doing something their own culture endorses. It is always wrong for a person from one culture to criticize the culturally sanctioned practices of a person from another culture. It is therefore morally wrong for environmentalists—who are not Makah themselves—to criticize a Makah person for hunting gray whales.

19. Placebos are pills or other substances that look like medications, but are designed to have no medical effect. Sugar pills, which look like prescription pills but are actually made of a small amount of sugar, are a classic example of a placebo. Doctors have known for a long time that if they offer patients placebos and tell them the pills are effective medication, placebos often do help. When patients *mistakenly believe* they are taking medically effective drugs, they often see improvement in their symptoms.

Some doctors believe it is morally permissible to use placebos. These doctors are wrong. Even if placebos are sometimes effective, it is always wrong for doctors to use placebos on patients, because it is always wrong for health care professionals to deceive their patients.

20. Physicians are bound by the principle of non-maleficence: they ought never harm. But physician-assisted suicide harms the patient—it ends their life. Thus, physician-assisted suicide is morally impermissible.

21. Physicians ought to respect patient autonomy. This is why voluntarily chosen physician assisted suicide is permissible: when a person has autonomously chosen to end their life, respecting the patient's autonomy requires assisting them in carrying out this decision.

22. I think you'll agree that it's always wrong to destroy someone else's property. But that's what you're doing when you commit suicide. Your life is the property of God, your creator. So, killing yourself is wrong.[9]

23. Everything naturally loves itself, and therefore it naturally seeks to preserve itself and to resist what would injure it as much as it can. Suicide, then, is contrary to a natural human inclination. So, suicide is wrong, because we should always act in conformity with natural human inclinations.[10]

24. Several Christian wedding-cake bakers have refused to bake cakes for same-sex weddings, citing their personal religious conviction that same-sex relationships are offensive to God. Some members and allies of the LGBTQ community have called for these Christian bakers to be fired, or sued, or otherwise penalized. These calls for punishment are misguided. No one should ever be penalized for acting according to their personal religious convictions.

25. Some Christian wedding-cake bakers believe that same-sex relationships are morally wrong. They are free to believe that, but they still have a moral obligation to bake wedding cakes for same-sex couples, and if they refuse to serve

---

[9]Adapted from an argument made by Saint Thomas Aquinas, in *Summa Theologiae* Q64, 5.
[10]Adapted from an argument by Saint Thomas Aquinas, in *Summa Theologica*, II–II.

same-sex couples they should be penalized. A business owner only has a right to refuse a customer if refusing is necessary to protect employees or other customers from harm.

26. Our hospital has an emergency situation: two patients are in the Emergency Department (ED) who need a ventilator due to severe cases of Covid-19. (We can't refer patients elsewhere, because all regional hospitals are similarly overloaded.) Unfortunately, there's only one ventilator left, and we need to decide whom to give it to.

    The first patient to arrive in the ED was Paul. Paul is an otherwise healthy single 56-year-old man who works in the human resources department for a large retail company. If we give the ventilator to Paul, doctors anticipate he will make a full recovery and have an estimated life expectancy of 80 years. The second patient, Lin, arrived and was assessed about fifteen minutes after Paul. Lin is a 30-year-old nurse and parent of two children who works at a local nursing home. If we give Lin the ventilator, doctors expect she will recover and have a life expectancy of at least 80 years.

    People in the hospital are acting like this is a tough choice. But, there's clearly only one fair way to make decisions like this. When medical resources are scarce, they should be distributed on a first-come, first-serve basis. For that reason, we should give the ventilator to Paul.

27. Look inside the mouth of a human being. You'll find canine teeth and incisors. These teeth are adapted for eating flesh, not vegetables. It isn't just our teeth—the general biological evidence is overwhelming: the human body is by nature able to eat meat. Look to the earliest cave paintings: they show humans hunting animals. It isn't just the cave paintings—the general archaeological evidence is also overwhelming: from our earliest days on Earth, human beings have eaten meat.

    In short, the scientific evidence from multiple disciplines proves that eating meat is natural for human beings. And surely behaviors that are *natural* for human beings are *morally permissible* for human beings—it would be absurd to claim otherwise. Therefore, eating meat is morally permissible for human beings.

28. In recent years, more school children have begun to identify as trans and to request accommodation of a gender identity that is not the identity they were assigned at birth. In practice, these accommodations usually amount to a request to be referred to using different pronouns, and a request to use the bathroom that corresponds to their gender identity. For example, a student who began elementary school as a boy might prefer to express the gender of a girl, and so request to be referred to with feminine pronouns and to be allowed to use the girls' bathroom.

    These requests for accommodation in pronouns and bathrooms have caused controversy, especially in conservative religious communities. But all too often, the argument against respecting a child's gender identity does nothing more than appeal to a religious text or edict. Public schools cannot avoid setting rules governing the behavior of the children who attend them—that is part of their job. But public schools should never set those rules based solely on highly contested religious premises, and it appears that the only way to argue against accommodating the requests of trans kids is to appeal to highly contested religious premises. That's why public schools should accommodate children's preferences about how they express their gender identity.

29. After asking and receiving assurance of confidentiality, a new client, full of remorse, tells his psychologist that two months earlier he gave his 73-year-old wife sleeping pills to end her life peacefully, and then he staged a bathtub drowning that resulted in an accidental death ruling by the medical examiner. His wife, he says, suffered from advanced Alzheimer's disease and was suffering greatly as the disease progressed. What should the psychologist do here? Should she report the client?

   She most certainly should not. The right action in a situation is the one that could be expected to produce the most total happiness when you weigh up the effects on everyone. In this case, keeping the patient's confidentiality would produce the most happiness, so that's what the psychologist should do.[11]

30. A fetus *potentially* has a right to life. (If allowed to develop, it will become a child, and children definitely have a right to life.) If someone *potentially* has a right, then we should treat them as though they already do have that right. For this reason, we should treat fetuses as if they have the same right to life that children have.

31. In most societies all over the world, women's primary role is in the home, while men are in charge of business, industry, and government. This division of labor between the sexes is so common that the examples dwarf the exceptions. Indeed, that this arrangement has been so long-held and so commonplace shows it to be justifiable. After all, if it wasn't best for society, then why would it be so universal a phenomenon?[12]

32. That women should primarily be in the home while men take responsibility for public offices and institutions is evident given the difference in men and women's natures. Women, as a group, have innate inclinations and abilities that better suit them for the important task of nurturing children and creating a loving home environment, while men are naturally better suited to public life and office due to their superior capacity for reasoning and emotional control. Thus, the natural differences in inclinations and abilities of men and women justify women's subordination to men and their exclusion from control of public life and office and justify enforcing this arrangement through law.[13]

33. Reginald Featherbottom is notorious for his view, explained in his book *The Implications of Racial Inferiority for Public Policy*, that different racial groups

---

[11]Adapted from case 6–2, page 119, in Koocher and Keith-Spiegel, *Ethics in Psychology: Professional Standards and Cases*, 2nd Ed. (London/New York: Oxford University Press, 1998).

[12]Adapted from an argument critiqued in J. S. Mill, *The Subjection of Women* (London: Longmans, Green, Reader, and Dyer, 1869).

[13]Adapted from an argument critiqued in J. S. Mill, *The Subjection of Women* (London: Longmans, Green, Reader, and Dyer, 1869).

are genetically disposed to have different levels of intelligence, and that, on average, Black people are inherently less intelligent than White and Asian people. Although the "science" of the book has been widely and repeatedly debunked, many white supremacists remain devoted fans of Featherbottom.

In 2017, Featherbottom gave a talk on an unrelated topic at Northern State College. Soon after he started, students in the audience began shouting over of him, which made it impossible for the audience to hear him and forced him to stop speaking. Afterward, student leaders of the protest said that they believed it was important to shut down the speech to avoid giving him a platform from which to spread bigoted views.

Featherbottom's case raises a challenging question: is it morally right to prevent a speaker from speaking on the grounds that they hold bigoted views?

At least in Featherbottom's case, the answer is no, it is not morally right. We should respond to the speech of others in a way that best helps the audience form true beliefs. Silencing Featherbottom's speech at Northern State didn't do that. Allowing him to speak, and then vigorously and rigorously *critiquing* his views would have been the morally better strategy. After all, vigorously critiquing his views would help the audience understand *why* his views are mistaken, while shutting down his speech only entrenches his supporters in their mistaken beliefs. It was wrong for Northern State students to shut down Featherbottom's talk.

34. Reginald Featherbottom has claimed, in print, that Black people are genetically inferior to White people. That kind of racist claim is totally unsupported by science but has nevertheless supported attitudes and policies of racial oppression throughout the history of the United States.

Students such as those at Northern State College, who have staged noisy protests to prevent Featherbottom from speaking at their college, deserve our moral respect. It is *always* right to prevent people from contributing to the oppression of minority groups, and that is what they did. Allowing Featherbottom a platform would contribute to the oppression of minority groups, and those students stepped in and stopped it.

CHAPTER 6

Evaluating Arguments from Principle

CHAPTER GOALS

By reading this chapter and completing the exercises, you will learn how to:

- Evaluate an Argument from Principle
- Raise objections to premise 1 by identifying counterexamples to the moral principle that grounds the argument.
- Raise objections to premise 2 by challenging the author's case claim.
- Evaluate objections to both premises.

EVALUATING ARGUMENTS FROM PRINCIPLE

When we come upon any argument, including an Argument from Principle, the first step in critically engaging it is to *understand* it. Chapter 5 demonstrated how to analyze Arguments from Principle by representing them in standard form. After we have understood an argument, we may evaluate it. When we evaluate an argument, we work to determine whether it is a *good* argument—an argument that *should* persuade us to accept its conclusion. This chapter demonstrates how to evaluate Arguments from Principle, with special focus on a method that philosophers use frequently: counterexamples to moral principles.

TWO WAYS ARGUMENTS FROM PRINCIPLE CAN GO WRONG

Recall the *General Form of Arguments from Principle*:

1. Cases of type A have moral status S.
2. Case x is of type A.

Therefore, case x has moral status S.

An argument of this form is structured well: if the premises are true, then the conclusion *must* be true. So, to evaluate an Argument from Principle, we need to figure out whether both premises are indeed true. If we have good reason to doubt the truth of either premise, then the argument fails to give us reason to accept its conclusion.

Consider, for example, an argument introduced in Chapter 5:

The medical necessity argument against sexual reassignment surgery (SRS)

1. Surgery is morally permissible only if it is necessary to promote the physical health of the body. (PRINCIPLE)
2. SRS does not promote the physical health of the body. (CASE)

So, SRS is not morally permissible. (CONCLUSION) [1]

Is the medical necessity argument a *good* argument? Answering that question requires us to evaluate both premises. Is it true that morally permissible surgeries must promote the physical health of the body? Is it true that SRS surgeries do not do that? If we have good reason to doubt the truth of either premise, then this argument fails to give us a reason to accept its conclusion.

Evaluating premise 2 requires us to gather some factual information. What are the typical effects of SRS on the human body? To answer that question requires careful attention to real-world data. But it is a notable feature of SRS that the surgery is typically performed on healthy tissues. So let us grant, for now, that premise 2 is true, and SRS is not necessary for the health of the *body*.

But what about the moral principle in premise 1? This principle, like all principles, attributes a moral status to a range of cases. It isn't just asserting that this or that surgery is morally permissible. It asserts that *only* surgeries that are necessary to promote the physical health of the body are morally permissible. An especially effective technique for testing general claims such as this one is the *method of counterexample*, introduced in Chapter 3. A counterexample to a moral principle is a description of a specific case in which the principle obviously gives morally wrong guidance.

A counterexample to premise 1 of the medical necessity argument, then, will be a specific, concrete example of a case in which the principle in premise 1 obviously gives the wrong guidance. To find a counterexample to premise 1, we must identify an example of a surgery that (a) is a surgery that is *not* necessary for the physical health of the body and (b) is a surgery that *is* morally permissible. If we can find such a counterexample, we will have shown that the general claim asserted by premise 1 is false.

Here's one possible counterexample: surgical repair of a cleft lip. Cleft lip is a condition in which the tissue forming the upper lip is split so that the teeth or

---

[1]As we noted in Chapter 5, there is some disagreement about which terms to use for this procedure. For instance, it is sometimes also known as "Gender Confirmation Surgery" or "Gender Affirmation Surgery."

other parts of the mouth are visible. Sometimes, this split can run deep into the hard palate, which can make it difficult or dangerous to swallow. But a shallowly cleft lip does not always affect a child's ability to eat, drink, or do other things that keep them healthy. Surgeons typically repair cleft lips in newborns before those babies are three months old. These surgeries are cosmetic procedures; they make no contribution to the physical health of the child's body. Are these surgeries morally wrong? We don't think so. And if cosmetic cleft lip surgeries are *not* morally wrong, then the principle asserted in premise 1 is false. We can see that it is false because it classifies surgical repair of cleft lip as morally wrong when it is clearly not morally wrong.

The medical necessity argument fails to give us reason to believe its conclusion is true. Note that critically evaluating an argument and finding it unpersuasive, as we have done here, is not the same thing as establishing that the argument's conclusion is false. We have shown that *this* argument does not give us good reason to accept the conclusion, but perhaps the argument could be salvaged by revising the moral principle in a way that addresses our counterexample. Cleft lip surgery pretty clearly increases the well-being of people who get it. So if we modify premise 1 to morally permit surgeries that promote well-being, then our upgraded principle would no longer be open to the cleft-lip counterexample. We would, of course, need to make a corresponding change in the second premise of the argument, which would leave us with a new version of the SRS argument:

The well-being argument against sexual reassignment surgery (SRS)
1. Surgery is morally permissible only if it effectively promotes the well-being of the person getting it.
2. SRS does not promote the well-being of the people who get it.

   So, SRS is not morally permissible.

Premise 1 now looks more plausible than it did in its original formulation; counterexamples to the upgraded version aren't *obvious*, and that's an improvement. But we've introduced a new problem: the new version of premise 2 now is probably false. The medical necessity version of the argument held that SRS is not necessary to promote the physical health of bodily tissues. That claim is plausible. But the claim that SRS does not promote the well-being of the people who get it is questionable. Although more research needs to be done on long-term outcomes of SRS, there is good evidence that for the majority of recipients "medical transition alleviates feelings of gender dysphoria and improves life satisfaction."[2] Barring other good evidence to the contrary, this gives us reason to reject premise 2. And if premise 2 of the well-being argument is false, then the argument fails to give us reason to accept its conclusion.

---

[2]Tim C. Van de Grift, "Surgical Satisfaction, Quality of Life, and Their Association after Gender-Affirming Surgery: A Follow-Up Study," *Journal of Sex & Marital Therapy*, 44, no. 2 (2017): 138–148.

These examples illustrate some general lessons about how to evaluate an Argument from Principle:

- An argument with the General Form of an Argument from Principle is a good one if, and only if, both premises are true. Thus, to evaluate the argument, we need to evaluate both premises.
- The standard method for evaluating the moral principle (premise 1) is the method of counterexample.
- Evaluating premise 2 requires establishing whether the case under discussion is, in fact, a case of the type covered by the principle. Settling this will often require you to gather information about the world.

COUNTEREXAMPLES TO MORAL PRINCIPLES

Though a complete evaluation of an Argument from Principle always requires critical evaluation of both premises, you will probably find that skill in locating counterexamples to moral principles is an especially useful method of evaluating Arguments from Principle found in philosophical texts, public debates, and friendly conversations.

An effective counterexample to a moral principle, like all effective counterexamples, must be _broadly accessible_ and _uncontroversial._ When you offer a counterexample, your goal is to come up with a concrete case that nearly everyone in your target audience nods along to and says, "yes, the moral principle obviously says the wrong thing about that case."

Example: Assisted suicide is illegal, therefore immoral.

There are some doctors who participate, illegally, in the underworld of assisted suicide. These doctors, in violation of the laws and their own professional codes, will write prescriptions they know patients plan to use to commit suicide. These doctors are doing something seriously morally wrong, and it is easy to explain why.

Breaking laws is morally wrong. It's as simple as that. It is often the case that law-breaking actions are themselves morally wrong—that's why we've outlawed them. But we don't even have to debate about whether this or that action is morally wrong in itself. If it's _illegal_ to do it, then it's _morally wrong_ to do it. For example, it's wrong to break into someone's house even if you don't take anything and the homeowners never know you've been there. It's wrong because you had to break the law to do it. It's wrong to run a stoplight, even if you're in the middle of nowhere and can see there's no one coming. It's wrong because it would break the law to do it.

In a state like Minnesota (for instance), there is absolutely no doubt that writing a suicide prescription is illegal. We don't even have to debate the abstract merits of euthanasia. The fact that we know these doctors are deliberately breaking the law is enough to establish that they are doing something morally wrong.

In standard form for Argument from Principle:

1. Breaking the law is morally wrong. (PRINCIPLE)
2. Writing a prescription for lethal drugs is breaking the law. (CASE)

Therefore, writing a prescription for lethal drugs is morally wrong. (CONCLUSION)

To evaluate the argument, we must evaluate both premises. In this case, premise 2 is uncontroversially true. What about premise 1?

Premise 1 asserts the general principle that *illegal* actions have the status *morally wrong*. An effective counterexample to this principle will thus be a broadly accessible and uncontroversial case of an action that *is* illegal, but is *not* morally wrong. Generating counterexamples to this principle is trivially easy, as there are many cases in which it is uncontroversially true that breaking the law is either morally permissible or morally required.

Counterexample 1: Before the Civil War, a collection of laws called Fugitive Slave laws required people who lived in free states to turn over to authorities any people they suspected were formerly enslaved but had escaped from slave states. Many Northerners defied these laws, and harbored escaped enslaved people in their homes. These people were breaking the law, and that was the morally right thing to do.

Counterexample 2: It is not morally wrong to drive as fast as you safely and responsibly can, instead of obeying the speed limit, to get a seriously injured friend to the hospital in time for doctors to save her life.

The general claim asserted by premise 1 is false. The illegal-therefore-immoral argument does not give us good reason to accept its conclusion.

Example: Campaigning is lying

No good person would ever enter a life of politics, because that life requires dishonesty. The problem is that politicians must campaign in order to be elected, and campaigning is a form of lying. In the best-case scenario, campaigns merely "spin" the truth. ("Spinning" is a deliberate misrepresentation of the facts, which is otherwise known as "lying.") In the worst case, campaigning politicians spew outright falsehoods. No matter how you slice it, political campaigning is always morally wrong, because it is a form of lying, and lying is always morally wrong.

In standard form for argument from principle:

1. Lying is always morally wrong. (PRINCIPLE)
2. Political campaigning is a form of lying. (CASE)

So, political campaigning is always morally wrong. (CONCLUSION)

An effective counterexample to the principle in premise 1 will be a broadly accessible and uncontroversial case of an action that *is* lying, but is *not* morally wrong.

Counterexample 1: Some Germans during World War II lied to Nazi police and claimed they were not hiding Jewish families when, in fact, they were. These were lies, but they were not morally wrong.

Counterexample 2: Imagine that you have been charged with delivering your friend to a surprise birthday party. You know that she's always wanted someone to throw her a surprise party, and she will be delighted if you can pull off the surprise. In this case, lying about where you are taking her is not morally wrong.

These counterexamples show that the moral principle that grounds the "campaigning is lying" argument is false; the argument does not give us good reason to accept its conclusion.

Premise 2 of the "campaigning is lying" argument makes a *descriptive* universal claim, and so the method of counterexample is an appropriate way to test it, as well. If we could find an example of a political campaign that nearly everyone agreed was an *honest* campaign, then we would have a counterexample to the general factual claim made by premise 2.

THE DISCUSSION CONTINUES: RESPONDING TO COUNTEREXAMPLES

Suppose you have offered someone an Argument from Principle, and they respond with a counterexample to the principle you have based your argument on. This is not necessarily the end of the discussion. It could be that they have put their finger on a serious flaw in your thinking. (This is a great result; figuring out we're wrong is how we learn.) But there are at least two other possibilities that would require that the discussion continue.

First, it might be the case that your interlocutor's counterexample is something you can explain away while still remaining committed to the principle you originally offered. Even if their counterexample meets the criterion of being uncontroversial, it might be the case that it *should be* controversial. Consider the surprise-party counterexample to the campaigning-is-lying argument, above. Is this actually a good counterexample? Lies are usually understood to be deliberate attempts to implant a false belief in someone else's mind, in order to get them to do what you want them to do. But that isn't really the case, here. Your friend is the one who wants to be surprised—you aren't manipulating her into doing what you want. She won't feel betrayed, or manipulated, or used once your true intentions come to light. So even though the surprise party example looks, at first blush, to be an example of a morally permissible lie, on closer inspection, that isn't obviously true. Maybe it is a lie, but maybe it's not; in order to decide if the counterexample actually shows premise 1 is false, the discussion needs to continue.

Second, it might be the case that the counterexample shows that your principle needs to be *modified* rather than abandoned. Perhaps a small modification would respond to the counterexample while still preserving your original argument. Consider the Nazi-police counterexample to the campaigning-is-lying argument, above. This is a good counterexample to premise 1, as premise 1 is written. But does the original argument need such a broad, sweeping principle in order to work? We might modify that principle to read: lying is wrong, unless it is necessary to prevent serious imminent harm. We could re-build the argument on that premise, because the kind of deception characteristic of political campaigns is not the kind that prevents serious, imminent harm to anyone. If we modified the argument to rest on this narrower and more plausible moral principle, then we would have to begin our counterexample efforts anew. The discussion continues as we search for a concrete case in which a lie is morally permissible, even though it is not necessary to prevent serious, imminent harm.

REVIEW

An Argument from Principle establishes its conclusion if, but only if, both of its premises are true. There are two ways to raise objections to Arguments from Principle, corresponding to their two-premise form.

One way to raise an objection is by identifying a counterexample to premise 1 (the moral principle). A counterexample is a specific kind of objection that is made to a moral principle.

> **Counterexample to a moral principle:** a specific (real or hypothetical) case that shows a moral principle is false because the principle clearly and uncontroversially attributes the wrong moral status to that case.

Another way to raise an objection to an Argument from Principle is to try to show that premise 2 is false. To do this, you must give reason to think the target case does not fall under the principle.

After raising an objection to an argument, the discussion must continue. Fully evaluating an Argument from Principle requires considering a variety of objections, and determining if any of those objections give us reason to modify or reject the argument.

To test your understanding of the material introduced in this chapter, complete the Demonstration Exercises and then check your answers against the solutions that follow.

Demonstration Exercises

Demonstration Exercises are designed to give you immediate feedback on your grasp of the skills introduced in this chapter. To use them effectively, you should attempt answers to all of them, then check your work against our suggested answers, which follow. For a detailed explanation of how best to use Demonstration Exercises, read the book's Introduction.

Demonstration Exercises 6A: Generating Counterexamples

Exercise Instructions: Offer a counterexample to each of the following moral principles.

1. It's always wrong to break a promise.
2. You should always do what's best for your child.

Demonstration Exercises 6B: Brainstorming Objections

Exercise Instructions: Each of the following passages makes an argument from principle. For each, do the following things:

- *First, represent the argument in standard form using the General Form of Argument from Principle.*
- *Second, suggest what you think is the best candidate for a counterexample to the principle that grounds the argument. "Premise 1 is false because . . . "*

1. Adultery is self-centered

There are few choices more transparently self-centered than the choice to cheat on your spouse. That's why we don't even have to delve deep into the various bad effects of adultery in order to declare it morally wrong. Yes, adultery is bad for the cheated-on spouse; yes, it's bad for any kids; yes, it's bad for the institution of marriage. But we don't need to establish any of that to establish that adultery is morally wrong. It's quite obviously a *self-centered* act, and self-centered acts are morally wrong.

2. Cloning is disgusting[3]

The human capacity to feel disgust is perhaps our greatest moral asset. Disgust, revulsion, and repugnance are, in people with properly tuned sensitivities, the expression of deep moral wisdom. A decent person feels disgust when exposed to immorality. In fact, I would hesitate to spend any time with someone who didn't feel overwhelming disgust at Adolf Hitler, or child pornographers, or slave traders, or incest, or cannibalism. People who feel appropriate disgust at these things ought to trust their reactions more generally: the disgust they feel, when they feel it, is a deep emotional response to immorality. In short, things that are disgusting are morally wrong.

Now, consider human reproductive cloning. When scientists clone a human, they scrape cells from an adult, penetrate those cells with a microscopic needle, and suck out the nucleus. They then take an egg that has been harvested from a probably unrelated woman, suck out that egg's nucleus, and squirt in the nucleus they scraped off an unrelated adult. All people of good conscience will find their stomachs churning in revulsion at this unnatural process. Human reproductive cloning is one of the most disgusting techniques currently discussed among medical researchers, and this is good evidence that human reproductive cloning is morally wrong.

3. A deathbed promise

The backstory: some years ago, a brother and a sister went through a difficult time after the death of their grandmother. On her deathbed, the grandmother had asked that they promise to keep in the family the remote cabin that she bequeathed to them in her will. The sibling grandchildren were happy to make that promise. It wasn't long, though, before it became clear that the cabin was a major liability. After decades of neglect it needed many fundamental repairs. They threw themselves into those repairs, physically and financially exhausting themselves for two summers. After the

---

[3]Adapted from an argument in Leon Kass, "The Wisdom of Repugnance," *The New Republic*, June 2, 1997.

(*continued*)

second summer, the sister concluded that they didn't have the resources to restore the cabin to a safe and stable condition, and that they should sell it to someone who could afford to repair and maintain it. The brother disagreed, and offered the following line of argument:

The passage:

> You made a deathbed promise to Grandma. You know as well as I do that she raised us to believe that keeping your promises is a moral obligation in all situations except where the person you promised lets you off the hook. And this wasn't just any promise, it was a deathbed promise! Obviously, you can't say Grandma has relieved you of the burden of your promise. If you break it, you'll be doing the wrong thing, end of story. It doesn't matter what you want, now, or what you didn't know, then. You made the promise, and now you're morally obligated to keep this cabin.

4. Liver transplants: an appeal to expected medical outcomes[4]

A huge number of cases can be marshaled in support of the ethical principle that scarce healthcare resources should be allocated in such a way that they go to the patients who will medically benefit the most from them. Consider just these few:

(1) Two people have dangerous bacterial infections, but the hospital has only a single course of a single antibiotic: penicillin. Patient A is not allergic to penicillin, and patient B is. (2) Two patients face imminent death from blood loss. There is only enough whole blood available to treat one of them. Patient A is likely to recover fully after the transfusion. Patient B will almost certainly die within hours from multiple organ damage, whether or not he gets the transfusion. (3) An EMT is called to the site of an accident. There are two casualties, both gravely injured: patient A is a 19-year-old woman and patient B is a 97-year-old woman. The EMT must pick one to treat first, and whoever she leaves to treat second is very likely to die.

In all these cases, it is Patient A who should receive the treatment. Why? Because scarce treatments should be allocated to the patients who will receive the most medical benefit from them. Donated livers are every bit as scarce as the resources in the fanciful examples described above. And alcoholics, who brought their liver failure on themselves, are likely to relapse and destroy any liver they are given. Allocating livers to alcoholics thus fails to provide the maximum medical benefit. That's why alcoholics should be de-prioritized on waiting lists for livers.

Demonstration Exercise 6C: Complete Argument Evaluation

Exercise Instructions: The following passage offers an Argument from Principle. Do the following things:

- *First, represent the argument in standard form using the General Form of Arguments from Principle.*
- *Second, offer what you believe to be the best objection to the argument. Clearly identify which premise you are engaging: "Premise 1 is false because ... " or "Premise 2 is false because ... "*

---

[4]Adapted from an argument in Alvin Moss and Mark Siegler (1991), "Should Alcoholics Compete Equally for Liver Transplantation?" *Journal of the American Medical Associa*tion 265, no. 10 (1991): 1295–1298.

- *Third, briefly explain how you believe the discussion should continue. What do you think is the author's best reply to the objection you have just raised?*

1. Lab-grown meat is a crutch[5]

Lab-grown meat [meat grown from cells in a laboratory rather than being produced by slaughtering animals] is being hailed as the solution to the factory farming of animals. The downside of factory farming for the cows, chickens, and pigs themselves is obvious enough. But it is also bad for human health, given the amount of antibiotics pumped into the animals, as well as for the environment, given the resources required to provide us with industrial quantities of meat.

By contrast, lab-grown meat need have none of these costs. Once the technology is perfected it will be indistinguishable in taste and texture from real meat, and will be cheaper to produce and purchase.

There is, however, a major problem with lab-grown meat: a moral problem. Factory farming causes billions of animals to live and die in great pain each year. Our response has been almost total indifference and inaction and, despite the rise of vegetarianism and veganism in some quarters, more animals are killed today for food than ever before. This does not reflect well on us, morally speaking, and history will not remember us kindly.

The moral problem stems from the fact that we will likely switch over to lab-grown meat because it is cheap, or thanks to its benefits for human health or the environment. That is, we will do it for our own sake and not for the sake of animals. . . . If we switch over to lab-grown meat just for our own sake, and not for the sake of animals, then the morally dubious part of us that is responsible for our inaction on factory farming will remain intact. If this part of us has other bad consequences, then we might have lost a valuable opportunity to confront it and avoid those outcomes. . . . People who are indifferent, thoughtless, complacent, lacking in curiosity, prepared to silence or turn away from qualms, blindly follow orders, and so on, may be more likely to ignore other groups who are in great need. Such people may also be more vulnerable to manipulation by morally unscrupulous leaders. In some circumstances, they could even be seduced by fascism.

---

[5]Quoted from Ben Bramble, "Lab-grown Meat Could Let Humanity Ignore a Serious Moral Failing," *The Conversation*, December 14, 2017. Online: https://theconversation.com/lab-grown-meat-could-let-humanity-ignore-a-serious-moral-failing-88909

Solutions to the Demonstration Exercises

Demonstration Exercises are most useful if you make your best attempt to complete them before you look at the answers. If you haven't yet attempted answers to all the Demonstration Exercises, go back and do that now.

Note: your standard form representation of the arguments should be the same as ours in spirit, but it's OK if you've used different words to express the same thoughts.

The range of possible good counterexamples is much broader. Thus, the counterexamples we offer here are merely samples. If your counterexamples function in the same way as ours, then you're in good shape. If our sample counterexamples appear to be doing something different than yours, then you should review the relevant portions of Chapter 6 to clarify your understanding.

(continued)

Solutions to Demonstration Exercises 6A: Generating Counterexamples

1. It's always wrong to break a promise.

To show this principle is false, we need an example of promise-breaking that is not morally wrong. For example:

- It is not morally wrong for a contract killer to refuse to kill someone they previously promised to kill.
- It is not morally wrong to break your promise to paint someone's house if they change their mind and tell you to forget it.

2. You should always do what's best for your child.

To show this principle is false, we need an example of something a parent shouldn't do even if it is best for their child. For example:

- It is wrong to give cheerleaders food poisoning, even if that would benefit your child by helping him make the cheerleading squad.
- It is wrong to help your child cheat on the SAT, even if that would help her get into an elite college.

Solutions to Demonstration Exercises 6B: Brainstorming Objections

1. Adultery is self-centered

In standard form for Argument from Principle:

1. Self-centered acts are morally wrong. (PRINCIPLE)
2. Adultery is a self-centered act. (CASE)

  Therefore, adultery is morally wrong. (CONCLUSION)

Counterexamples to the principle:

To show premise 1 is false, we need an example of an act that *is* self-centered but lacks the feature of being morally wrong. For example:

- It is self-centered, but not morally wrong, to take a vacation from work to recharge your metaphorical batteries.
- It is self-centered, but not morally wrong, for parents to hire a sitter for the evening so they can go out with friends and spend some time with adults.
- It is self-centered, but not morally wrong, to apply for competitive scholarships to fund your own studies.
- It is self-centered, but not morally wrong, to ask your friends to help you move so you don't have to pay for movers.

2. Cloning is disgusting

In standard form for Argument from Principle:

1. Things that are disgusting are morally wrong. (PRINCIPLE)
2. Human reproductive cloning is disgusting. (CASE)

  So, human reproductive cloning is morally wrong. (CONCLUSION)

Counterexamples to the principle:

To show premise 1 is false, we need an example of something that *is* disgusting but *lacks* the feature of being morally wrong. For example:

- When a paramedic reaches into the throat of a choking person and pulls out a big bolus of half-chewed food, that's disgusting but not morally wrong.

- When a heart surgeon cracks open the ribcage of an anesthetized patient to replace a malfunctioning heart valve, that's disgusting but not morally wrong.

- When parents wash their baby's bedding after an episode of explosive diarrhea, that's disgusting but not morally wrong.

- When a plumber uses a drain-snake to remove a giant ball of rotting human hair, that's disgusting but not morally wrong.

Note: premise 2 of this argument also invites critical engagement. Is it actually true that moving a nucleus from one cell to another is *disgusting*? Complete argument evaluation might reveal that both premises of this argument are false.

3. A deathbed promise

In standard form for Argument from Principle:

1. Keeping your promises is a moral obligation unless the person you promised says you need not keep it anymore. (PRINCIPLE)

2. You promised Grandma you'd keep the cabin, and she hasn't said you need not keep the promise. (CASE)

   So, keeping the cabin is a moral obligation. (CONCLUSION)

Counterexamples to the principle:

To show premise 1 is false, we need an example of a situation in which keeping a promise is *not* a moral obligation, even though the person you promised hasn't told you that you don't need to keep your promise anymore. For example:

- You promise to buy a bicycle from a person at a garage sale, but before you hand over the money you learn that the bike is stolen. You ought not keep your promise to buy it.

- You promise to loan your best friend $1,000, but then you find out he plans to use the money to hire a hitman to assassinate his bookie. You ought not keep that promise. (And you ought to find a different bestie!)

- You promise to meet your lab partner by 10 a.m., but on your way you see a bad car accident. So, you stop to help care for the injured, which makes you late. You did the right thing, even though helping the injured required breaking your promise to your lab partner.

4. Liver transplants: an appeal to expected medical outcomes

In standard form for Argument from Principle:

1. Scarce treatments should be allocated to the patients who will medically benefit the most from them. (PRINCIPLE)

2. De-prioritizing recovering alcoholics for liver transplants allocates scarce liver transplants to the people who will medically benefit the most from them. (CASE)

   So, alcoholics should be de-prioritized for liver transplants. (CONCLUSION)

(continued)

Counterexamples to the principle:

To show premise 1 is false, we need an example of a scarce treatment that ought to be allocated to someone *other than* the person who will benefit medically the most from it.

For the following counterexamples, imagine that a hospital has a single dose of Drug A, which works within minutes of taking it. They also have Drug B, which treats the same condition, but requires a two-week course to be as effective as Drug A. Now, imagine the following pairs of people, both of whom need the same treatment (and both of whom would prefer to have Drug A).

- The Governor and a high school student working a summer job need the same treatment in order to be able to return to work. Drug A will be somewhat more medically effective on the high school student, because he's significantly younger than the Governor. But State operations will be seriously disrupted if the Governor has to settle for the inferior treatment, and thus can't return to work for two weeks, whereas the high school student is in a good position to take two weeks off of work. In this case, Drug A should go to the Governor, even though its *medical* benefit to the student would be more significant.

- The lone caregiver for 5 children and an independently wealthy single man need the treatment. It will be somewhat more effective on the wealthy single man, but it will still allow the caregiver to resume his caregiving immediately. In this case, Drug A should go to the caregiver, even though its medical benefit to the wealthy single man is more significant.

- The reason Drug A is at the hospital is because Millicent has gone to significant trouble to order and pay for it. When she arrives at the hospital to receive her treatment, she finds Gertie has beaten her there and asked that Drug A be given to her, instead. Even though Millicent paid for it, Gertie has a good case that the drug would be somewhat more medically effective for her. Still, the hospital should give Drug A to Millicent.

- Suppose Drugs A and B (somehow) treat gunshot wounds. Two patients arrive at the hospital at the same time: a man who was shot and wounded by police after he opened fire in a crowded nightclub, and an innocent bystander who was wounded by the shooter. Even if Drug A would be more medically effective on the shooter, it should go to the innocent victim.

Note 1: remember that the conversation doesn't stop with the offering of a counterexample. There are some bioethicists who accept premise 1 as true, and so they would rightly want to respond to the counterexamples offered here. The discussion should continue, focused on whether or not these counterexamples illuminate a problem with premise 1.

Note 2: complete argument evaluation requires evaluating both premises. In this argument, premise 2 is probably false. To determine that, we need to investigate the empirical evidence about transplant outcomes for recovering alcoholics.

Solution to Demonstration Exercise 6C: Complete Argument Evaluation
As in previous exercises, your standard-form representation of the argument should be the same as ours in spirit, but it's OK if you've used different words to express the same thoughts. The objections we offer are merely samples; there are probably other objections not listed here that are worth thinking more about.

1. Lab-grown meat is a crutch

In standard form for argument from principle:

1. It is morally wrong to forgo opportunities to improve morally dubious parts of our character. (PRINCIPLE)

2. Eating lab-grown meat forgoes an opportunity to improve a morally dubious part of our character. (CASE)

So, eating lab-grown meat is wrong. (CONCLUSION)

Candidate objections to each premise:

A counterexample to premise 1:

To show premise 1 is false, we need an example of a case where someone forgoes an opportunity to improve morally dubious parts of their character but forgoing this opportunity is *not* wrong.

> Annoying coworker: Suppose you are at an important work party, and so is a co-worker you find unbearably annoying. You worry that if you talk to this co-worker, you will not be able to control yourself and will end up being rude, even insulting. You recognize that this is a flaw in your character, and you should try to practice politeness, even when it is difficult. But because the work party is so important, and because it will ruin everyone's night if you lose control and are rude or insulting, you decide to avoid interacting with your annoying co-worker at the party. This forgoes an opportunity to improve a morally dubious part of your character by practicing politeness in a difficult situation, but it's nevertheless morally permissible. Since premise 1 says otherwise, premise 1 must be false.

An objection to premise 2:

Premise 2 is false, because not everyone who might eat lab-grown meat is thereby forgoing improvement of a morally dubious part of their character. For instance, someone who is vegan for ethical reasons (and so consumes no animal products at all) might choose to add lab-grown meat to their diet because it helps them sustain a healthy cruelty-free diet more easily. It's hard to see how this would count as refusing to fix a morally important character flaw, so this example therefore shows that the general claim made in premise 2 is false.

The discussion continues/author's best reply:

The annoying coworker counterexample does seem to show that premise 1, as it is stated, is false. I think the author's best reply would be to concede that we aren't morally obligated to take *every possible opportunity* for self-improvement, and to try to narrow the principle accordingly. The principle might be more plausible if it focused on *easy* opportunities for self-improvement, or opportunities that *don't* expose other people to risk of harm. A revised, narrower principle might still support the author's argument.

The vegan objection to premise 2 also shows a problem with that premise, as written. I think this objection is easier for the author to respond to, though. The argument appears to be targeted at meat eaters who are indifferent to the suffering of farm animals. The author could just make it explicit that that's all the argument is about. It isn't an argument that lab-grown meat is *always* wrong, but rather an argument that eating lab-grown meat is wrong when a person uses it in a way that makes it easier for them to maintain their callous attitude toward animals. That response from the author does not change the argument much at all, but it does effectively address the objection to premise 2.

CHAPTER 6 PRACTICE EXERCISES

EVALUATING ARGUMENTS FROM PRINCIPLE

Exercises 6A: Generating Counterexamples

Exercise Instructions: *Offer a counterexample to each of the following moral principles.*

1. You should never hurt your friends.
2. If an action is unnatural, then it's morally wrong.
3. Human beings should never make decisions that lead to another person's death.
4. If stealing doesn't harm anyone physically or emotionally, then it's not wrong.
5. Stealing is morally permissible when it results in benefits that outweigh the harms.
6. If a person isn't mad at you for breaking your promise, then breaking your promise is morally permissible.
7. Performing a treatment on someone without their consent is always wrong regardless of the good it will do.
8. Nurses ought to protect patient confidentiality unless breaking it could be expected to save someone's life.

Exercises 6B: Brainstorming Objections

Exercise Instructions: *In this section you will revisit the arguments you analyzed in the* Chapter 5 *Practice Exercises 5B. For each of the arguments in Practice Exercises 5B, do the following things. (Number your answers with the corresponding numbers from Practice Exercises 5B. For example, label your answer 6B7 when examining the argument from 5B7.)*

- *First, represent the argument in standard form using the General Form of Argument from Principle.*
- *Second, suggest what you think is the best candidate for a counterexample to the principle that grounds the argument. "Premise 1 is false because. . ."*

Exercises 6C: Complete Argument Evaluation

Instructions: *for each of the following passages:*

- *First, represent the argument in standard form using the General Form of Arguments from Principle.*
- *Second, offer what you believe to be the best objection to the argument. Clearly identify which premise you are engaging: "Premise 1 is false because. . ." or "Premise 2 is false because. . ."*
- *Third, briefly explain how you believe the discussion should continue. What do you think is the author's best reply to the objection you have just raised?*

1. Any activity teachers can provide that safely promotes student practice and learning is morally permissible. Extra credit assignments do that, so they're morally permissible for teachers to assign.[6]

2. In an effort to ensure that students who missed or did poorly on course assignments can pass the class, some teachers offer extra credit assignments that were not on the original syllabus. Extra credit opportunities like this promote habits that are not conducive to success in the world students will enter after college. Extra credit allows students to get away with procrastination or minimal effort and thus discourages accountability. Since teachers should design courses in ways that do not promote bad habits, they should not assign extra credit.

3. When teachers give extra credit opportunities for students who attend optional activities outside of class time, these opportunities are not equally accessible to all students. Some might not have that time available due to work or other classes, and some might be unable to get to the assigned locations. It is always unfair for a teacher to base course grades on assignments that are not equally available to all students. Therefore, extra credit points for attending activities outside of class time and/or off campus are unfair.

4. Teachers should design their courses so that grades are assigned in a way that accurately reflect students' academic skills, grasp of class content, and motivation and dedication to their studies. But extra credit opportunities don't contribute to the accurate assignment of grades. After all, if the extra credit opportunity is easy, then it allows some people to earn the same grade as someone who is more skilled or dedicated. And if the extra credit opportunity is hard, then it only widens the gap between the scores of the most skilled and motivated students and the rest of the class. So, teachers shouldn't assign extra credit opportunities.

5. Some women have hyperandrogenism, a medical condition characterized by much higher than average testosterone levels. Women with this condition should not be allowed to compete in professional athletics against women with average levels of testosterone, because athletes should never be allowed to benefit from unfair competitive advantages.

6. You should always refer to people in whatever way they prefer. If Abdirahman wants to be called Abdi, or if Lester wants to be called by his middle name (Robert), you should use the name they have asked you to use. If your spouse prefers you to refer to her as your "partner" rather than your "wife," you should do that. If a colleague asks to be referred to as an "autistic person" rather than a "person with autism," you should do as they ask.

---

[6]Passages 1–4 are adapted from arguments discussed in Nathan Nobis, "Ethics and 'Extra Credit'," https://1000wordphilosophy.com/2018/02/25/ethics-and-extra-credit/ which is itself adapted from Pynes, Christopher A. "Seven Arguments Against Extra Credit," *Teaching Philosophy* 37, no. 2 (2014): 191–214.

The same principle applies to the use of pronouns in classrooms. When a student asks to be referred to with she/her pronouns, or they/them pronouns, you should use whatever pronouns that student prefers.

7. Teachers should not be required to call trans students by their preferred gender pronouns, because that would be requiring people to lie.[7]

8. A being deserves to have its interests taken into consideration only if the being cares about its own interests. So, non-conscious organisms (such as plants) don't deserve consideration, since they don't care about their own interests.

9. Many species today, such as the leatherback turtle, pied tamarin, black rhinoceros, and northern hairy-nosed wombat, are on the brink of extinction. Fortunately, the extinction of these marvelous species is often something we can prevent. Indeed, we ought to preserve every species possible. This follows from a clear and compelling principle: if something could possibly be of use to us in the future, then we ought to preserve it.[8]

10. Some people have racial preferences when it comes to dating: they prefer to date only people of a particular race. But acting on this kind of racial dating preference is wrong. It's always wrong to act on discriminatory preferences—that is, preferences that treat a person differently based upon their racial group—and that is precisely what people do when they act on racial dating preferences.[9]

11. Some people have racial preferences when it comes to dating: they prefer to date only people of a particular race. And, if you really look into this, you'll see that such preferences are based upon a superficial and shallow perspective. A person of good character does not have sexual or relationship preferences that rule out whole groups of people based upon physical appearance. So, because people who have racial dating preferences exhibit exactly this sort of shallow preference when they prefer dating someone because of their race, they to that extent lack good character.[10]

12. Dr. P has just determined that patient X has Multiple Sclerosis. But patient X also has a history of depression and anxiety, and Dr. P has reason to think that knowing her actual diagnosis would not help patient X and would in fact cause her to go into a depression that would negatively impact the course of her condition. Should Dr. P tell patient X their actual diagnosis? No. A healthcare

---

[7]Adapted from an argument by Dale O'Leary, as reported at http://www.mfc.org/the-issue-gender-sexuality/. Accessed Jan. 10, 2019.

[8]Adapted from an argument evaluated in Elliott Sober, "Philosophical Problems for Environmentalism," in *The Preservation of Species*, ed. B. Norton (Princeton: Princeton University Press, 1986), 173–194.

[9]Adapted from an argument discussed in Raja Halwani, "Racial Sexual Desires," in *The Philosophy of Sex*, 7th Edition, ed. Raja Halwani, Alan Soble, Sarah Hoffman, and Jacob M. Held (London: Rowman & Littlefield, 2017).

[10]Adapted from an argument discussed in Raja Halwani, "Racial Sexual Desires," in *The Philosophy of Sex*, 7th Edition, ed. Raja Halwani, Alan Soble, Sarah Hoffman, and Jacob M. Held (London: Rowman & Littlefield, 2017).

practitioner should only tell a patient the truth if it won't be likely to cause the patient clear and immediate harm.

13. Several companies now offer a startling new service: for a substantial portion of money, they will make a clone of your dog. By taking cells from your dog they can produce a genetic duplicate. Some people say this is morally wrong to do, but they are misguided. Cloning a recently deceased pet helps a pet owner manage their grief without harming their pets, and that's why it's perfectly morally permissible.[11]

14. Parents should help their children develop the traits that will allow them to live the best life they can. Parents are living up to this principle when they send their kids to school, and feed them nutritious food, and teach them to develop self-control. This plausible principle has interesting implications given recent technological advances. In the near future, we will probably be able to use genetic manipulation to alter an embryo's genetic traits in ways that increase their innate intelligence and impulse control. Because increased intelligence and impulse control would lead to a better life, parents should use genetic manipulation to ensure their child has these traits if this procedure is safe and available to them.[12]

15. In some countries and jurisdictions, convicted sex offenders are offered chemical castration—that is, medications that reversibly lower testosterone and sex drive—as an alternative to prison time. This is clearly not morally justifiable, because it coerces people into making choices that could potentially harm them. After all, the drugs used have a risk, however small, of causing serious side-effects such as depression or bone demineralization.

16. A number of public libraries across the country have recently hosted a controversial event: drag queen story hour. Although organizers and participants emphasize the ways they could help combat invidious bias against LGBT people, some library patrons find these events morally problematic. Some have gone so far as to suggest that drag queen story hour should be banned.

   I think this is correct: public libraries should not be allowed to host drag queen story hour. This follows from the fact that a publicly-funded institution should never be allowed to host an event that offends a large portion of the public. Since hosting drag-queen story-hour at a public library does that, it should clearly not be allowed.

17. Pre-implantation genetic diagnosis (PGD) is a procedure in reproductive medicine that allows doctors to test an embryo to be implanted in a woman using in-vitro fertilization to see if it is genetically predisposed to a particular medical condition. Some parents who are Deaf want to use PGD to ensure that they have a deaf child. They do this by identifying and implanting only those embryos that carry the gene for deafness.

---

[11]Argument inspired by a comment by Barbara Streisand, reported at https://parade.com/653333/leahingram/why-barbra-streisand-cloned-her-dog/

[12]Adapted from an argument in Julian in Savulescu, "Procreative Beneficence: Why We Should Select the Best Children," *Bioethics*, 15, no. 5–6 (2001): 413–426.

I believe that doctors and genetic counselors should not assist Deaf parents in identifying and implanting deaf embryos. A deaf child will have many fewer options as an adult—fewer career options, fewer relationship options, fewer options for hobbies. Genetic counselors should never help parents constrain the future options of the children they are helping to create.[13]

18. A health care practitioner has a right to conscientious objection—a right to be protected from punishment for refusing to perform a job-related treatment or procedure—if their objection to the practice is motivated by values that are fundamental to the legal system. So, a health care practitioner has a right to conscientious objection to performing abortion, euthanasia or medically-assisted reproduction, because objections to those practices are motivated by respect for life, and that's a value that's fundamental to the legal system.[14]

19. On Santa Cruz Island, island foxes are endangered because they are killed by golden eagles, and golden eagles are on the island because their competitors (bald eagles) were killed off by a chemical pollution from humans. Feral pigs are present in large numbers because they were originally brought by settlers, and now the pigs destroy and threaten large numbers of plant species on the island. The golden eagles stay on the island because the pigs are a good source of food. One response to this situation would be to stabilize the ecosystem by killing off lots of the feral pigs, capturing and re-locating golden eagles, bringing in bald eagles, and breeding and reintroducing island foxes.

This restoration plan, although it is complicated, is the right thing to do. As environmentalist Aldo Leopold has argued, "A thing is right when it tends to preserve the integrity, stability, and beauty of the biotic community. It is wrong when it tends otherwise."[15] Leopold's principle plausibly emphasizes that is the functioning of the *ecosystem as a whole* that matters, and our efforts should be to do what will promote it functioning stably and well. The restoration would clearly help in that regard.

20. The Earth can only absorb a finite amount of greenhouse emissions without those emissions changing the climate. Beyond that threshold, any additional greenhouse emissions damage the environment. That means that non-damaging emissions—those that occur beneath the threshold—are a strictly limited global resource.

The United States and other countries in the Global North emit the greatest share of global emissions—far more than the finite amount the Earth can absorb without damage. For that reason, we in the Global North ought to bear the biggest share of the burden of reducing emissions: those who use up a

[13]Adapted from Dena S. Davis, "Genetic Dilemmas and the Child's Right to an Open Future," *Hastings Center Report*, 27, no. 2 (1997): 7–15.

[14]Adapted from Meaney et al., "Objective Reasons for Conscientious Objection in Health Care," *National Catholic Bioethics Quarterly*, 12, no. 4 (2012): 611–620.

[15]Aldo Leopold, *A Sand County Almanac* (New York, NY: Ballantine Books, 1966), 262.

finite resource and deprive others of the ability to use it owe compensation to those who were deprived.[16]

21. Many people across the globe suffer from Vitamin A deficiency, which can cause blindness or even death. Some suggest that the solution is to have people plant and eat Golden Rice, which is a genetically engineered rice that is high in Vitamin A. Researchers in the Philippines are working to develop a strain that is both high in vitamin A and that grows as easily and well as regular rice. Some worry that the rice is still not rich enough in Vitamin A to solve the problem. Others worry that genetically modified Golden Rice could have unintended bad effects on the environment or human health. While preliminary evidence (mainly, comparisons to other crops we already know are safe) suggests there's no reason to think Golden Rice is likely to cause serious harms, we do not yet have direct tests of how safe it is to use.

    Given our current ignorance, we should ban the use of Golden Rice. Failing to do so could possibly lead to disastrous consequences, because Golden Rice could contaminate other rice crops. This would lead to massive food insecurity if Golden Rice is later revealed to have some harmful effects on human health. We should ban any practice that could possibly cause catastrophic harm to humans or the environment. We should ban Golden Rice.[17]

22. Although many people find the taste of meat more pleasing than the taste of vegetarian alternatives, for almost all of us in the United States, our preference for the taste of meat is disconnected from any underlying health concerns. What I mean is that people eat meat because they like it, not because they need it to be healthy. (In fact, most people would be healthier if they stopped eating meat!)

    Let us not forget, though, that meat comes from animals. In the case of factory farmed meat, those animals suffer for their entire life, and then suffer even more during the moments leading up to slaughter.

    In our lives away from the dinner table, we all acknowledge that causing suffering to other creatures—whether human or animal—can only be morally justified if that suffering is necessary to prevent some greater harm. We are obviously violating that basic moral principle at the dinner table, where we tacitly inflict massive suffering on animals for no reason other than that we like the way their tissues taste. When we eat meat, we inflict suffering for reasons that have nothing to do with the prevention of greater harms. That's why it's morally wrong to eat meat.

---

[16]Adapted from an argument discussed in Stephen M. Gardiner, "Ethics and Climate Change: An Introduction." *Wiley Interdisciplinary Reviews: Climate Change* 1, no. 1 (2010): 54–66.

[17]This description of potential problems with Golden Rice is loosely adapted from a statement by Greenpeace, as expressed on their website: https://www.greenpeace.org/archive-international/en/campaigns/agriculture/problem/Greenpeace-and-Golden-Rice/. The principle applied is a version of the so-called "precautionary principle" that is discussed in Neil A. Manson, "Formulating the Precautionary Principle." *Environmental Ethics* 24, no. 3 (2002): 263–274.

23. [Background: Nelson Mandela was a leader of the African National Congress and a key figure in the struggle to end South Africa's racist system of Apartheid. In 1961, Mandela and several others formed uMkhonto we Sizwe, an armed wing within the previously non-violent African National Congress. uMkhonto we Sizwe carried out acts of sabotage, such as the bombing of power stations. In 1963 Mandela was arrested and tried for crimes related to these acts of sabotage. The following is an excerpt from a speech Mandela gave at his trial. In this speech, which has since become known as the "I Am Prepared to Die" speech, Mandela explains and defends uMkhonto's violent tactics.][18]

> I have already mentioned that I was one of the persons who helped to form Umkhonto. I, and the others who started the organisation, did so for two reasons. Firstly, we believed that as a result of Government policy, violence by the African people had become inevitable, and that unless responsible leadership was given to canalise and control the feelings of our people, there would be outbreaks of terrorism which would produce an intensity of bitterness and hostility between the various races of the country which is not produced even by war.
>
> Secondly, we felt that without sabotage there would be no way open to the African people to succeed in their struggle against the principle of white supremacy. All lawful modes of expressing opposition to this principle had been closed by legislation, and we were placed in a position in which we had either to accept a permanent state of inferiority, or to defy the Government. We chose to defy the Government. We first broke the law in a way which avoided any recourse to violence; when this form was legislated against, and when the Government resorted to a show of force to crush opposition to its policies, only then did we decide to answer violence with violence.
>
> But the violence which we chose to adopt was not terrorism. We who formed Umkhonto were all members of the African National Congress, and had behind us the ANC tradition of non-violence and negotiation as a means of solving political disputes. We believed that South Africa belonged to all the people who lived in it, and not to one group, be it black or white. We did not want an inter-racial war, and tried to avoid it to the last minute. [. . .]
>
> Our problem, My Lord, was not whether to fight, but was how to continue the fight. We of the ANC had always stood for a non-racial democracy, and we shrank from any action which might drive the races further apart than they already were. But the hard facts were that fifty years of non-violence had brought the African people nothing but more and more repressive legislation, and fewer and fewer rights.
>
> It may not be easy for this Court to understand, but it is a fact that for a long time the people had been talking of violence—of the day when they

---

[18]The following passage is excerpted from the transcript of Mandela's "I Am Prepared to Die" speech. Available online: http://db.nelsonmandela.org/speeches/pub_view.asp?pg=item&ItemID=NMS010

would fight the white man and win back their country, and we, the leaders of the ANC, had nevertheless always prevailed upon them to avoid violence and to pursue peaceful methods. When some of us discussed this in June of 1961, it could not be denied that our policy to achieve a non-racial state by non-violence had achieved nothing, and that our followers were beginning to lose confidence in this policy and were developing disturbing ideas of terrorism. [. . .]

At the beginning of June 1961, after a long and anxious assessment of the South African situation, I, and some colleagues, came to the conclusion that as violence [in this country—inaudible] was inevitable, it would be unrealistic and wrong for African leaders to continue preaching peace and non-violence at a time when the Government met our peaceful demands with force.

This conclusion, My Lord, was not easily arrived at. It was when all, only when all else had failed, when all channels of peaceful protest had been barred to us, that the decision was made to embark on violent forms of struggle, and to form Umkhonto we Sizwe. We did so not because we desired such a course, but solely because the Government had left us with no other choice. In the Manifesto of Umkhonto published on the 16th of December 61, which is Exhibit AD, we said, I quote:

"The time comes in the life of any nation when there remain only two choices—submit or fight. That time has now come to South Africa. We shall not submit and we have no choice but to hit back by all means in our power in defence of our people, our future, and our freedom."

This was our feeling in June of 1961, when we decided to press for a change in the policy of the National Liberation Movement. I can only say that I felt morally obliged to do what I did.

24. Black Lives Matter (BLM) protesters have been working to promote awareness and change in response to unjust policing practices that have resulted in wrongful harassment, injury, and death for many people of color. So when groups of counter-protesters push back against BLM by yelling "All lives matter!" this has unsurprisingly led to fierce debates about whether these White counter-protesters are doing something racist.

An action is racist if it is based upon false or unjustified beliefs that contribute to oppression or subordination of some racial group.[19] This principle provides a resolution to the debate: chanting "All lives matter!" is indeed racist. White counter-protesters who yell "All lives matter!" at a Black Lives Matter demonstration reveal that they believe that Black people are just whining or making up problems. This belief is unjustified and clearly contributes to racial oppression by perpetuating an unwillingness to face up to serious injustices.

---

[19]Adapted from a principle defended in Tommie Shelby, "Is Racism in the Heart?" *Journal of Social Philosophy*, 33, 3 (2002): 411–420.

CHAPTER 7

Developing an Argument from Principle

CHAPTER GOALS

In this chapter, you will learn how to:

- Develop an original Argument from Principle.
- Prepare your argument for presentation to others.

DEVELOPING AN ARGUMENT FROM PRINCIPLE

In previous chapters we analyzed Arguments from Principle by representing them in standard form and evaluated them by identifying and assessing objections. If you are able to effectively analyze and evaluate Arguments from Principle written by others, then you already understand the key features of these arguments. That means you already know what goal you seek in creating your own Arguments from Principle.

Developing an original Argument from Principle requires a combination of creative and logical thinking that takes practice to develop. In this chapter, we'll discuss some strategies for developing Arguments from Principle worthy of the serious critical engagement you practiced in the previous chapter.

DEVELOPING A PLAUSIBLE MORAL PRINCIPLE

Imagine yourself in the following situation. Many years ago you promised your grandmother on her deathbed that you'd take care of her cabin so that your extended family could use it as a place to gather for reunions. After she died, you threw yourself into the project of maintaining the cabin. But over the years, it became increasingly physically and financially challenging for you to continue that work. You ask your family for help, but they live too far away to help, and they have no money to spare. You feel trapped between your promise to your grandmother and your personal need to let go of responsibility for her cabin.

This scenario raises a moral question: is it morally permissible to break your deathbed promise and sell the cabin? The process of developing an Argument from Principle that addresses the question involves three steps. First, brainstorm moral principles that seem relevant in this case. Second, identify the most promising principle from your list of brainstormed principles. Third, refine that principle until it satisfies two criteria: (i) the principle avoids obvious counterexamples and (ii) the principle gives guidance about this case.

What moral principle is most relevant in the case of Grandmother's cabin? Keeping promises is morally important, so the following simple principle might have occurred to you already:

Candidate A: Failing to do what you've promised to do is always morally wrong.

This principle satisfies the second criterion—it gives guidance about the case. Applied to the case of Grandmother's cabin, the principle says that breaking your promise by selling the cabin is morally wrong.

Unfortunately, Candidate A fails to satisfy the first criterion, because it is open to many obvious counterexamples:

- It is not wrong for a young mafioso to decide *not* to kill someone he'd promised his family he'd kill.
- It is not wrong for you to fail to paint your neighbor's fence, as you promised you would, if she has since decided that she wants to wait until next summer.
- It is not wrong to break a promise to a friend to ride the roller coaster if you find out later that you have a heart condition.
- It is not wrong to break a promise to go out drinking with friends if you find out you're pregnant.

You can probably generate half a dozen more with a few minutes' thought. This principle is too broad.

Still, what prompted us to offer our first-pass moral principle is that in *most* situations it is indeed morally wrong to fail to do something you promised to do. In response to these counterexamples, we should modify the principle so that it better specifies when promise-breaking is wrong and when it is permissible. Here's one possible upgrade of the principle that attempts to do that:

Candidate B: Breaking a promise is morally permissible in cases in which keeping the promise would require you to do something that is itself seriously morally wrong.

A counterexample to Candidate B would be a case where it is *not* morally permissible to break a promise even though keeping the promise would require you to do something seriously morally wrong. None of the obvious counterexamples we offered against Candidate A meets that condition, and it is relatively difficult to think up *any* examples of cases in which you ought to do something seriously morally wrong just because you promised you would. Candidate B thus satisfies the first criterion of a useful principle: it is not open to obvious counterexamples.

However, Candidate B fails to satisfy the second criterion: it gives no guidance about the case we're interested in. We want to know whether it is permissible to break the deathbed promise to Grandma. But maintaining her cabin is not itself seriously morally wrong, so a principle that focuses on promises to do immoral things is beside the point. We need, instead, to identify a principle that clearly applies to the kind of promise you made to Grandma.

Candidate C: Breaking a promise is morally permissible in cases in which the person to whom you made the promise would not want you to keep it.

A counterexample to Candidate C would be a case in which it is *not* morally permissible to break a promise even though the person you made the promise to does not want you to keep it. None of the obvious counterexamples we offered against Candidate A meets that condition, and it is relatively difficult to think up *any* examples of cases in which you have a moral obligation to keep a promise that your promisee does not want you to keep. Candidate C thus satisfies the first criterion of a useful principle: it is not open to obvious counterexamples.

Candidate C also has clear implications for your promise to Grandma. Presumably, your grandma would not want you to endure financial hardship in order to maintain her cabin. Because she cares about you, she wouldn't want you to keep your promise. Candidate C thus gives you guidance about your promise to grandma: it's morally permissible to break it.

It took a bit of brainstorming, and a careful search for counterexamples, but we have now identified a principle, Candidate C, that has the two features we're looking for: it avoids obvious counterexamples and gives clear guidance in the case of the deathbed promise to Grandma.

The lesson: when developing an Argument from Principle, do not be too wedded to the first principle that occurs to you. Test that principle by looking for counterexamples. If you discover counterexamples, refine your first-draft principle to address them. Continue until you identify a principle that (i) avoids obvious counterexamples and (ii) gives guidance about the case you're interested in. Once you have a principle that satisfies both criteria, you are ready to move ahead.

USING THE PRINCIPLE IN AN ARGUMENT

Once you've refined a plausible principle, the next step is to outline it in the *General Form of Arguments from Principle*:

1. Cases of type A have moral status S.
2. Case x is of type A.

    Therefore, case x has moral status S.

In the case of the deathbed promise, a standard form representation of the argument looks like this:

1. Breaking a promise is morally permissible in cases in which the person to whom you made the promise would not want you to keep it.
2. Your grandmother wouldn't want you to keep your promise about the cabin.

Therefore, breaking your promise to your grandmother is morally permissible.

Is this a good argument? There is work yet to be done before we decide: we must evaluate both premises. Note that while premise 1 is not open to *obvious* counterexamples, careful thought suggests some possibilities. For example, suppose you have promised your friend that you will attend her parents' funeral, but on the day you decide you'd rather stay home and watch TV. Suppose also that your friend has such low self-esteem that she believes her needs are not as important as yours, and so she would not want you to keep your promise. In this case, it seems obviously wrong for you to break that promise, but the principle in premise 1 says it is permissible. Further discussion will help determine if this counterexample undermines the argument.

So what should you do? Should you break your deathbed promise to your grandmother? There is even more work to do before you settle on an answer to that question. We have so far developed a single argument that is worth considering. Before you settle on a course of action, you should generate and vigorously evaluate the best arguments *on both sides* of the question, and then decide which arguments are the most persuasive. Developing one Argument from Principle is only the first step in that process.

PREPARING YOUR ARGUMENT FOR PRESENTATION

With a properly structured, well-refined argument in hand, the last step is to prepare your argument for presentation to others. Whether you are planning to explain and defend your argument in an academic paper, a letter to the editor, or a public discussion, you will need more than your standard form representation. Those bare bones of your argument, on their own, give your audience little reason to accept the premises you offer and may in fact confuse them. Supplementary information is usually needed in order to make your argument accessible and persuasive to others.

In general, useful supplementary information contributes to one of two interrelated goals: helping your audience understand what your premises mean, and helping your audience see why they should believe those premises are true. Doing this well will often require three kinds of supplementary information. First, you should define and explain any unusual or unfamiliar terms you use. Second, you should illustrate your generalizations with examples. Third, if you make any empirical claims that are not obviously true, you should supply the evidence that leads you to believe those claims are, in fact, true.

Example: Climate change reparations

1. An individual or group ought to bear the burdens of fixing a problem to the extent that they are responsible for causing it.[1]
2. The United States, more than any other nation, is responsible for the greenhouse gas emissions that have resulted in global climate change.

Therefore, the United States ought to bear the greatest burdens of addressing global climate change.

This standard-form presentation makes clear the key components of the argument, but this alone does not make for an effective piece of persuasive writing. Faced with this skeletal presentation, it is unlikely that readers will be able to come away with a complete and charitable understanding of the argument. Both premises require supplementary information to make clear their meaning and explain their appeal.

In providing supplementary information in support of premise 1, our goals are to help readers *understand* what the principle means and to *persuade* them that the principle is probably true. Illustrative examples help achieve both those goals. For example:

> **Explanation of premise 1:** Justice requires that those who are primarily responsible for a wrong ought to bear the greatest burdens of fixing it. For instance, suppose you and your friends rented a car together, and you negligently left your ice cream sandwich to melt on the seat. In that case, you clearly ought to be the one who bears most of the responsibility for fixing the mess, either by cleaning it up yourself or paying the cleaning fee. Or, suppose that a manufacturing company knowingly uses chemicals that pollute the local drinking water. The polluting company, rather than the locals who drink the water, should bear the primary burden of clean-up, because the company is responsible for causing the mess in the first place.

Although it is brief, this explanation effectively uses illustrative examples to show how the principle applies in particular cases. This not only makes it clear what the principle means but also helps to show why the principle is plausible. Depending on the situation, you may need to include more detailed supplementary information. If your principle is especially complex, or contains terms that need defining, or if you are writing an academic paper in which the standards of argumentation are high, you'll often need more supplementary information in order to support premise 1 effectively.

Premise 2 also requires supplementary information to explain to readers what the premise means and why they should think it is true. Because premise 2 makes an empirical claim that is not universally known to be true, it should be supported with reliable evidence.

> **Explanation of premise 2:** There is good evidence that the United States is responsible for more of the carbon emissions that have produced global climate

---

[1]For an in-depth discussion of a version of this argument, see Stephen M. Gardiner, "Ethics and Climate Change: An Introduction," *WIREs Climate Change* 1, no. 1 (2010): 54–66.

change than any other nation. According to a report by the World Resources Institute, the United States is responsible for 27% of all the CO_2 emissions from 1850–2011, which is more than any other nation, including all the nations of the European Union combined.[2]

This brief explanation of the premise is enough to explain the main idea and to give some initial reason to accept the claim as true. Depending on the situation, you may want to provide more detail. Is there any other apparent evidence *against* premise 2? Does it matter that the explanation only discusses CO_2 emissions but not other greenhouse gas emissions? Why are the years 1850 to 2011 significant? A complete discussion or defense of the argument would likely need to address these questions.

The lesson: supplementary information is usually needed to turn a standard-form representation of an argument into an effective piece of persuasive writing. In the case of Arguments from Principle, supplemental material will typically involve examples illustrating the principle that grounds the argument and empirical support for the claim that the target case is governed by that principle.

COMMON PITFALLS IN DEVELOPING ARGUMENTS FROM PRINCIPLE

In our experience, students asked to write an original Argument from Principle for the first time most commonly stumble in one of two specific ways. As you begin to develop your argument-writing skills, be especially on the lookout for these two problems in your early drafts.

Pitfall 1: Your principle is open to obvious counterexamples

Particularly when we are writing an argument for a conclusion we already believe is true, we are at risk of too-readily accepting a moral principle that appears to get us the conclusion we want. In such a situation, it can be difficult to recognize counterexamples, even when those counterexamples should be obvious. This pitfall is easily avoided if you develop two habits.

First: when you write, *always* imagine that you are writing for an audience that will critically engage your work. Imagine how your suggested principle sounds to an intelligent person who has never heard it before or who disagrees with the conclusion you're arguing for. What counterexamples would such a person probably suggest?

Second: discuss your work with friends and classmates. Explain your candidate principle to them. Do they understand it? Do any counterexamples strike them as obvious?

---

[2]See "6 Graphs Explain the World's Top 10 Emitters," Nov. 25, 2014. http://www.wri.org/blog/2014/11/6-graphs-explain-world%E2%80%99s-top-10-emitters. Accessed July 11, 2018.

Pitfall 2: The connection between your principle and the case under discussion is dubious

Some moral principles are so plausible that it seems unlikely that they're open to any realistic counterexamples, and they might even be immune to fanciful examples. Philosophers sometimes use the following principle as an example of an unassailable moral principle: torturing children for fun is morally wrong.

Although this moral principle is plausible, imagine it employed in the following argument:

The Teacher Torture Argument:

1. Torturing children for fun is morally wrong.
2. Philosophy essays are painful to read.

Therefore, it is morally wrong for professors to assign philosophy readings.

As written, premise 2 isn't obviously false. But does it actually have anything to do with the principle in premise 1? One way to test it is to rephrase it so that it better matches the General Form of Argument from Principle. Premise 2 should assert that the case at hand (professors assigning philosophy readings) is an action of type *A* (torturing children for fun). That yields a more clearly expressed version of the argument:

The Teacher Torture Argument	General Form of Arguments from Principle
1. Torturing children for fun is morally wrong.	1. Cases of type *A* have moral status *S*.
2. Professors who assign philosophy readings are torturing children for fun.	2. Case *x* is of type *A*.
So, assigning philosophy readings is morally wrong.	So, case *x* has moral status *S*

Once the case is properly framed to match the principle, a variety of problems become obvious. Even if it's true that philosophy essays are painful to read, they aren't *torture*. Reading philosophy is in several important ways *not* relevantly similar to waterboarding, electrocution, stress positions, and solitary confinement. Also, relatively few college students are appropriately characterized as children. Finally, philosophy professors assign philosophy readings because they believe students will benefit from struggling with them—they don't assign them for fun. These problems were obscured by the poor structure of the initial draft of the argument. Structuring the argument properly, in a way that frames the case as an instance of the principle, makes the problems immediately clear.

To ensure that the connection between your case and your principle is tight, structure your argument to match the General Form of Argument from Principle. If the second premise seems plausible after doing so, then this is evidence that your principle indeed applies to the target case.

REVIEW: ARGUMENT FROM PRINCIPLE STEP-BY-STEP

We've recommended the following steps for developing Arguments from Principle worth taking seriously:

1. Think carefully through the details of the target case, and articulate the principle you think determines what is right (or wrong) in that kind of case.
2. Test your principle by looking for counterexamples.
3. If necessary, modify the principle to avoid counterexamples.
4. Repeat steps (2) and (3) until you are reasonably sure you have a principle that avoids obvious counterexamples and gives guidance about the target case.
5. Use the General Form for Argument from Principle to represent your argument in standard form.
6. Brainstorm objections to both premises of your argument, on your own and with the input of others who might disagree with you. Revise your argument as needed to address any objections that seem important.
7. Prepare your argument for presentation by including the supplementary information that will best help others understand the persuasive force of your argument.

Developing your own Arguments from Principle requires both creative and logical thinking. It is a worthwhile challenge to undertake, because the process of writing and refining your own arguments almost always has good outcomes. You might discover that an issue you thought was simple and obvious is more complicated than you thought. You might discover that your initial answers to a controversial question were simply wrong, and you need to change your mind. Or you might discover a clearer and more persuasive way to defend your views. In each of these cases, the process of developing your own arguments leaves you with better considered, articulated, and defended views about what matters.

CHAPTER 8

Analyzing Arguments from Analogy

CHAPTER GOALS

By reading this chapter and completing the exercises, you will learn how to:
- Represent an Argument from Analogy in Standard Form using the General Form of Argument from Analogy
- Recognize and articulate implicit premises in an Argument from Analogy.
- Distinguish premises from the supplementary information that supports them.

ANALYZING ARGUMENTS FROM ANALOGY

On September 19, 2016, Donald Trump, Jr., the son of President Trump, posted a tweet that went viral. Appended to the picture (Figure 8.1), Trump, Jr. tweeted "This image says it all. Let's end the politically correct agenda that doesn't put America first."[1]

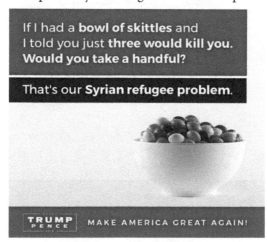

---

[1]https://twitter.com/DonaldJTrumpJr/status/778016283342307328/. The post was subsequently removed because of apparent copyright violations.

This picture offers an Argument from Analogy: it seeks to establish a controversial conclusion about American refugee policy by drawing an analogy to our broadly shared judgments about what to do with poisoned candy.

Public debates and published philosophy both regularly feature Arguments from Analogy. This form of argument draws its appeal, and its power, from a background commitment nearly everyone shares: we ought to treat morally similar cases similarly, and like cases alike.

As always, we must understand arguments before we can evaluate them. This chapter demonstrates how to understand Arguments from Analogy by analyzing their structure. The following chapters demonstrate how to evaluate Arguments from Analogy and how to develop your own.

THE GENERAL FORM OF ARGUMENTS FROM ANALOGY

In their most basic form, Arguments from Analogy are two-premise arguments: they assert a broadly accepted judgment about an uncontroversial case, and they assert that the uncontroversial case and the controversial case under discussion are so morally similar that we should treat them alike. They are all instances of this general form:

General Form of Argument from Analogy
1. Case x has moral status S.
2. Case y is relevantly similar to case x.

Therefore, case y has moral status S.

Look again at the poisoned Skittles Argument from Analogy that begins this chapter. We represent that visual argument in General Form of Argument from Analogy this way:

1. We ought not eat any Skittles from a bowl that includes some poisoned Skittles. (JUDGMENT)
2. Allowing Syrian refugees into the United States is relevantly similar to eating from a bowl containing some poisoned Skittles. (ANALOGY)

Therefore, the United States ought not allow any Syrian refugees into the country. (CONCLUSION)

The first premise asserts a moral judgment about an uncontroversial case: it says that case x (choosing to eat from a bowl of poisoned Skittles) has a clear moral status (we shouldn't do it). Second, it asserts that the choice about whether to embrace Syrian refugees fleeing civil war is so morally similar to the decision to eat from a poisoned candy bowl that we should treat these two cases alike. If both premises are true, then the author's conclusion follows: we shouldn't embrace any Syrian refugees.

REPRESENTING ARGUMENTS FROM
ANALOGY IN STANDARD FORM

The process of faithfully representing any argument in standard form involves three phases. First, identify the *conclusion* the author is arguing for. Second, articulate the key claims the author appeals to in order to justify that conclusion; that is, articulate the argument's *premises*. Third, reread both your standard-form representation and the author's original passage to confirm that you have accurately and charitably represented the author's argument. (For a more detailed discussion of standard form, see Chapter 4.)

If you recognize that you are working with an Argument from Analogy, phase two of this process becomes easier, because you know exactly what key components you need to find. First, you must articulate the *judgment* the author asserts about an uncontroversial described case (case *x*). Second, you must articulate the author's claim about the *analogy* between the uncontroversial described case and the controversial target case (case *y*).

Example: Jewish refugees in World War II

The Nazi attempt to eliminate Jewish people from Europe generated a wave of Jewish refugees during World War II. Throughout the 1930s, and well into the 1940s, the United States refused to accept significant numbers of Jewish refugees.[2] Jewish refugees were stereotyped as insidious agents of un-American ideologies and religions, a drain on State resources, and as a possible Trojan Horse for Nazi agents attempting to sneak into the country. A particularly egregious consequence of this fear-mongering occurred in 1939, when the *MS St. Louis*, a German ship carrying more than 900 Jewish refugees fleeing imprisonment and execution, was turned away by American authorities at a Florida port. The ship eventually had no choice but to return to Europe, where 254 of its passengers were eventually killed in the Holocaust.

American cold-heartedness toward Jewish refugees in World War II, motivated by ignorant bigotry and groundless fear, is one of the great stains on this nation's history. We are, right now, seeing exactly the same kind of cowardice and bigotry driving President Trump's attempts to categorically exclude Syrian refugees from the United States. Syrians today, like European Jews in the 1930s, are fleeing a war zone in which the threats to their lives are urgent and constant. Syrians today, like European Jews in the 1930s, are caricatured as insidious agents of foreign ideologies, a drain on State resources, and potential terrorist infiltrators. We should not forget the lessons of the past. Just as it was morally wrong to turn away the *MS St. Louis* and other desperate refugees in 1939, it is morally wrong to close our borders to Syrian refugees today.

---

[2]The following passage paraphrases a common argument for welcoming Syrian refugees. For a readable overview of this kind of argument, see: http://www.vox.com/policy-and-politics/2017/1/27/14412082/refugees-history-holocaust. For a well-sourced and detailed catalog of the historical points of correspondence, see: https://theintercept.com/2015/11/18/syrian-jews-refugees/. For an interview that focuses on the lessons to be learned from the plight of the MS St Louis, see: https://www.theatlantic.com/politics/archive/2017/01/jewish-refugees-in-the-us/514742/.

To represent the argument in standard form, first ask: What conclusion is the author arguing for? In this case, the conclusion is clearly stated right at the end: it is morally wrong for the United States to close its borders to Syrian refugees.

Second, ask: What components are essential to the author's case for that conclusion? There are two components, characteristic of all Arguments from Analogy. First, the author asserts a judgment about an uncontroversial case. Here, the author describes the plight of Jewish refugees in World War II, expecting that readers will agree that American treatment of those refugees was morally wrong. Second, the author asserts that Trump-era attempts to exclude Syrian refugees are relevantly similar to our historical exclusion of Jewish refugees. The implication is that we should transfer our moral condemnation of WWII-era policies excluding Jewish refugees to present-day policies excluding Syrian refugees. The remainder of the passage is supplementary information aimed at explaining and clarifying those two premises. In standard form for Argument from Analogy:

1. American exclusion of Jewish refugees during World War II was morally wrong. (JUDGMENT)
2. American exclusion of Syrian refugees today is relevantly similar to the exclusion of Jewish refugees during WWII. (ANALOGY)

   Therefore, American exclusion of Syrian refugees is morally wrong. (CONCLUSION)

Third, ask: have we accurately and charitably represented the argument? Would the author of the above passage accept this standard-form representation of the argument?

ANALYZING ARGUMENTS WITH IMPLICIT PREMISES

Arguments published in essays or offered in public debates often include implicit premises and supplementary information. When an author relies on implicit premises, you should explicitly state those premises in your standard-form representation of the argument. If you have recognized that the passage you are analyzing contains an Argument from Analogy, it is easy to recognize and articulate implicit premises.

Example: sharing Netflix passwords
You shouldn't share your Netflix password with your friends. That's no different than picking the pockets of the artists who make the shows.

The argument draws an analogy between picking pockets and sharing passwords, but it leaves implicit a key premise. We can represent the explicitly stated portions of the argument like so:

1. . . .
2. Sharing Netflix passwords is relevantly similar to picking artists' pockets. (ANALOGY)

   Therefore, sharing Netflix passwords is wrong. (CONCLUSION)

Articulating the implicit premise is easy once we have understood the General Form of Argument from Analogy, because that form highlights for us exactly what is missing from this passage.

The Passwords Argument	General Form of Argument from Analogy
1. . . .	**1.** Case x has moral status S.
2. Sharing Netflix passwords is like picking pockets.	**2.** Case y is relevantly similar to case x.
Therefore, sharing Netflix passwords is wrong.	Therefore, case y has moral status S.

The original passage left implicit the judgment the author expects us to form about the morality of pick-pocketing. This is perfectly sensible—we all, presumably, believe that picking pockets is morally wrong. But when representing an argument in standard form, we make these implicit assumptions explicit, both to check our understanding of the argument and to promote careful evaluation of *all* of its premises:

1. Picking pockets is morally wrong. (JUDGMENT)
2. Sharing Netflix passwords is relevantly similar to picking pockets. (ANALOGY)

Therefore, sharing Netflix passwords is morally wrong. (CONCLUSION)

The lesson: understanding the General Form of Argument from Analogy makes it easy to recognize and articulate premises authors have left unstated.

ANALYZING PASSAGES WITH SUPPLEMENTARY INFORMATION

Arguments in the real world typically include supplementary information. We've encountered a few main types of supplementary information in previous chapters: *background information* that helps a reader understand a moral argument by describing context or defining relevant terms, and *illustration and/or justification of premises*. Sorting premises from supplementary information is easy if you recognize that you are working with an Argument from Analogy.

Example: Against pets

Domesticated animals are completely dependent on humans, who control *every* aspect of their lives.[3] Unlike human children, who will one day become autonomous, non-humans never will. That is the entire point of domestication—we *want* domesticated animals to depend on us. [. . .] We might make them happy

---

[3]Quoted from Francione and Charlton, "The Case Against Pets." Available online: https://aeon.co/essays/why-keeping-a-pet-is-fundamentally-unethical

in one sense, but the relationship can never be 'natural' or 'normal.' They do not belong in our world, irrespective of how well we treat them. This is more or less true of all domesticated non-humans. They are perpetually dependent on us. We control their lives forever. They truly are 'animal slaves.' Some of us might be benevolent masters, but we really can't be anything more than that . . . .

We love our dogs, but recognize that, if the world were more just and fair, there would be no pets at all [because holding animals as property is fundamentally unjust and unfair].

The authors are clearly drawing an analogy between two particular practices: pet-ownership and slave-ownership. As soon as you recognize that they are offering an Argument from Analogy, you can re-read the passage with the General Form of Argument from Analogy in mind. Once you do that, it becomes clear that most of this passage is supplementary information intended to illustrate and support the claim that owning pets is like owning slaves. The judgment, which the authors have left implicit because it is so obviously true, is that slave-ownership is unjust and unfair. In standard form:

1. Owning slaves is unjust and unfair. (JUDGMENT)
2. Owning pets is relevantly similar to owning slaves. (ANALOGY)

So, owning pets is unjust and unfair. (CONCLUSION)

The lesson: understanding the General Form for Argument from Analogy makes it easy to sort premises from the supplementary information that supports them.

WHY USE ARGUMENTS FROM ANALOGY?

A good analogy walks a fine line: it presents us with a new described case that's different enough from the controversial subject to allow us to get a "clean read" on what we actually believe, but similar enough to allow us to transfer our judgment from the analogous case to the controversial case. It draws our attention to cases in which our moral sensitivities are probably functioning well, and allows us to use that case as a guide to a controversial issue, in which our moral sensitivities might be confused or in conflict.

Consider, for example, the controversy surrounding Physician-Assisted Death. In Oregon, California, and several other states, doctors may prescribe a lethal dose of pain medication to terminal patients who request that. In most other states, doctors are not permitted to prescribe a lethal dose of those drugs under any circumstances. Which states have it right? Is it ever morally permissible for doctors to prescribe lethal medication to terminal patients who have asked for help in dying? That is the controversy of Physician-Assisted Death.

Part of the reason this controversy invites so much passion on both sides is that each side tends to have a different image in mind when they imagine doctors administering lethal drugs. Those who believe Physician-Assisted Death is always morally wrong tend to think that the job of doctors is to sustain life, and deliberately ending life tears at the very foundation of medical practice.

Is it *true* that participating in Physician-Assisted Death tears at the foundation of medical practice? Argument from Analogy is one way to think critically about this question.

Example: the analogy of euthanasia for pets

One of the sad jobs veterinarians must do is euthanize beloved pets when those animals become so sick that they are suffering with no prospect of improvement. Virtually everyone accepts that in certain circumstances, euthanizing a beloved pet can be an act of compassion. In fact, virtually everyone acknowledges that there are some circumstances in which refusing to euthanize a hopelessly suffering pet is selfish and cruel. If, when it comes to the proper care of pets, euthanasia can be an act of compassion (and a necessary part of good veterinary care) why can't the same be true of people? If someone is hopelessly suffering badly enough that they ask to be "put to sleep" (to use the veterinary parlance), why wouldn't that be an act of compassion, and an aspect of good medical practice?

In standard form for Argument from Analogy:

1. In some cases, euthanizing a terminally ill pet is an act of compassion and a component of good veterinary practice. (JUDGMENT)
2. Some instances of Physician-Assisted Death for people are relevantly similar to euthanasia for terminally ill pets. (ANALOGY)

   Therefore, some instances of Physician-Assisted Death are acts of compassion and a component of good medical practice. (CONCLUSION)

Arguing by analogy in this case allows us to take stock of our moral commitments in an area of minimal controversy—the compassionate treatment of beloved pets—and to consider whether those are the commitments that should guide us in the controversial area of end-of-life decisions for beloved family members or, for that matter, ourselves. Understanding and critically evaluating this argument focuses our attention on morally important features of euthanasia even if we disagree about which moral principles are central to the euthanasia debate.

In general, analogies allow us to access controversial topics through the door of less controversial topics. They allow us to make philosophical and moral progress in difficult terrain by carefully transferring moral judgments we're very confident about to relevantly similar topics we are less sure about.

This, at least, is the promise of Argument from Analogy. Of course, not all analogies are *good* analogies. In the next chapter you'll learn strategies for evaluating them.

REVIEW

An Argument from Analogy suggests that we should transfer our moral judgment about an uncontroversial case to a morally similar controversial case. Arguments from Analogy share a common structure.

The general form of Arguments from Analogy

1. Case x has moral status S. (JUDGMENT)
2. Case y is relevantly similar to case x. (ANALOGY)

Therefore, case y has moral status S. (CONCLUSION)

To test your understanding of the material introduced in this chapter, complete the Demonstration Exercises and then check your answers against the solutions that follow.

Demonstration Exercises

Demonstration Exercises are designed to give you immediate feedback on your grasp of the skills introduced in this chapter. To use them effectively, you should attempt answers to all of them, then check your work against our suggested answers, which follow. For a detailed explanation of how best to use Demonstration Exercises, read the book's Introduction.

Demonstration Exercises 8A: Identifying Premises and Conclusions

Exercise Instructions: Supply the missing premise or conclusion to make a properly structured Argument from Analogy.

1.
    1. Stealing a CD from a band's merchandise table at a concert is wrong.
    2. ...

       So, illegally downloading music is wrong.

2.
    1. ...
    2. Plagiarizing a college paper is relevantly similar to a professional athlete using prohibited performance-enhancing drugs.

       Thus, plagiarizing a college paper is morally wrong.

3.
    1. Getting a copy of a band's album from a friend who purchased it is morally permissible.
    2. Illegally downloading a band's album is relevantly similar to getting a copy of the album from a friend who purchased it.

       Therefore, ...

Demonstration Exercises 8B: Representing Arguments from Analogy in Standard Form

Exercise Instructions: Represent the following arguments in standard form using the General Form of Argument from Analogy.

(continued)

1. Corvino's defense of same-sex sex[4]

Many people who object to gay and lesbian romantic relationships do so by appealing to the fact that gay and lesbian sex can't be *procreative* sex. But this objection quite obviously misunderstands the role of sex in romantic relationships. To see this, imagine a committed, loving, and happy heterosexual couple who cannot have procreative sex because the woman has had a hysterectomy. Everyone can agree that there's nothing morally wrong with those two continuing their romantic relationship, and no moral problem when they have non-procreative sex. Babies, after all, aren't the only reason heterosexual couples have sex.

Gay and lesbian relationships are no different. Even though sex in gay relationships can't produce babies, it can produce lots of other good things, such as intimacy, pleasure, trust, and emotional support. Just as non-procreative heterosexual sex is morally permissible, so too is gay sex.

2. In favor of kidney markets

As the law stands right now, you are legally permitted to sell your own blood plasma to a blood bank, but you are not allowed to sell one of your kidneys to a kidney bank. This makes no sense—the two types of sale are so similar that they should be treated the same way. Volunteers can recover fully after selling plasma, and they can recover fully after selling a kidney, too. Volunteers in both cases are healthy and clear-headed, so it is easy to obtain informed consent. Other patients benefit significantly from a healthier supply of both plasma and kidneys. I am (and should be) allowed to sell my plasma because the law recognizes that selling plasma benefits everyone. I should be allowed to sell one of my kidneys, too.

3. A defense of race-based affirmative action in college admissions

Elite universities seek a wide variety of forms of diversity in their freshmen classes. The varieties of diversity universities seek includes, among others, geographical diversity, athletic diversity, and diversity of extra-curricular interests. If the University of Minnesota gets only a small handful of applications from California, those Californian applicants have a better chance of getting in. If the overwhelming majority of applicants served on student government in high school, that's no longer a distinguishing factor, and students with less common activities are more likely to get in. All of these various diversity considerations are a long-standing part of the college admissions process, and no one complains about them. And people *shouldn't* complain about them, because these various dimensions of diversity contribute to a thriving, interesting, and balanced student body.

But if it is morally permissible to seek all of these other-than-racial kinds of diversity in assembling a freshman class, then why on earth would it be wrong to seek *racial* diversity in assembling a freshman class? It wouldn't.

4. Against imitation meat[5]

Most people think it is morally permissible to eat imitation meat products, such as veggie burgers that look like beef burgers and imitation chicken nuggets made out of tofu. These people are mistaken. It is, in fact, morally wrong to eat realistic imitation meat.

---

[4]Adapted from a passage in John Corvino, "Why Shouldn't Tommy and Jim Have Sex? A Defense of Homosexuality." Available online: http://johncorvino.com/academic/

[5]Adapted from Bob Fischer and Burkay Ozturk, "Facsimiles of Flesh," *Journal of Applied Philosophy*, 34(4): 489–497.

Imagine a detective who captured a serial killer who had made a lampshade from the skin of his victims. Suppose, as a keepsake to remember the case, the detective commissions a perfect replica of the lamp—the replica is not actually made of human skin but otherwise appears to be exactly the same as the killer's lamp. It is clearly wrong for the detective to commission a replica of the human skin lamp, even if the replica is not made of real human skin. Eating realistic imitation meat products is morally no different than commissioning an imitation human skin lamp, so eating imitation meat is wrong, too.

5. Texting while driving is wrong

It is not uncommon today to see someone texting on their smartphone while they're driving.[6] Whether they're unable to wait to read the next text from a friend or eager to see the latest updates on their social media feeds, many people seem to think there's nothing wrong with picking up their phone and actively texting while driving their car. Even though it is socially accepted, texting while driving is morally wrong. Morally speaking, texting while driving is no different than driving drunk. Driving drunk is wrong because impairs attentiveness and reaction times. There is ample evidence that texting while driving does the same thing, so it is wrong, too.

6. Graphical analogy: National Congress of American Indians on the Cleveland Indians

Background: The Cleveland Indians is a real baseball team, and their actual mascot is represented on the rightmost cap. For decades, the team refused requests to change their name and mascot, though in 2019 they did retire the "Chief Wahoo" logo from their official uniforms.

In 2001, the National Congress of American Indians commissioned this poster, which offers an argument from analogy in graphical form:

The poster achieved viral internet fame in 2013, when a CBS affiliate in Cleveland published a story featuring it. Many viewers reacted with offense, as if the *poster* is racist. If you properly represent the poster in standard form for Argument from Analogy, you'll easily be able to explain why this poster is not racist.

---

[6]Adapted from an argument discussed in Jason Swartwood, "Drinking, Texting, and Moral Arguments from Analogy," *Think* 16, no. 45(2017): 15–26.

Solutions to Demonstration Exercises

Demonstration Exercises will be most useful if you make your best attempt to complete them before you look at the answers. If you haven't yet attempted answers to all the Demonstration Exercises, go back and do that now.

Solutions to Demonstration Exercises 8A: Identifying Premises and Conclusions

1.

　1. Stealing a CD from a band's merchandise table at a concert is wrong.

　2. *Illegally downloading music is relevantly similar to stealing a CD from a band's merchandise table.*

　So, illegally downloading music is wrong.

2.

　1. *It is morally wrong for professional athletes to use prohibited performance-enhancing drugs.*

　2. Plagiarizing a college paper is relevantly similar to a professional athlete using prohibited performance-enhancing drugs.

　Thus, plagiarizing a college paper is morally wrong.

3.

　1. Getting a copy of a band's album from a friend who purchased it is morally permissible.

　2. Illegally downloading a band's album is relevantly similar to getting a copy of the album from a friend who purchased it.

　Therefore, illegally downloading a band's album is morally permissible.

Solutions to Demonstration Exercises 8B: Putting Arguments into Standard Form

Note: your standard-form representations should identify the same judgment, analogy, and conclusion as we have, but variation in wording or expression is perfectly fine.

1. **Corvino's defense of homosexuality**

　1. Non-procreative heterosexual sex is morally permissible. (JUDGMENT)

　2. Gay and lesbian sex is relevantly similar to non-procreative heterosexual sex. (ANALOGY)

　So, gay and lesbian sex is morally permissible. (CONCLUSION)

2. **In favor of kidney markets**

　1. People should be allowed to sell their blood plasma. (JUDGMENT)

　2. Allowing people to sell their kidneys is relevantly similar to allowing people to sell their blood plasma. (ANALOGY)

　Therefore, people should be allowed to sell their kidneys. (CONCLUSION)

3. **A defense of race-based affirmative action policies in college admissions**
   1. It is not morally wrong to seek geographic diversity in assembling a freshman class. (JUDGMENT)
   2. Racial diversity is relevantly similar to geographic diversity. (ANALOGY)

   Thus, it is not morally wrong to seek racial diversity in assembling a freshman class. (CONCLUSION)

4. **Against imitation meat**
   1. It is morally wrong for the detective to purchase a replica lamp made out of realistic imitation human skin. (JUDGMENT)
   2. Buying realistic imitation meat products is relevantly similar to buying a fake human-skin lamp. (ANALOGY)

   Therefore, buying realistic imitation meat products is morally wrong. (CONCLUSION)

5. **Texting while driving is wrong**
   1. Driving while drunk is morally wrong. (JUDGMENT)
   2. Texting while driving is relevantly similar to driving while drunk. (ANALOGY)

   So, texting while driving is morally wrong. (CONCLUSION)

6. **National Congress of American Indians on the Cleveland Indians**
   1. The NY Jews and the SF Chinamen are demeaning names and mascots that should not be used. (JUDGMENT)
   2. The Cleveland Indians name and mascot are relevantly similar to the NY Jews and SF Chinamen. (ANALOGY)

   Thus, the Cleveland Indians is a demeaning name and mascot that should not be used. (CONCLUSION)

CHAPTER 8 PRACTICE EXERCISES

ANALYZING ARGUMENTS FROM ANALOGY

Exercises 8A: Identifying Premises and Conclusions
Exercise Instructions: *Supply the missing premise or conclusion to make a properly structured Argument from Analogy.*

1.
   1. Throwing your trash in the street is wrong.
   2. . . . .

   Therefore, failing to recycle is wrong.

2.

   1. . . .

   2. Consuming factory-farmed meat is relevantly similar to paying to watch a dog fight.

   So, consuming factory-farmed meat is wrong.

3.

   1. Denying people the vote based upon their race is unjust.

   2. Denying people the vote based upon their sex or gender is relevantly similar to denying people the vote based upon their race.[7]

   Therefore, . . .

4.

   1. It is morally permissible for a taxi driver to protect themselves by refusing to transport a violent passenger.

   2. . . .

   Thus, it is morally permissible for a nurse to protect themselves by refusing to care for a patient with a highly contagious deadly disease (such as Ebola).

5.

   1. It would be morally wrong for a firefighter to refuse to fight a fire just because it is dangerous.

   2. A nurse refusing to treat an Ebola patient out of concern for his own well-being is relevantly similar to a firefighter refusing to fight a fire just because it is dangerous.

   Therefore, . . .

6.

   1. . . .

   2. Internet service providers selling information about your browsing habits without your consent is relevantly similar to your roommate making and selling videos of you showering without your permission.

   So, internet service providers selling information about your browsing habits without your consent is wrong.

7.

   1. Despite the serious risk of injury to their body and brain, people should be allowed to take paying jobs as players in the NFL.

   2. . . .

   Thus, people should be allowed to be paid to participate in dangerous clinical trials.

---

[7]Adapted from W. E. B. Du Bois, "Heckling the Hecklers," *Crisis*, 3, no. 5(1912): 195.

Exercises 8B: Representing Arguments from Analogy in Standard Form

Exercise Instructions: *represent each of the following arguments in standard form using the General Form of Argument from Analogy.*

1. It would be wrong to end the life of a person in a temporary coma, even if they are currently totally unconscious. Abortion is like ending the life of someone in a coma: a fetus cannot currently think, feel or experience anything right now, but at some point it will be able to do those things. Even if the fetus isn't yet conscious, abortion is wrong.

2. First trimester abortions are morally permissible. That early in a pregnancy, the fetus lacks the brain capacity required for even the most minimal conscious experiences, including pleasure and pain. An abortion that removes a cluster of fetal tissues that can't possibly have conscious experiences is not morally different than a surgery that removes a benign tumor.

3. Some people argue that it's wrongful cultural appropriation—wrongful use of the ideas or practices of another culture—for a white person to wear dreadlocks. But that condemnation is totally unjustified. No one says it's wrongful cultural appropriation for a black woman with kinky hair to straighten it. But this is relevantly similar to a white person wearing dreadlocks: both are cases where a person is adopting practices from another culture. So, it's not wrongful cultural appropriation for a white person to wear dreadlocks.

4. When Victoria's Secret sent a white model out on the runway in a turquoise and suede bikini with a feathered Native American war bonnet headdress, that was morally wrong. Among the Native American tribes who wear them, war bonnets are used to recognize feats of bravery in battle. A white lingerie model wearing a war bonnet is morally no different than a non-veteran wearing as casual jewelry a Medal of Honor or a Purple Heart that they did not earn.[8]

5. I think you'll agree that it's wrong to drive around with a car that heavily pollutes the air, because doing that unnecessarily puts others at increased risk of harm. But that's morally no different than refusing to get your child vaccinated: an unvaccinated child puts other people (especially those with compromised immune systems who can't be vaccinated) at increased risk of harm. It follows that it's wrong to refuse to get your child vaccinated when there's no medical reason they can't get a vaccine.

6. People should be allowed to do stupid and dangerous things like skydive if that's what they want to do. It's their right to take whatever risks they want. Similarly, with people who refuse to vaccinate themselves or their children. Jumping out of a plane and refusing vaccines—I personally think they are both pointless risks. But just as you should be allowed to skydive, you should be allowed to refuse vaccines for yourself or your kids.

---

[8]Adapted from an argument described in https://www.theatlantic.com/entertainment/archive/2015/10/the-dos-and-donts-of-cultural-appropriation/411292/.

7. Some Deaf couples intentionally choose to have a deaf child using preimplantation genetic diagnosis: they create embryos in the lab and identify and implant only those which are genetically predisposed to deafness. But this is wrong, because it's like drinking alcohol during pregnancy. In both cases, you're intentionally doing something that could lead to having a disabled child just because it gives you some sort of pleasure or satisfaction.[9]

8. Clearly, it's wrong to drive a gas-guzzling car. After all, driving a gas-guzzling car is, morally speaking, no different than driving drunk: in both cases you put yourself and others at increased risk of harm (in the former by contributing to global warming and the latter by increased risk of causing traffic accidents) merely for your own pleasure. Therefore, since drunk driving is wrong, driving a gas-guzzling car is, too.

9. It would clearly be unjust if a society failed to provide women with the same educational opportunities it provides to men. Women should have the same chance to secure the kinds of skills and credentials that will help them succeed in their lives and careers. But if failing to educate women is unjust, then it is also unjust for a society to fail to ensure that women have access to birth control. If the former unfairly and unnecessarily denies women control and opportunity in important aspects of their work and social life, then so does the latter.

10. Imagine the parents of an anorexic daughter did everything they could to help their child starve herself. Those parents are not being *supportive* of their daughter. Rather, they are *harming* her by nurturing in her a misguided self-conception. Parents should not help their children be anorexic.

    Schools who accommodate transgender students by allowing them to express whatever gender identity they choose are doing the same kind of thing. Schools shouldn't help children be trans.[10]

11. The fact that there aren't any short players in the NBA *obviously* isn't evidence that the NBA unjustly excludes short people. Similarly, the fact that women aren't allowed to serve in combat roles in the military isn't evidence the military unjustly excludes women. In both cases, members of some groups simply don't meet the performance-based qualifications required for the job.

12. Imagine that you are a famous concert pianist. One day, while walking along the train tracks, you see a stranger about to be crushed by a train. You know you could save them but in the process you'd lose your hand. Now, it would certainly be nice of you to sacrifice your hand, and thus your career, to save the life of this stranger. But this much is clear: the law should not *require* you to sacrifice your hand for the sake of the stranger.

    Carrying a pregnancy to term likewise involves significant physical sacrifice. If the law shouldn't require you to sacrifice your hand for a stranger, the law shouldn't require you to carry a pregnancy to term, either.

---

[9]Adapted from arguments in Peter Singer, "Ethics and Disability: A Response to Koch," *Journal of Disability Policy Studies*, 16, no. 2 (2005): 133; and Jeff. McMahan, "The Morality of Screening for Disability," *Reproductive Biomedicine Online* 10 (2005): 129–132.

[10]Adapted from an argument in: https://mnchildprotectionleague.com/2015/gender-radicalism/a-defining-moment-for-our-kids/. Accessed Sept. 2, 2016.

13. Suppose there were a suburban dentist with an odd hobby: he likes to capture stray dogs, then torture and kill them in his basement. He likes to take pictures of himself with their bloody bodies and display those pictures in his home. It makes him feel like a big man.

    Some rich people pay large amounts of money to hunt lions in Zimbabwe and other African countries. Even in countries where such trophy hunting is legal, it is morally wrong. Trophy hunters are morally no different than the cruel suburban dentist: both practices cause suffering and death to animals for sick entertainment.[11]

14. Clearly, a vegetarian cafe owner has a right to refuse to serve meat without being punished or fined. An owner of a private hospital refusing to prescribe or dispense birth control is relevantly similar: both are refusing to offer a service they have moral objections to. So, the owner of the private hospital has a right to refuse to prescribe or dispense birth control without being punished or fined by the state.

15. Commercial surrogacy is a practice in which a woman—the surrogate—is paid to carry a baby to term on behalf of another woman who cannot, or does not want to, carry a pregnancy to term. Commercial surrogacy should be illegal. The reason is simple: legalizing commercial surrogacy is, morally speaking, no different from legalizing prostitution. In both cases, women are renting their bodies to people willing to pay to use them as they please. Thank goodness prostitution is illegal! Prostitution exploits women by treating their bodies like commodities, and it disrespects women by treating them as objects to be used instead of persons deserving of respect. This is exactly what commercial surrogacy does.

16. Let's say I break into your house. Let's say that when you discover me in your house, you insist that I leave. But I say, "No! I like it here. It's better than my house. I've made all the beds and washed the dishes and did the laundry and swept the floors. I've done all the things you don't like to do. I'm hard-working and honest (except for when I broke into your house).[12] [In these circumstances you are morally permitted to expel me from your house. That's what the United States is doing when it deports undocumented immigrants.]

17. Doctors should never even consider helping a patient die, even if the patient has requested it, for the same reasons doctors should never even consider having sex with their patients. A total prohibition on doctors having sex with patients, even in situations in which the patient requests it, removes any temptation a doctor might feel to seduce a vulnerable patient. A total prohibition on assisted suicide removes any temptation a doctor might feel to urge a vulnerable patients to prematurely end their lives.[13]

18. Some religious pharmacists object to the use of birth control and further believe that, because of their moral objection, they have a moral right to refuse to fill birth control prescriptions. I believe these pharmacists are wrong—all

---

[11]Adapted from an argument in Alastair Norcross, "Puppies, Pigs, and People: Eating Meat and Marginal Cases," *Philosophical Perspectives* 18 (2004): 229–245.

[12]Quoted from https://conservativecolloquium.wordpress.com/2008/03/15/lets-say-i-break-into-your-house-illegal-immigration-analogy/. Accessed August 17, 2019.

[13]Adapted from an argument in Paul Weithman, "Of Assisted Suicide and 'The Philosophers' Brief'," in *Ethics*, 109, no. 3 (1999): 548–578.

pharmacists have a duty to fill birth control prescriptions, whether or not they personally object to birth control.

Think about it this way. Ethical vegans are people who have moral objections to meat, dairy, eggs, fur, leather, and all other animal products. What if a bunch of ethical vegans took jobs as checkout clerks in grocery stores? Do they have a moral right to refuse to ring up any customers who are trying to purchase non-vegan food? I don't think they do. Vegans are welcome to their own beliefs, and welcome not to use animal products themselves. But if they choose to take a job that sometimes involves letting non-vegan people buy non-vegan food, they have a duty to do their job. Pharmacists who object to birth control have a moral obligation to fill those prescriptions for the same reason.[14]

19. Some bakers refuse to bake wedding cakes for same-sex couples on the grounds that same-sex relationships violate their religious values. The law should not protect these bakers from sanctions for their refusal; they *should* face penalties for refusing service on religious grounds. We can see this by looking at other cases.

For instance, in 2007 there was some controversy at Minneapolis/St. Paul International Airport, when many Muslim taxi drivers, citing their own religious objections to alcohol, refused to transport passengers who were carrying alcohol (such as wine from a trip to California, or duty-free alcohol from an international flight). Some passengers were refused by many taxi drivers in a row and left standing in the cold waiting for a taxi that would take their money. After receiving many complaints, the airport commission imposed a penalty of a thirty-day suspension for drivers who refused fares for religious reasons. That is what the airport commission should have done. When someone voluntarily takes a job providing taxi service to the public, they should not be allowed to impose their religious beliefs on others by refusing to provide taxi service to those who do not share their religious values. Taxi drivers who do that should not be protected from sanctions.

Bakers refusing to bake cakes for same-sex couples are morally no different from taxi drivers who refuse service to people carrying alcohol. Bakers shouldn't be protected from sanctions either.[15]

20. Suppose a photographer takes pictures for all sorts of different events but refuses to do children's birthday parties, because they don't feel comfortable around children. Clearly, this photographer has a right to refuse to do children's birthday parties without being penalized. Some Christian bakery owners have refused to sell cakes to same-sex couples because they don't feel comfortable around gay people. These cases are morally identical. Therefore, Christian bakers have the right to refuse to sell cakes to same-sex couples without being penalized.[16]

[14]Adapted from cases discussed in Eva LaFollette and Hugh LaFollette, "Private Consciences, Public Acts," *Journal of Medical Ethics*, 33(2007): 249–254.

[15]Adapted from an argument in "Of Christian Bakers & Muslim Cab Drivers," *The American Spectator*, Dec. 12, 2013. http://spectator.org/57069_christian-bakers-muslim-cab-drivers/> http://spectator.org/57069_christian-bakers-muslim-cab-drivers/. Accessed March 1, 2016.

[16]Adapted from a case discussed in John Corvino, Ryan T. Anderson, and Sherif Girgis, *Debating Religious Liberty and Discrimination* (London/New York: Oxford University Press, 2017), 192.

21. [Some people believe that it is morally wrong to hunt and kill wild animals. They are mistaken. Consider an analogy.] No one thinks that [a veterinarian] putting a suffering dog to sleep is inhumane. The same logic applies to hunting . . . .

    Usually, these [wild] animals are in for a painfully slow natural death [due to starvation or disease] or a painfully quick natural death by being eaten alive by other predators . . .

    This may sound harsh, but sometimes ending an animal's misery is the most humane thing to do. That's why it happens in American veterinarian offices every day.[17]

22. Someday we may be able to use genetic manipulation to alter a fetus's genetic code so that it will live a better life. For instance, suppose that one day it is possible for people to increase their child's healthy life-span well beyond the current average. Suppose we have developed the ability to do this safely, with no risk of adverse side-effects for the child. In that situation, parents who can afford it would be morally obligated to use genetic manipulation to extend their child's health span. After all, parents are morally obligated to provide healthy food to their children, because that increases the child's chances for living a longer, healthier life. Genetic manipulation to increase a child's healthy life-span is no different.[18]

23. [Some animal-rights activists object to the use of animals in medical research. They think it is wrong to hurt or kill non-human animals in order to benefit our own species. I believe these animal-rights activists are mistaken. Consider an analogy.]

    A mother is faced with the choice of saving one of two small children from a fire, knowing that the other will die. Suppose that one of the children is her own and that, as is most likely, this is the one she saves. Few would find this choice morally reprehensible; the alternative choice would likely be seen as a failure in the mother's primary duty to her own child; the alternative choice would likely be seen as a failure in the mother's primary duty to her own child . . .

    The mother's choice in the example just given is not as different as it may at first seem from the choices that have to be made with regard to the proper human use of animals . . .

    [J]ust as a mother owes a special duty to her child (and for the same kind of biologically based reasons), so we owe a special duty to members of our own species . . . It would therefore . . . be morally right to carry out the experiments [that cause animal suffering or death with the goal of preventing human suffering or death].[19]

---

[17]Quoted from Wayne Bisbee, "In Defense of Legal Hunting," cnn.com (2017). Available online: http://www.cnn.com/2015/08/11/opinions/bisbee-legal-hunting/.

[18]Adapted from an argument in Julian Savulescu, "Genetic Interventions and the Ethics of Enhancement of Human Beings," in *The Oxford Handbook of Bioethics*, ed. Bonnie Steinbock (London/New York: Oxford University Press, 2007).

[19]Quoted from J. A. Gray, "In Defence of Speciesism," *Behavioral and Brain Sciences*, 13, no.1 (1990): 22–23.

24. During the 2016 election, Republican presidential candidate Rick Santorum argued that we should deport people who are in the United States illegally, even if it means splitting them from their children who, because they were born in the United States, are US citizens.

    He said: "It's like someone who robs a bank because they want to feed their family," . . . "Do I feel bad that they don't have enough money and they felt the need to rob a bank and provide for their family? Of course I feel bad, we all feel bad. . . . But that doesn't obviate the fact that they've broken the law and that there are consequences to breaking the law."[20]

25. We legally prohibit discrimination against people based upon their race or religion when they are searching for a job, a home, or trying to access off-the-rack sales and services. We have good reason for prohibiting these forms of racial discrimination—we have seen for ourselves that allowing them leads to the kind of racial oppression common in the American South before the Civil Rights Act of 1968.

    Many states currently allow similar forms of discrimination based on sexual orientation or gender identity. In many states, for instance, there is no law prohibiting someone from being fired because they are gay or lesbian, being rejected for apartment rental because they are queer or trans, and so on.

    Discriminating against someone based upon their sexual orientation or gender identity is, morally speaking, no different than discriminating based upon their race or religion. That's why we should prohibit discrimination based on sexual orientation and gender identity in employment, housing, and the sale of goods and services.[21]

26. Suppose that Jones lives in a time of serious inequality between racial groups. One racial group has much more wealth, many opportunities for better jobs, better living conditions, better food. Jones, luckily for him, is a member of the much-better-off racial group. Imagine that Jones consistently gives preference to members of his own racial group. When he has jobs to offer, he offers them to people of his race. When he gives to charities, he gives to charities that benefit people of his race. Jones's behavior, it seems to me, is morally offensive.

    American patriotism, understood as the practice of giving preference to the interests of one's own country and compatriots over those of people in other countries, is not importantly different. Patriotism perpetuates unjust inequality between groups by giving preference to people who are already benefiting from that inequality. Patriotic, "Americans first" behavior, like Jones's behavior, is morally offensive.[22]

---

[20]The quotation in the second paragraph is from Elise Foley, "Rick Santorum Compares Undocumented Parents to Bank Robbers," *Huffington Post*, August 20, 2015. http://www.huffington-post.com/entry/rick-santorum-immigration_us_55d60d88e4b0ab468da02dbf)

[21]Adapted from an argument discussed by John Corvino, Ryan Anderson, and Sherif Girgis in *Debating Religious Liberty and Discrimination* (London/New York: Oxford University Press, 2016).

[22]Adapted from an argument in Paul Gomberg (1990), "Patriotism Is Like Racism," *Ethics*, 101(1): 147–148.

27. That a morally acceptable form of patriotism is possible can be seen by comparing patriotism to love or family loyalty. People may (and, one hopes, typically do) have a special interest and concern for their parents, spouses, and children. They really do care more about those "near and dear" than about strangers. Yet, so long as this concern is not an exclusive concern, there is nothing the matter with it. That is, so long as family loyalty does not violate the rights of nonmembers of one's family, then actions inspired by family loyalty or love are perfectly permissible and may reveal important virtues in a person . . .

    Patriotism is exactly like other forms of loyalty. My loyalty to my family may lead me to strive for its well-being in many laudable ways and so may be counted as a virtue. Nonetheless, I may not do anything on behalf of my family's well-being. I may not legitimately kill my child's competitor for a school prize or threaten a neighbor whose house we would like to own. When one engages in immoral actions in order to promote one's own family's well-being, then family devotion is excessive and is no virtue. It remains a virtue so long as it is constrained by other moral principles.[23]

28. [Present-day white men, as innocent beneficiaries of historical injustice, do not owe compensation, including preferential treatment in hiring for desirable jobs, to the non-white victims of historical injustice.] Suppose my parents, divining that I would grow up to have an unsurpassable desire to be a basketball player, bought an expensive growth hormone for me. Unfortunately, a neighbor stole it and gave it to little Michael, who gained the extra 13 inches—my thirteen inches—and shot up to an enviable 6 feet 6 inches. Michael, better known as Michael Jordan, would have been a runt like me but for his luck. As it is he profited from the injustice, and excelled in basketball, as I would have done had I had my proper dose.

    Do I have a right to the millions of dollars that Jordan made as a professional basketball player—the unjustly innocent beneficiary of my growth hormone? I have a right to something from the neighbor who stole the hormone, and it might be kind of Jordan to give me free tickets to the Bull's basketball games, and perhaps I should be remembered in his will. As far as I can see, however, he does not owe me anything, either legally or morally.

    Suppose further that Michael Jordan and I are in high school together and we are both qualified to play basketball, only he is far better than I. Do I deserve to start in his position because I would have been as good as he is had someone not cheated me as a child? Again, I think not. But if being the lucky beneficiary of wrong-doing does not entail that Jordan (or the coach) owes me anything in regards to basketball, why should it be a reason to engage in preferential hiring in academic positions or highly coveted jobs?[24]

---

[23]Quoted from Stephen Nathanson, "In Defense of Moderate Patriotism," *Ethics*, 99, no. 3 (1989): 538.

[24]Quoted from Louis Pojman, "The Case Against Affirmative Action," in *The Ethical Life*, 3rd Ed., ed. Russ Shafer-Landau (New York: Oxford University Press, 2015), 466.

29. Preferential hiring and admissions policies (PHA) give preference to qualified candidates from disadvantaged groups. Daniel M. Hausman uses an analogy to argue that these policies are justifiable. "Suppose that in the local elementary school there are two first-grade and two second-grade classes. One of the first-grade teachers is excellent, and one is terrible. One of the second-grade teachers is also excellent, and one is terrible. The socioeconomic status of families in this community is uniform, and the children have had similar preschool experiences. The school board assigns students to first grade teachers by lottery on the grounds that the fairest policy gives every student an equal chance at a good first-grade experience . . .

   Some school board members argue that every child should have one good and one bad teacher. Those children who had the good first-grade teacher should get the bad second-grade teacher, and vice versa. These board members say, 'If every child has both a good teacher and a bad teacher, then the children's schooling and overall future opportunities will be as close to equal as we can make them . . .

   [I]nsuring that every child has one good teacher and one bad one promotes equality of opportunity, just as PHA does (on the assumption that the opportunities and resources available previously to black applicants have, on average, been worse than those available to white applicants) . . .

   The school analogy also makes clear that PHA does not punish white applicants, just as assigning children who had the good first-grade teacher to the bad second-grade teacher does not punish them.[25]

30. Bob is close to retirement. He has invested most of his savings in a very rare and valuable old car, a Bugatti, which he has not been able to insure. The Bugatti is his pride and joy. In addition to the pleasure he gets from driving and caring for his car, Bob knows that its rising market value means that he will always be able to sell it and live comfortably after retirement.

   One day when Bob is out for a drive, he parks the Bugatti near the end of a railway siding and goes for a walk up the track. As he does so, he sees that a runaway train, with no one aboard, is running down the railway track. Looking farther down the track, he sees the small figure of a child very likely to be killed by the runaway train. He can't stop the train and the child is too far away to warn of the danger, but he can throw a switch that will divert the train down the siding where his Bugatti is parked. Then nobody will be killed—but the train will destroy his Bugatti. Thinking of his joy in owning the car and the financial security it represents, Bob decides not to throw the switch. The child is killed. For many years to come, Bob enjoys owning his Bugatti and the financial security it represents.

   Bob's conduct, most of us will immediately respond, was gravely wrong . . . . But . . . we, too, have opportunities to save the lives of children. We can give to organizations like UNICEF or Oxfam America. How much would we

---

[25]Quoted from Daniel M. Hausman, "Affirmative Action: Bad Arguments and Some Good Ones," in *The Ethical Life*, 3rd Ed., ed. Russ Shafer-Landau (New York: Oxford University Press, 2015), 476–489.

have to give to one of these organizations to have a high probability of saving the life of a child threatened by easily preventable diseases? . . . $200 in donations would help a sickly two-year-old transform into a healthy six-year-old—offering safe passage through childhood's most dangerous years . . .

If you still think that it was very wrong of Bob not to throw the switch that would have diverted the train and saved the child's life, then it is hard to see how you could deny that it is also very wrong not to send money to one of the organizations listed above.[26]

31. Think about it. Facebook, YouTube and Google, Twitter and others—they reach billions of people. The algorithms these platforms depend on deliberately amplify the type of content that keeps users engaged—stories that appeal to our baser instincts and that trigger outrage and fear. It's why YouTube recommended videos by the conspiracist Alex Jones billions of times. It's why fake news outperforms real news, because studies show that lies spread faster than truth. And it's no surprise that the greatest propaganda machine in history has spread the oldest conspiracy theory in history—the lie that Jews are somehow dangerous. As one headline put it, "Just Think What Goebbels Could Have Done with Facebook." [. . .]

[Facebook CEO Mark] Zuckerberg claimed that new limits on what's posted on social media would be to "pull back on free expression." This is utter nonsense. The First Amendment says that "Congress shall make no law" abridging freedom of speech, however, this does not apply to private businesses like Facebook. We're not asking these companies to determine the boundaries of free speech across society. We just want them to be responsible on their platforms.

If a neo-Nazi comes goose-stepping into a restaurant and starts threatening other customers and saying he wants kill Jews, would the owner of the restaurant be required to serve him an elegant eight-course meal? Of course not! The restaurant owner has every legal right and a moral obligation to kick the Nazi out, and so do these internet companies.[27]

32. If we divide the world crudely into rich nations and poor nations, two thirds of them are desperately poor, and only one third comparatively rich, with the United States the wealthiest of all. Metaphorically each rich nation can be seen as a lifeboat full of comparatively rich people. In the ocean outside each lifeboat swim the poor of the world, who would like to get in, or at least to share some of the wealth. What should the lifeboat passengers do? [. . .]

So here we sit, say 50 people in our lifeboat. To be generous, let us assume it has room for 10 more, making a total capacity of 60. Suppose the 50 of us in the lifeboat see 100 others swimming in the water outside, begging for

---

[26]Quoted from Peter Singer, "The Singer Solution to World Poverty," *New York Times Magazine*, Sept. 5, 1999, pp. 60–63. The "Bob's Bugatti" argument was originally developed by Peter Unger.

[27]Quoted from Sacha Baron Cohen's Keynote Address at the Anti-Defamation League's "Never Is Now 2019" Summit on Anti-Semitism and Hate. Available online: https://www.adl.org/news/article/sacha-baron-cohens-keynote-address-at-adls-2019-never-is-now-summit-on-anti-semitism

admission to our boat or for handouts. We have several options: we may be tempted to try to live by the Christian ideal of being "our brother's keeper," or by the Marxist ideal of "to each according to his needs." Since the needs of all in the water are the same, and since they can all be seen as "our brothers," we could take them all into our boat, making a total of 150 in a boat designed for 60. The boat swamps, everyone drowns. Complete justice, complete catastrophe.

Since the boat has an unused excess capacity of 10 more passengers, we could admit just 10 more to it. [. . .] If we do let an extra 10 into our lifeboat, we will have lost our "safety factor," an engineering principle of critical importance. [. . .]

Suppose we decide to preserve our small safety factor and admit no more to the lifeboat. Our survival is then possible although we shall have to be constantly on guard against boarding parties. . . .

[T]his last solution clearly offers the only means of our survival. [. . .]

Every human born constitutes a draft on all aspects of the environment: food, air, water, forests, beaches, wildlife, scenery and solitude. Food can, perhaps, be significantly increased to meet a growing demand. But what about clean beaches, unspoiled forests, and solitude? If we satisfy a growing population's need for food, we necessarily decrease its per capita supply of the other resources needed by men. [. . .]

[T]he world's resources are inequitably distributed. But we must begin the journey to tomorrow from the point where we are today. We cannot remake the past. We cannot safely divide the wealth equitably among all peoples so long as people reproduce at different rates. To do so would guarantee that our grandchildren, and everyone else's grandchildren, would have only a ruined world to inhabit.[28]

---

[28]Quoted from Hardin, G., 1974. Lifeboat Ethics: The Argument Against Helping the Poor. *Psychology Today*, 8, pp.38–43. Available online: https://www.garretthardinsociety.org/articles/art_lifeboat_ethics_case_against_helping_poor.html

Evaluating Arguments from Analogy

CHAPTER GOALS

By reading this chapter and completing the exercises, you will learn how to:

- Evaluate an Argument from Analogy
- Raise objections to premise 1 by challenging the author's evaluation of the described case that grounds the argument.
- Raise objections to premise 2 by identifying disanalogies.
- Evaluate candidate disanalogies with relevance tests.

EVALUATING ARGUMENTS FROM ANALOGY

Arguments from Analogy draw a connection between two cases: they try to justify a judgment about a controversial case by comparing it to an uncontroversial, but morally similar, case. The previous chapter demonstrated how to understand Arguments from Analogy by analyzing their structure. This chapter demonstrates how to evaluate Arguments from Analogy, with special focus on a technique for testing the moral similarity of different cases.

TWO WAYS ARGUMENTS FROM ANALOGY CAN GO WRONG

Recall the General Form of Argument from Analogy:

1. Case x has moral status S. (JUDGMENT)
2. Case y is relevantly similar to case x. (ANALOGY)

Therefore, case y has moral status S. (CONCLUSION)

An argument with this form gives us reason to accept its conclusion if, and only if, both premises are true. There are thus two ways an Argument from Analogy can go wrong.

First, an Argument from Analogy fails if premise 1 is implausible. If we can show that the judgment the author asserts about case x is (or should be) controversial, we can show that an Argument from Analogy is weak.

For example, suppose a student has bought a term paper on the internet and handed it in as their own work. They offer this argument in defense of the moral permissibility of their behavior:

1. It's morally permissible for professional athletes to use banned performance-enhancing drugs (PEDs).
2. Handing in a purchased term paper is relevantly similar to athletes' using banned PEDs.

Therefore, it's morally permissible to hand in a purchased term paper.

The judgment asserted in premise 1 is highly controversial, and so cannot ground an effective Argument from Analogy. The consensus view, which is plausible, is that using banned PEDs is a form of wrongful cheating.

Second, an Argument from Analogy fails if premise 2 is false. To show that premise 2 is false, we must show that cases x and y are morally different in such a way that we cannot or should not transfer our judgment from one to the other other.

For example, suppose the term-paper purchaser tried out a different argument:

1. It is morally permissible to borrow someone else's wrench to fix your bike before a race.
2. Handing in a purchased term paper is relevantly similar to borrowing someone else's wrench.

Therefore, handing in a purchased term paper is morally permissible.

This is a bad argument because its second premise is implausible. There are obvious morally relevant differences between borrowing a wrench to fix your bike and purchasing a term paper. For example, handing in a purchased term paper involves dishonesty, while borrowing a wrench does not. (Other important differences probably occur to you as well.) It is true that borrowing someone else's wrench before a race is morally permissible, but that case is so morally unlike purchasing a term paper that we have no reason to transfer our moral judgment from one case to the other.

In more thoughtful and carefully crafted Arguments from Analogy, authors will have taken care to construct cases that are more plausibly similar, so raising an objection to the second premise is a subtler task. The remainder of the chapter explains how to identify and evaluate differences to see if they undermine the second premise of an Argument from Analogy.

DISANALOGIES IN DETAIL

To raise the objection that two cases are not morally similar, we must do more than merely identify a difference between them. We must identify a *disanalogy*: a difference between case *x* and *y* that is both (a) *genuine* and (b) *morally relevant* in the context of the argument.

Disanalogies must be genuine: the case of Jewish refugees in World War II

In the previous chapter, we introduced a sample argument that draws an analogy between American treatment of Jewish refugees from Germany during World War II and American treatment of Syrian refugees today. In standard form:

1. American exclusion of Jewish refugees in World War II was morally wrong.
2. American exclusion of Syrian refugees today is relevantly similar to exclusion of Jews in WWII.

Therefore, American exclusion of Syrian refugees is morally wrong.

One popular criticism of this argument asserts that an important difference between the cases is the threat posed by these different refugee populations: many Americans worry that ISIS terrorists will slip into the United States posing as Syrian refugees, but Americans did not worry about terrorists slipping into the United States posing as Jewish refugees in WWII. We would more formally present the objection this way:

Objection: Premise 2 is false because there is a disanalogy—unlike with Jewish refugees during WWII, many Americans fear that terrorists will infiltrate the United States posing as Syrian refugees.

This objection fails because it is demonstrably untrue. Fear of communist and Nazi infiltration was regularly cited as a reason for excluding Jewish refugees during WWII.[1] It is understandable that many Americans know little about this aspect of history, because it is rarely taught in standard history classes, but the fear of infiltrators posing as refugees is, in fact, one of the many points of *similarity* between past and present refugee crises.

In sum: the claimed difference between Jewish and Syrian refugees doesn't actually exist. Because this objection fails to cite a *genuine* difference between the two cases, it fails to undermine the argument.

There are some genuine differences between (most) Jewish refugees in WWII and (most) Syrian refugees today. For example, most Syrian refugees today speak some dialect of Arabic, while Jewish refugees spoke a variety of

---

[1]For one respected academic source, see especially pages 213–215 of Max Paul Friedman, 2003, *Nazis and Good Neighbors: The United States Campaign Against the Germans of Latin America in World War II*, Cambridge University Press. See also the United States Holocaust Memorial Museum's page on President Roosevelt, which includes a discussion of the refugee crisis: https://www.ushmm.org/wlc/en/article.php?ModuleId=10007411

Germanic and Slavic languages, often in addition to Yiddish. Most religiously observant Jewish refugees practiced some form of Judaism, while most religiously observant Syrian refugees practice some form of Islam. These are genuine differences between case x and case y. But do these differences matter in a way that undermines the argument? To answer that question, we need a way to test if a difference is morally relevant.

Interlude: the idea behind relevance tests

Suppose you have on your desk an antique clock full of many gears and other moving parts. You identify one tiny gear, g, and wonder if it is part of what makes the clock work. To investigate, you remove that gear without disturbing any other parts of the clockwork. After the removal, the clock runs exactly the same as it did before. If the clock functions identically with or without it, this is excellent evidence that gear g is irrelevant to the functioning of the clock.

A *relevance test* uses a similar strategy to determine whether a difference between cases is morally relevant in the context of an argument. One genuine difference between Jewish refugees in WWII and Syrian refugees today is that Jewish refugees did not tend to speak Arabic, but contemporary Syrian refugees do. Does this difference between the cases constitute a flaw in the argument? Was it the language they spoke that made it morally wrong to exclude Jewish refugees? To figure that out, we reimagine the case in a way that eliminates that specific difference, then check to see if eliminating that difference changes our moral evaluation of the case.

For example, imagine that all was the same with Jewish refugees in WWII except that they tended to speak Arabic. Would it have been morally permissible to exclude Jewish refugees fleeing Nazi genocide if they were Arabic speakers? Obviously not. Imaginatively changing the language spoken by Jewish refugees has no effect on our judgment that it was wrong to exclude them. Like the superfluous gear in the clock, the fact that Jewish refugees spoke Yiddish and other languages plays no role in generating our moral judgment that excluding them was wrong. That is excellent evidence that the language spoken by refugees is not morally relevant in the context of this argument.

Notice two features of this initial example of a relevance test. First, the question we seek to answer is: does the language spoken by Jewish refugees play a role in shaping our judgment that it was wrong for the United States to exclude them? It is the *uncontroversial* case of Jewish refugees that is the "clockwork" whose functioning we seek to explore with a relevance test.

Second, notice that we are careful to reimagine *only* the specific difference we are testing for relevance. In the case of clockwork, if we want to know whether gear g plays a role in the functioning of the clock, we must remove *only* gear g. We cannot learn anything about gear g if we remove other gears at the same time. Similarly, if we want to know whether it was the languages they spoke that made it wrong to exclude Jewish refugees, we must change *only* that detail of the case.

Pay special attention to these features in the examples that follow: an effective relevance test reimagines the *uncontroversial* case that grounds the argument, and it reimagines it in a way that changes *only* the difference whose relevance we aim to test.

Disanalogies must be relevant I: Legalizing marijuana

Consider this version of a popular argument for legalizing recreational marijuana:

> Recreational alcohol is potentially dangerous and prone to abuse. Nevertheless, nearly everyone agrees that alcohol ought to be legal for recreational consumption—the potential risks of alcohol use are the sorts of risks people ought to be allowed to choose for themselves. But in every way that matters, marijuana is similar to alcohol. Since recreational alcohol ought to be legal, so too should recreational marijuana.

In standard form for Argument from Analogy:

1. Recreational alcohol use should be legal.
2. Recreational marijuana use is relevantly similar to recreational alcohol use.

   Therefore, recreational marijuana use should be legal.

Evaluating premise 1 requires us to ask: is it true that recreational alcohol use ought to be legal? After the disastrous experiment with alcohol prohibition in the United States in the 1920s, we accept that it is.

Evaluating premise 2 requires us to ask: are there differences between recreational alcohol and marijuana, such that our judgment about the appropriate legal status of alcohol should *not* be transferred to marijuana?

In our classroom discussions, students typically suggest, as objections to the argument, the following four differences between alcohol and marijuana:

- Alcohol and marijuana are different substances.
- It is possible to consume alcohol without becoming intoxicated, while it is not possible to consume marijuana without becoming intoxicated.
- Alcohol poses a significantly higher risk of dangerous or fatal overdose than marijuana.
- Alcohol is more broadly socially accepted than marijuana.

In order to constitute an effective criticism of the second premise, an alleged difference must be both genuine and morally relevant. Let us check each of our candidate objections in turn.

Objection 1: Premise 2 is false because there's a disanalogy—alcohol and marijuana are different substances, so we're talking about legalizing two totally different things.

This objection fails because it does not identify any candidate disanalogy at all. The original passage suggests that we can learn something about marijuana policy by looking at alcohol policy. The author believes alcohol use and marijuana use are *similar in the morally relevant respects*; the author does not believe that alcohol and marijuana are *identical* substances. To raise an objection to premise 2, we must identify some specific difference between these two substances that makes alcohol a poor analogy for marijuana.

Imagine trying to run a relevance test for this objection. That would require re-imagining case *x* (legal recreational alcohol) as legal recreational marijuana—which is case *y*. In attempting this relevance test, we haven't re-imagined the analogy; we have eliminated it. That is a red flag that this objection is not actually taking the analogy seriously. To count as a candidate disanalogy, an objection must do more than assert that the two cases are different. Of course they are. A candidate disanalogy must identify a *specific* difference that challenges the author's claim that these two different cases are *morally similar.*

For example:

Objection 2: Premise 2 is false because there's a disanalogy—it is impossible to consume marijuana without intoxication, while it is possible to drink alcohol without intoxication.

This objection fails to identify a *genuine* difference between alcohol and marijuana. Both drugs have intoxicating effects above a certain threshold dose, and minimal effects below it. Because this candidate objection has failed to identify a genuine difference, it is no good; we can discard it.

Objection 3: Premise 2 is false because there's a disanalogy—recreational alcohol use is significantly more dangerous to users than recreational marijuana use.

This objection has probably identified a genuine difference between alcohol and marijuana. (To verify that, we would need to investigate the relevant empirical research.) Is it a morally *relevant* difference? To determine that, we rebuild the original case in our imaginations in a way that eliminates the suggested difference; we need to imagine a version of alcohol that is as safe as marijuana.

Relevance test: Imagine a version of alcohol which, like marijuana, has no known lethal dose and, like marijuana, is minimally damaging to the liver, and so on. Imagine, in other words, a version of alcohol that is much safer than our real-world alcohol.

Should this less-dangerous version of alcohol be legal? We think so. If real-world alcohol should be legal, then the imaginary, safer version of alcohol should be legal too.

The original case—real-world alcohol—and its re-imaged safer version have the same moral status: both of these intoxicants ought to be legal. Our relevance shows that our judgment that alcohol ought to be legal does not depend on the relative dangerousness of alcohol; the relative safety of marijuana is therefore not morally relevant in the context of this argument.

Objection 4: Premise 2 is false because there's a disanalogy—recreational alcohol use is more broadly socially accepted than recreational marijuana use.

This difference was more clearly a genuine difference a decade ago, but it is still plausibly true that recreational marijuana use carries more social stigma than alcohol use. Let us grant that this is a genuine difference and test it for moral relevance. To do that, we need to imagine public attitudes toward alcohol were more like public attitudes toward marijuana.

> **Relevance test:** Imagine a world in which a larger fraction of people tend to frown on those who drink alcohol, even if they only have a glass of beer or wine with dinner every once in a while. Everything else about recreational alcohol use is the same.

In that world, should recreational alcohol use still be legal? Yes, it should. (Indeed, we don't have to be particularly imaginative here—alcohol was more strongly stigmatized during the era of prohibition, and it seems clear, at least in retrospect, that prohibition was a moral mistake despite alcohol's social stigma at the time.)

The relevance test shows that our judgment about the appropriate legal status of alcohol does not depend on its level of social stigma; social stigmatization of marijuana is not morally relevant in the context of this argument.

We have so far been unable to locate a genuine and morally relevant difference between recreational alcohol and marijuana that could undermine this argument. Are there differences we have overlooked?

Disanalogies must be relevant II: Thomson's burglar

In "A Defense of Abortion," Judith Jarvis Thomson argues that consenting to sex (particularly sex using contraception) doesn't itself grant an accidental and unwanted fetus the right to use your body. She offers this Argument from Analogy to make her case:

> If the room is stuffy, and I therefore open a window to air it, and a burglar climbs in, it would be absurd to say, "Ah, now he can stay, she's given him a right to the use of her house—for she is partially responsible for his presence there, having voluntarily done what enabled him to get in, in full knowledge that there are such things as burglars, and that burglars burgle." It would be still more absurd to say this if I had had bars installed outside my windows, precisely to prevent burglars from getting in, and a burglar got in only because of a defect in the bars.[2]

In standard form for Argument from Analogy:

1. Voluntarily opening a window does not grant a burglar the right to burgle my house.
2. A fetus resulting from consensual sex is relevantly similar to a burglar who has slipped in through an open window.

Therefore, consenting to sex does not grant a fetus the right to use my body.

---

[2]Judith Jarvis Thomson, 1971, "A Defense of Abortion," *Philosophy and Public Affairs,* 1(1): 58–59.

Premise 1 is uncontroversial. Are there genuine, morally relevant disanalo-gies that call into question premise 2? In classroom discussions, students have raised the following worries about the argument:

- Burglars are big and threatening; fetuses are tiny and non-threatening.
- Burglars are strangers, but fetuses are genetically related to you.
- Burglars exist independently of you and *choose* to burgle you. Fetuses only exist because you chose to have sex—they did not choose to set up shop in your uterus.

To identify a disanalogy that undermines the argument, we need to identify a difference that's both genuine and morally relevant. Let us check each of our candidate objections in turn.

Objection 1: Premise 2 is false because there's a disanalogy—burglars are big and fetuses are small.

This is a genuine difference. Is it morally relevant? To test for relevance, check to see if our judgment about the burglar case changes when we re-imagine it in a way that eliminates this specific difference.

Relevance test: Imagine that scientists invented a shrink ray, and that this technology became popular among burglars, who shrink themselves down to about the size of a raspberry or plum before they go out burgling. Their small size makes it easier to slip into houses, to hide there, and to explore the nooks in which people stash their jewelry.

Would opening your window grant one of these tiny burglars the right to use your home? No, it wouldn't. Even if burglars were tiny, that wouldn't give them the right to burgle your house.

Our judgment about the rights of burglars does not depend on their size; differences of size are not morally relevant in the context of this argument. We can discard this objection.

Objection 2: Premise 2 is false because there's a disanalogy—pregnant women are genetically related to their fetuses, and victims are not genetically related to their burglars.

This is (usually) a genuine difference between fetuses and burglars. Is it morally relevant? To test for relevance, check to see if our judgment about the burglar case changes when we re-imagine it in a way that eliminates this specific difference.

Relevance test: Suppose you have an adult son who, since moving out of your house, has turned to a life of burglary. One day you open your window for some fresh air and—bad luck—you are burgled.

Does it matter whether it was *your* estranged son who did the burgling or rather someone else's child? Do you need to know something about the burglar's DNA before you can determine whether or not opening the window gave the burglar the right to take your things? We expect your answer is, "no."

Our judgment about the rights of burglars does not depend on the presence or absence of shared DNA; genetic relationships not morally relevant in the context of this argument. We can discard this objection.

Objection 3: Premise 2 is false because there's a disanalogy—a fetus comes into existence as a result of my choice, not because they chose to take advantage of me of their own free will. Burglars exist independently of my choices and they choose to rob me of their own free will.

This is a genuine difference between burglars and fetuses. Is it morally relevant? To test for relevance, we must re-imagine burglars and windows to look more like fetuses and consensual sex in this specific way. This one requires some creativity.

Relevance test: Imagine that we live in a fantasy world in which burglars are strange creatures. They are a kind of instinct-driven imp that is occasionally created when someone opens a window. If no one ever opened a window, there would be no burglar-imps, and everyone knows that if they *do* open a window, there is a 1-in-100 chance that will create a mindless burglar-imp who will ransack their house for jewelry and then flee.

Does opening your window in imp-land, in full knowledge that it might create a mindless jewelry-thieving imp, give that mindless imp the right to steal your jewelry? We expect you have some difficulty answering this question. It seems at least possible that, if the world worked like this, you should only open your windows if you're willing to risk losing your jewels.

The original described case—real world burglars—and the re-imagined world of burglar imps do not obviously have the same moral status. It is undoubtedly the case real-world burglars do something morally wrong when they burgle through an open window, but it isn't nearly so clear that instinct-driven burglar-imps are doing anything wrong when they follow their instincts after being created by the opening of a window. That suggests this is a morally relevant difference between fetuses and burglars: we cannot transfer our judgment about the rights of burglars through to rights of fetuses.

In sum: to test whether or not a *genuine* difference is a *morally relevant* difference, we re-imagine the original, uncontroversial case in a way that eliminates the difference. If our moral evaluation of the case doesn't change when we re-imagine it, then the identified difference isn't playing a role in shaping our moral evaluation of the case. On the other hand, if re-imagining the case to eliminate the identified difference *does* change our evaluation of the case, then that suggests the identified difference is indeed playing an important role in shaping our evaluation of the described case. If there is a morally relevant difference between the two cases, then our convictions about case *x* cannot reliably guide us in case *y*.

THE DISCUSSION CONTINUES: RESPONDING
TO DISANALOGIES

Suppose you have offered someone an Argument from Analogy, and they respond with a disanalogy, supported with a relevance test. This is not necessarily the end of the discussion. It could be that they have put their finger on a serious flaw in your thinking. (This is great. That's how we learn.) But there are at least two other possibilities that would require the discussion to continue.

First, it might be the case that their relevance test deserves some critical examination of its own. Consider, for example, the third objection to Thomson's burglar argument, discussed above. Thomson's critic holds that burglars have free will and exist independently of homeowners' actions, and fetuses do not. This is supported by a relevance test in which the critic imagines burglar-imps that share these features with fetuses. If opening your window was what caused burglars to be called into being, then (says the critic) we *would* be responsible for being burgled when we chose to open our windows.

Thomson would likely respond that this suggested disanalogy misunderstands her point. The judgment she seeks to elicit with the burglar example is that opening your window doesn't grant burglars *the right to take your jewelry*. But that remains true even in the re-imagined burglar-imp scenario. Even if you are responsible for calling the burglar-imp into being by opening a window, that doesn't grant it the right to your jewelry. You can still hide your jewelry before opening the window, or try to shoo the imp away before it can steal any of your things. The fact that your voluntary act of opening the window called the imp into existence doesn't change anything about the way *rights* work.

Who has the better case, here: Thomson or her critic? The discussion should continue.

Second, the appropriate response to a disanalogy might be to modify the described case to better target the specific judgment the case is intended to elicit. This is the appropriate response when the disanalogy, though legitimate, focuses on a detail of the original described case that is not centrally important to its function in the argument.

This is exactly what happens in Thomson's "A Defense of Abortion." She anticipates the free-will disanalogy as a criticism of her original burglar analogy, and responds by offering an upgraded version of the same Argument from Analogy. (The upgraded version is her famous "people-seeds" analogy.)[3] Does Thomson's upgraded version of the burglar argument succeed in establishing that consenting to sex doesn't grant a fetus a right to use your body? The discussion should continue.

REVIEW

An Argument from Analogy establishes its conclusion if, but only if, both of its premises are true. There are two ways to raise objections to Arguments from Analogy, corresponding to their two-premise form.

---

[3]Judith Jarvis Thomson, "A Defense of Abortion," *Philosophy and Public Affairs*, 1, no. 1 (1971): 59.

To raise an objection to premise 1, a critic must give reason to think the author's judgment about the allegedly uncontroversial case x is mistaken.

To raise an objection to premise 2, a critic must identify a special kind of objection: a disanalogy between the uncontroversial case x and the controversial target case y.

Disanalogy: an identified difference between cases x and y that makes it clear that our judgment about case x cannot provide reliable moral guidance in controversial case y.

To count as a disanalogy, an identified difference between cases x and y must satisfy two criteria: it must be both a genuine difference and a relevant difference.

Genuine difference: a feature that case x actually has but case y actually lacks (or vice versa).

Relevant difference: in the context of an Argument from Analogy, a genuine difference is relevant if, and only if, that feature is (at least part of) the reason we judge that uncontroversial case x has moral status S.

One standard way to demonstrate the moral relevance of a difference between cases x and y is to perform a relevance test.

Relevance test: a technique to determine if a proposed disanalogy constitutes a (morally) relevant difference. To do a relevance test, re-imagine case x in a way that eliminates the proposed difference. If the re-imagined case x still has moral status S, the difference is *not* relevant. If the re-imagined case x no longer has moral status S, the difference *is* relevant.

To test your understanding of the material introduced in this chapter, complete the Demonstration Exercises and then check your answers against the solutions that follow.

Demonstration Exercises

Demonstration Exercises are designed to give you immediate feedback on your grasp of the skills introduced in this chapter. To use them effectively, you should attempt answers to all of them, then check your work against our suggested answers, which follow. For a detailed explanation of how best to use Demonstration Exercises, read the book's Introduction.

Demonstration Exercises 9A: Applying Relevance Tests

Exercise Instructions: each exercise below presents an Argument from Analogy along with a proposed disanalogy. For each proposed disanalogy, complete a relevance test to determine if the difference is morally relevant.

   1. Hunting deer for sport[4]

     1. It's morally permissible to chop down a tree in order to carve it into a decorative sculpture.

---

[4] Adapted from an argument in Timothy Hsiao, "A Moral Defense of Trophy Hunting," *Sport, Ethics and Philosophy,* 14, no. 1 (2020): 26–34.

(*continued*)

2. Hunting deer for sport (so you can display a deer head on your wall) is relevantly similar to chopping down a tree in order to carve it into a decorative sculpture.

So, it's morally permissible to hunt deer for sport.

Proposed disanalogy: Premise 2 is false because there's a disanalogy—unlike chopping down trees, hunting deer causes suffering to beings capable of feeling pleasure and pain.

2. Living kidney sales

1. People should be allowed to sell their blood plasma.

2. Allowing people to sell their kidneys is relevantly similar to allowing people to sell their blood plasma.

Therefore, people should be allowed to sell their kidneys.

Proposed disanalogy: Premise 2 is false because there's a disanalogy—unlike blood plasma, kidneys are not something your body can regrow on its own.

Demonstration Exercises 9B: Brainstorming Disanalogies

Exercise Instructions: For each of the following passages, do the following things.

- *First, represent the argument in standard form using the General Form of Argument from Analogy.*
- *Second, suggest what you think is the best candidate for a genuine and morally relevant disanalogy between the cases being compared. "Premise 2 is false because..."*
- *Third, test your suggested disanalogy for moral relevance.*

1. Texting while driving is wrong[5]

It is not uncommon today to see someone texting while they're driving. Whether they're unable to wait to read the next text from a friend or eager to see the latest updates on their social media feeds, many people seem to think there's nothing wrong with picking up their phone and actively texting while driving their car. But despite its social acceptance, this practice is morally wrong because, morally speaking, it's no different from driving drunk. Driving drunk is wrong because it puts you and others at unnecessary risk when you're behind the wheel. There is ample evidence that texting while driving does the same thing, so it is wrong, too.

2. All Syrian refugees should be excluded from the United States [6]

The civil war in Syria has displaced many people, some of whom would like to re-settle in the United States as refugees. Though some of them are probably lovely people, it could easily be the case that a handful of these putative refugees are actually ISIS terrorists trying to sneak into the United States. The fact that we can't tell the "real" refugees from the terrorists means that the United States should exclude all refugees. Think of the issue this way. Suppose you had a big

---

[5]For a discussion and demonstration of relevance tests for a variety of objections to this argument, see Jason Swartwood, "Drinking, Texting, and Moral Arguments from Analogy," *Think* 16, no. 45 (2017): 15–26.

[6]This Argument from Analogy was introduced, in visual form, in a previous chapter. The image was originally posted on Donald Trump, Jr.'s twitter feed but has since been removed: https://twitter.com/DonaldJTrumpJr/status/778016283342307328/

bowl of Skittles, and someone told you that just a few of them were laced with a deadly poison. Would you eat a handful? Would you force your children, or your neighbors, to eat a handful? Of course you wouldn't. The only morally appropriate response to a bowl with a few poisoned Skittles is to throw out the entire bowl.

3. The case against pets[7]

Domesticated animals are completely dependent on humans, who control *every* aspect of their lives. Unlike human children, who will one day become autonomous, non-humans never will. That is the entire point of domestication – we *want* domesticated animals to depend on us. [. . .] We might make them happy in one sense, but the relationship can never be "natural" or "normal". They do not belong in our world, irrespective of how well we treat them. This is more or less true of all domesticated non-humans. They are perpetually dependent on us. We control their lives forever. They truly are "animal slaves". Some of us might be benevolent masters, but we really can't be anything more than that . . . .

We love our dogs, but recognize that, if the world were more just and fair, there would be no pets at all . . . [Just as holding humans as property is fundamentally incompatible with justice and fairness, so too is it fundamentally unjust and unfair for humans to hold animals as property.]

4. Watching gorefest films is morally wrong

Imagine this story about a teen named Jones. Jones first heard urban legends about snuff films—mythical films in which an actor is murdered on camera—when he was fourteen. He was fascinated by the stories and sought out every available book, novel, and article about snuff films. When he was sixteen, Jones decided to settle, to his own satisfaction, whether snuff films exist. He learned how to use the encryption and onion-routing software needed to access the darknet, and he went searching. Though he didn't find anything that matches the urban legends, what he did find was shocking: videos of real beheadings and animal killings, photos of crime scenes and car accidents, dash-cam videos of police shootings and extended arias of self-mutilation. Jones was disturbed; but there was also something gripping about these scenes of suffering and death, and Jones soon found that he craved the emotional rush he got from viewing and processing them. For the first time in a while, he was excited to come home from school, so he could log in and see what new footage of real violence his Internet friends had posted.

If Jones's parents discovered his hobby, should they intervene to stop him from watching these videos? Of course they should. He's doing something seriously damaging to his own psychological well-being and (not unrelatedly) he's doing something seriously morally wrong. Would it matter, though, if Jones got the same emotional rush from watching gorefest films, which feature simulations of the same kinds of violence? It's hard to see how it could. That's why it's wrong to watch gorefest films devoted to the display of images of suffering and death.

Demonstration Exercises 9C: Complete Argument Evaluation

Exercise Instructions: for the following passage:

- *First, represent the argument in standard form for Argument from Analogy.*
- *Second, offer what you believe to be the best objection to the argument. Clearly identify which premise you are engaging: "Premise 1 is false because . . . " or*

---

[7]Quoted from https://aeon.co/essays/why-keeping-a-pet-is-fundamentally-unethical

(continued)

"Premise 2 is false because . . . " If the objection is to premise 2, be sure to include a relevance test.

• *Third, briefly explain how you believe the discussion should continue. What do you think is the author's best reply to the objection you have just raised?*

1. Spanking children is morally permissible[8]

Although the practice of spanking children as a form of corrective punishment has a long history, it has recently become fashionable to condemn this practice in moral terms. But the truth is that prior generations had it right: spanking children is morally permissible, and maybe even morally required. Perhaps the best way to see why is to consider the analogy of dogs. Dogs and small children share many features. Two of the most important similarities: 1. both dogs and children adapt their behaviors so as to avoid pain, and 2. it is the responsibility of adults to shape both dog and child behavior into socially acceptable patterns.

Everyone accepts that the judicious application of pain is a morally acceptable tool in the dog-trainers toolbox. That's why we have choke collars, shock collars, and invisible fences. These are appropriate tools because they are effective means of training a dog into a *good* dog, and it is the responsibility of dog owners to train good dogs. Spanking misbehaving children is relevantly similar. Just as dog owners morally ought to judiciously inflict physical pain in order to train well-behaved dogs, parents ought to judiciously inflict physical pain in order to raise good children.

---

[8]Adapted from an argument in: http://philosophy.hku.hk/think/value/analogy.php

---

Solutions to Demonstration Exercises

Demonstration Exercises are most useful if you make your best attempt to complete them before you look at the answers. If you haven't yet attempted answers to all the Demonstration Exercises, go back and do that now.

   Note: the relevance tests we offer here are examples of good work. Since relevance testing is usually a creative effort, your own tests may differ from ours. If so, you must ask yourself if your relevance tests *function in the same way* as ours. Have you re-imaged the original case *x*? Have you done it in a way that eliminates the proposed difference between case *x* and case *y*? If you have, you're probably in good shape. If your relevance tests are doing something else, that's evidence that you need to review this chapter and try again.

Solutions to Demonstration Exercises 9A: Applying Relevance Tests

1. Hunting deer for sport

Proposed disanalogy: Premise 2 is false because there's a disanalogy—unlike chopping down trees, hunting deer causes suffering to beings capable of feeling pleasure and pain.

A relevance test: To test this difference for moral relevance, we must re-imagine the original described case in a way that eliminates the difference. In this case, that means imagining that the trees chopped down in order to make a sculpture are conscious, sentient beings.

Suppose it were like this: you're part of a landing party for a space exploration team that is exploring a new habitable planet. After establishing a base camp, you decide to commemorate your landing with a sculpture. The planet is packed with what appear to be trees, which seem like excellent prospects for carve-able wood. But your resident astrobiologist notes that the trees appear to be sentient. On close examination, everyone in the party agrees: though they look like trees, these life-forms are conscious beings, capable of feeling pleasure and pain. Cutting them down causes them to suffer and die!

Is it morally permissible to cut down these "trees" to make your commemorative sculpture? We suspect you'll agree it would not, especially since there are other non-sentient things you could use to make the sculpture.

Since our moral evaluation of case x changes when we re-imagine it to be more like case y, this difference appears to be relevant. Premise 2 is probably false.

2. Living kidney sales

Proposed disanalogy: Premise 2 is false because there's a disanalogy—unlike blood plasma, kidneys are not something your body can regrow on its own.

A relevance test: To test this difference for moral relevance, we must re-imagine the original described case in a way that eliminates the difference. In this case, that means imagining that blood plasma was, like kidneys, something our bodies have in surplus, but cannot regrow.

Suppose it were like this: human bodies cannot regenerate blood plasma. Instead, we are born with a fixed amount of plasma that is roughly double what we actually need to be healthy. Some companies would like to pay people to buy their surplus plasma, which the companies would then sell to hospitals, which would use that plasma to save lives. This system does pose some risks for the plasma sellers. If they are ever severely injured and lose a lot of blood, they will not have enough surplus plasma to survive.

Should this system of plasma sales be legal? It is hard to say. That is a controversial, contentious question. Though payment for plasma in the real world is uncontroversial, if people couldn't regenerate it, payment for plasma would be morally much more complicated. Since our moral evaluation of case x changes when we re-imagine it to be more like case y, this difference appears to be relevant. Premise 2 is probably false.

Solutions to Demonstration Exercises 9B: Brainstorming Disanalogies

Note: your standard-form representations should identify the same judgment, analogy, and conclusion as we have, but variation in wording or expression is perfectly fine.

1. Texting while driving is wrong

In standard form for Argument from Analogy:

1. Drunk driving is wrong. (JUDGMENT)
2. Texting while driving is relevantly similar to drunk driving. (ANALOGY)

Thus, texting while driving is wrong. (CONCLUSION)

(continued)

Proposed disanalogy 1:

Objection to premise 2: Premise 2 is false because there's a disanalogy—when a person drives drunk, they are impaired for the duration of the drive; when someone texts, they are only impaired briefly and intermittently.

Relevance test: To test this difference for moral relevance, we must re-imagine the original described case in a way that eliminates the difference. In this case, that means imagining the drunk driving as a temporary, intermittent impairment.

Suppose you have just been introduced to an amazing new party beer that is exactly like regular alcohol except that, after drinking it, you can turn the intoxication on and off with a specific head movement. Excited about the possibilities of this new drink, you down a sizeable amount and then hop into the car. You start out inebriated but then start to feel self-conscious, so you do the head movement and the intoxication goes away. After a while, you feel bored, so you do the head movement again and are blissfully intoxicated. In this case, you did something that didn't impair you for the whole duration of the drive. Is driving while intermittently intoxicated morally wrong? We think it is.

Our moral evaluation of drunk driving doesn't change when we imagine an intermittent version of drunk driving. That suggests that the fact that drunk drivers are impaired for the duration of the drive, instead of only parts of it, is not a factor in generating our moral evaluation that drunk driving is wrong. This candidate disanalogy is not morally relevant in the context of this argument, and fails to undermine premise 2.

Proposed disanalogy 2:

Objection to premise 2: Premise 2 is false because there's a disanalogy—unlike drunk driving, you're not intoxicated when you text while driving.

Relevance test: To test this difference for moral relevance, we must re-imagine the original described case in a way that eliminates the difference. In this case, that means imagining that drunk driving has similar consequences as it does in reality, but it does not involve intoxication. This will take some imagination. Suppose it were like this:

You have just been introduced to an amazing new party drink. Instead of getting you intoxicated, the drink makes you very pleasantly distracted—it makes you more likely to bounce from one thought to the next in a way you enjoy but in a way that makes it hard to give sustained focus to other tasks. So, the drink is not intoxicating, though it does impair your ability to drive safely to the same degree as alcohol. Suppose you drink this fancy new drink and go out for a drive. Your attention pleasantly flits from looking at various buildings outside, to examining the details of your car's upholstery, to thinking about your dinner plans, to looking for a book you lost in your back seat, and so on. This distraction is enjoyable for you, though it puts you and others at increased risk. Is driving while distracted by a non-intoxicating drink morally wrong? We think it is.

Our moral evaluation of drunk driving doesn't change when we imaginatively remove the element of intoxication. That suggests that the chemical state of intoxication is not what leads us to evaluate drunk driving as morally wrong.

This candidate disanalogy is not morally relevant in the context of this argument, and fails to undermine premise 2.

2. All Syrian refugees should be excluded from the United States

In standard form for Argument from Analogy:

1. We ought not eat any Skittles from a bowl in which some are poisoned. (JUDGMENT)

2. The United States allowing Syrian refugees into the country is relevantly similar to eating Skittles from the bowl in which some are poisoned. (ANALOGY)

   So, the United States ought not allow any Syrian refugees into the country. (CONCLUSION)

Proposed disanalogy:

Objection to premise 2: Premise 2 is false because there's a disanalogy— unlike Skittles, refugees have thoughts and feelings, and can suffer and die.

Relevance test: To test this difference for moral relevance, we must re-imagine the original described case in a way that eliminates the difference. In this case, that means re-imagining Skittles as things that can think, feel, suffer, and die. This will take some imagination. Suppose it were like this:

You have before you an enormous bowl filled with tens of thousands of Skittles. Each Skittle is connected to a specific person living somewhere in the world. When you eat a Skittle, the person assigned to that Skittle is saved. When you decline to eat a Skittle, the person assigned to that Skittle suffers or dies. But there's a catch: there are one or two poisoned Skittles in the bowl, and so there is a tiny, miniscule chance that the next Skittle you eat will kill *you*. Should you eat any Skittles?

Even though the experience would be more psychologically fraught than eating most other candy, there is powerful moral reason to eat as many Skittles as you can handle. When there is almost no chance of you being poisoned, and a certainty that you can save someone from suffering or death with each Skittle you eat, to refuse to eat *any* Skittles is to respond with cowardice and callousness to the plight of the people whose fate is determined by those Skittles.

Our moral evaluation of the original described case changes when we imagine that eating Skittles prevents suffering and death. That suggests that the fact that Skittles can't think, feel, suffer, or die plays a role in shaping our moral judgments about how to treat them. This candidate disanalogy is morally relevant in the context of this argument, and undermines premise two. We can learn little about how best to treat people by thinking about how best to treat candy.

3. The case against pets

In standard form for Argument from Analogy:

1. Owning humans as slaves is morally wrong. (JUDGMENT)

2. Owning animals as pets is relevantly similar to holding humans as slaves. (ANALOGY)

   Thus, owning animals as pets is morally wrong. (CONCLUSION)

(*continued*)

Proposed disanalogy 1:

Objection to premise 2: Premise 2 is false because there's a disanalogy—unlike holding humans as slaves, keeping animals as pets is legal.

Relevance test: To test this difference for moral relevance, we must re-imagine the original described case in a way that eliminates the difference. In this case, that means imagining that owning humans as slaves was legal.

Imagine the community you live in suddenly legalized slavery. Would it be morally permissible for you to go buy yourself a slave? Surely not.

Our moral evaluation of slavery as morally wrong does not change when we imagine legalized slavery. That suggests that the fact that slavery is illegal is not what leads us to evaluate it as morally wrong. This candidate disanalogy is not morally relevant in the context of this argument, and fails to undermine premise 2.

Proposed disanalogy 2:

Objection to premise 2: Premise 2 is false because there's a disanalogy—the control and dependence characteristic of slavery harms humans, who have the capacity to develop and pursue their own conception of happiness. The control and dependence characteristic of pet ownership does not harm pets, because they do not have that capacity.

Relevance test: To test this difference for moral relevance, we must re-imagine the original described case in a way that eliminates the difference. In this case, that means imagining a human relationship of dependence and control, at slavery-like levels, which does not harm the person who is dependent and controlled because they lack the capacity to develop and pursue their own conception of happiness.

In fact, this is the usual relationship between parents and young children. Young children, who do not yet have the capacity to develop and pursue their own conception of happiness, are dependent on and controlled by their parents. So, imagine the parents of a two-year-old son. It is true that he is dependent on them and they control him. But they are good parents, and they always make decisions with his well-being as their central concern. They keep him healthy, happy, challenged, stimulated, and safe. Their treatment of their son—which centrally features dependency and control—is *not* morally wrong. Young children who cannot yet form or pursue their own conception of the good life *should* be dependent on and controlled by their parents.

Our moral evaluation of the original case changes when we imagine it to be more like pet ownership. This suggests that the fact that slavery denies people the ability to develop and pursue their own conception of happiness is part of the reason we evaluate slavery as morally wrong. Since pets cannot develop and pursue their own conception of happiness, we cannot transfer our judgments about the morality of human slavery through to the morality of pet-keeping. This candidate disanalogy undermines premise 2.

4. Watching gorefest films is morally wrong

In standard form for Argument from Analogy:

1. It is morally wrong to watch real footage of suffering and death. (JUDGMENT)
2. Gorefest films are relevantly similar to real videos of suffering and death. (ANALOGY)

Therefore, it is morally wrong to watch gorefest films. (CONCLUSION)

Proposed disanalogy:

Objection to premise 2: Premise 2 is false because there's a disanalogy—unlike watching real videos of suffering and death, no one was actually hurt in the making of gorefests, and everyone in the audience knows that.

Relevance test: To test this difference for moral relevance, we must re-imagine the original described case in a way that eliminates the difference. In this case, that means imagining Jones enjoys watching internet videos that feature staged scenes of suffering and death that everyone knows is fake.

Suppose that instead of finding real footage on the darknet, Jones goes in search of classic tragedy films like *Titanic, Schindler's List,* and *Requiem for a Dream.* These films include realistic footage of people suffering and dying, but Jones, like everyone else, knows that the films are *simulations* of these tragedies; the actors are not actually suffering and dying. Jones finds he really enjoys the emotionally intense experience of watching a good tragedy, and he looks forward to coming home from school so he can watch more of them. Is it wrong for Jones to watch classic films that feature scenes of simulated suffering and death? We don't think so.

Our moral evaluation of the original described case changes when we re-imagine Jones's films as a closer analogy to gorefest films (in that the suffering in them is *simulated* suffering). That suggests that the fact that real people suffered and died in the original example played a role in leading us to evaluate watching those films as morally wrong. Since gorefests do not have this feature, which is morally relevant in the context of this argument, we cannot transfer our judgments about viewing real suffering to viewing gorefests. This candidate disanalogy undermines premise 2.

Solutions to Demonstration Exercises 9C: Complete Argument Evaluation

1. Spanking children is morally permissible

Part 1: In standard form for Argument from Analogy:

1. Corporal punishment (e.g. a shock collar) is a morally permissible tool to use in the training of dogs. (JUDGMENT)
2. Using corporal punishment (e.g. spanking) on children is relevantly similar to using corporal punishment on dogs. (ANALOGY)

   Thus, corporal punishment (e.g. spanking) is a morally permissible tool to use in the raising of children. (CONCLUSION)

Part 2: The best objection to this argument:

I do not think premise 1 is true. It isn't morally permissible to use shock collars on dogs—there are many gentler, kinder ways to train dogs that are at least as effective as shock collars. However, I recognize that many people do use them and think they are fine, so I'll focus my attention on premise 2, which is also false.

(continued)

Premise 2 is false because there is a disanalogy: unlike dogs, children are capable of more effectively learning through the clear communication of expected behavior and (nonviolent!) consequences for misbehavior.

Relevance test: To test for relevance, we must imagine dogs, like children, learn more effectively from clear communication and non-violent consequences for misbehavior. So, imagine that your dog is able to speak English. You can explain to your dog why she should not leave the yard, pee in the house, or menace the neighbor's cat, and your dog will understand your explanation. You can arrange consequences that your dog will understand: if she leaves the yard, she will be grounded for two days. If you could train your dog in these ways, would it be permissible to use a shock collar or choke collar on her? Even current users of shock collars would agree that using a shock collar on a dog who can understand expectations, reasons, and consequences, would be pointlessly cruel. People who use shock collars do it because they believe their dogs can't understand reasons, and the only way to shape their behavior is by inflicting pain. Since children do not share this feature, no one should transfer their judgment about the appropriate way to treat dogs through to how to treat children. This disanalogy is genuine and relevant; it undermines premise two.

Part 3: Discussion continues/Author's reply:

Although I think most people, in response to the relevance test, will think that it would be wrong to use a shock collar on a dog that could understand spoken explanations, I'm not sure the author would think that. My guess is that he thinks any form of training that is effective is morally permissible, and so he would defend using shock collars even on dogs of child-like intelligence. Although I think that will be a difficult case for him to make, that's probably his best response to my objection.

CHAPTER 9 PRACTICE EXERCISES

EVALUATING ARGUMENTS FROM ANALOGY

Exercises 9A: Applying Relevance Tests

Exercise Instructions: *each exercise below presents an Argument from Analogy along with a proposed disanalogy. For each proposed disanalogy, complete a relevance test to determine if the difference is morally relevant.*

1. The argument:
   1. It's permissible for a surgeon to perform breast augmentation on a competent adult who wants it.
   2. Performing a clitoridectomy (that is, the surgical excision of the clitoris) on a competent adult who wants it is relevantly similar to performing breast augmentation on a competent adult who wants it.

   Thus, it's permissible for a surgeon to perform a clitoridectomy on a competent adult who wants it.

Proposed disanalogy: unlike breast augmentation, clitoridectomy removes part of a person's body.

2. The argument:
  1. It's permissible for a surgeon to perform breast augmentation on a competent adult who wants it.
  2. Performing a clitoridectomy (that is, the surgical excision of the clitoris) on a competent adult who wants it is relevantly similar to performing breast augmentation on a competent adult who wants it.

  Thus, it's permissible for a surgeon to perform a clitoridectomy on a competent adult who wants it.

Proposed disanalogy: Unlike breast augmentation, clitoridectomy deprives a person of the ability to feel sexual pleasure.

3. The argument:
  1. It's wrong for a professional athlete to use illegal performance-enhancing drugs.
  2. A college student handing in a paper they bought on the internet is relevantly similar to a professional athlete using illegal performance-enhancing drugs.

  So, it's wrong for a college student to hand in a paper they bought on the internet.

Proposed disanalogy: Unlike performance-enhancing drugs, a purchased paper doesn't improve a person's abilities.

4. The argument:
  1. It's wrong for a professional athlete to use illegal performance-enhancing drugs.
  2. A college student handing in a paper they bought on the internet is relevantly similar to a professional athlete using illegal performance-enhancing drugs.

  So, it's wrong for a college student to hand in a paper they bought on the internet.

Proposed disanalogy: While performance enhancing drugs could directly prevent others from placing as well in a race (there is only one first place medal), a student doing well on a paper assignment because they turn in a purchased paper doesn't prevent others from doing as well on the paper.

5. The argument:
  1. A state should provide all citizens with access to basic education.
  2. A state providing access to basic health care is relevantly similar to a state providing access to basic education.

  Therefore, a state should provide all citizens with access to basic health care.

Proposed disanalogy: While everyone needs the same amount and type of basic education, people don't all need the same type and amount of basic health care.

6. The argument:
    1. Entering your dog into a dog fight for money is morally wrong.
    2. Eating factory-farmed meat is relevantly similar to entering your dog into a dog fight for money.

Therefore, eating factory-farmed meat is morally wrong.

Proposed disanalogy: a person who enters a dog in a fight is trying to make money from their dog's suffering and death; people who eat factory-farmed meat are not trying to make money from the suffering and death of the animals they eat.

7. The argument:
    1. It's wrong for members of a book club to stop people from leaving the group to start another club.
    2. A state (like Canada) stopping a territory (like Quebec) from seceding is relevantly similar to members of a book club stopping people from leaving to start another club.

So, it's wrong for a state to stop a territory from seceding from it.

Proposed disanalogy: while you're leaving a book club wouldn't require anyone else to leave it who didn't want to, a whole territory seceding would require people to stop being part of the state even though they didn't want to.[9]

8. Case: Some adults have developmental disabilities that leave them unable to care for themselves. In the recent past, developmentally disabled adults who did not have family members able or willing to care for them were often confined in institutions. These institutions were often stifling: overcrowded, devoid of opportunities for stimulation or genuine interpersonal connection. We now recognize that these stifling institutions were cruel and abusive to the people confined in them.
    The argument:
    1. It's wrong to confine developmentally disabled people in stifling institutions.
    2. Confining orangutans in small, urban zoos is relevantly similar to confining developmentally disabled people in stifling institutions.

Therefore, it's wrong to confine orangutans in small, urban zoos.

Proposed disanalogy: unlike the stifling institutions, zoos provide educational opportunities for visitors.

9. Case: many art museums are teetering on the brink of bankruptcy; the money they collect from visitors and donors is not sufficient to cover their

---

[9]Adapted from David Miller, "Like most secessionist movements, Brexit shows that breaking up is hard," *New Statesman America*, 1 April 2019. https://www.newstatesman.com/politics/brexit/2019/04/most-secessionist-movements-brexit-shows-breaking-hard

operating costs. Imagine a consortium of art museums lobbies for government subsidies, so that they can remain open. They offer the following argument for the permissibility of spending tax dollars to subsidize struggling art museums.

The argument:

1. Spending tax dollars to clean up and prevent serious air pollution is morally permissible.
2. Spending tax dollars to support art museums is relevantly similar to spending tax dollars to clean up and prevent serious air pollution.

So, spending tax dollars to support art museums is permissible.

Proposed disanalogy: everyone gets a benefit from clean air, but only art lovers benefit from art museums.

10. Case: Hugh G. Coffers, who is very rich, buys vastly more food than he could possibly eat, because he likes the convenience of having a wide variety of convenient options for any meal. As a result, he ends up throwing away 1,000 pounds of food a week, while there are many people in his community who do not get adequate nutritious food because they can't afford it.

The argument:

1. It is morally wrong for Coffers to waste 1,000 pounds of food a week.
2. Driving a car to work when you could bike or ride public transport is relevantly similar to Coffers' actions.

Therefore, it's morally wrong to drive a car to work when you could bike or ride public transportation.

Proposed disanalogy: driving a car to work when you could bike or use public transport wastes a small amount of fuel that would make little difference to anyone else; Coffers wastes a huge amount of food that would make a big difference to many families.

Exercises 9B: Brainstorming and Testing Disanalogies

Exercise Instructions: *In this section you will revisit the arguments you analyzed in the* Chapter 8 *Practice Exercises 8B. For each of the arguments in Practice Exercises 8B, do the following things. (Number your answers with the corresponding numbers from Practice Exercises 8B. For example, label your answer 9B12 when examining the argument from 8B12.)*

- *First, represent the argument in standard form using the General Form of Argument from Analogy.*
- *Second, suggest what you think is the best candidate for a genuine and morally relevant disanalogy between the cases being compared. "Premise 2 is false because . . . "*
- *Third, test your suggested disanalogy for moral relevance.*

Exercises 9C: Complete Argument Evaluation

Exercise Instructions: *for each of the following passages:*

- *First, represent the argument in standard form for Argument from Analogy.*
- *Second, offer what you believe to be the best objection to the argument. Clearly identify which premise you are engaging: "Premise 1 is false because . . . " or "Premise 2 is false because . . . " If your objection is to premise 2, be sure to include a relevance test.*
- *Third, briefly explain how you believe the discussion should continue. What do you think is the author's best reply to the objection you have just raised?*

1. We require people to have a license to do all sorts of things. For instance, we require people to have a license to drive a car. This is clearly a license we *should* require. Cars are potentially dangerous machines that, if operated incompetently, can seriously harm or kill innocent people. For the same reasons, we should license gun ownership. Requiring people to pass a basic skills and safety test before they are allowed to buy a gun would mitigate the harms of irresponsible gun ownership without depriving responsible people of the opportunity to own firearms.

2. Human reproductive cloning is the use of artificial reproductive technology in the laboratory to produce a baby that is the genetic duplicate of a donor. This practice could enable some people who otherwise couldn't have a baby to have one. Currently, reproductive cloning cannot be done safely—there are still significant health risks for the clone. But someday we will be able to produce perfectly healthy clones. Once cloning technology has become safe and reliable, it will be morally permissible for people to use reproductive cloning to have a baby.

   We already commonly use a non-sexual medical technique to help couples have a baby when they are otherwise unable to: artificial insemination. There is nothing morally wrong with the non-sexual introduction of donor sperm into a woman's vagina to have a baby. Using reproductive cloning is relevantly similar: it enables people who otherwise aren't able to have a baby to have one.

3. People these days don't even bat an eye at violence in video games. Millions of people play video games that simulate all manner of wrongful killing: drug dealers killing innocent bystanders, pirates butchering whales and orcas, and street fighters tearing the spines from their opponents. Violence in video games is the norm. But people fail to realize that engaging in *simulated* murder is still morally wrong. It would, after all, be wrong for someone to watch simulated child pornography. If watching simulated child porn is wrong, even though no actual minors were sexually abused to produce it, then committing simulated murder in video games is wrong, too.[10]

---

[10]Adapted from an argument discussed in Morgan Luck, "The gamer's dilemma: An Analysis of the Arguments for the Moral Distinction between Virtual Murder and Virtual Paedophilia." *Ethics and Information Technology*, 11, no. 1 (2009): 31–36.

4. Imagine that I have founded a charity organization that helps the poor. But not enough people are voluntarily contributing to my charity, so many of the poor remain hungry. I decide to solve the problem by approaching well-off people on the street, pointing a gun at them, and demanding their money. I funnel the money into my charity, and the poor are fed and clothed at last.

In this scenario, I would be called a thief. Why? The answer seems to be: because I am taking other people's property without their consent . . .

Now compare the case of taxation. When the government "taxes" citizens, what this means is that the government demands money from each citizen, under a threat of force: if you do not pay, armed agents hired by the government will take you away and lock you in a cage. This looks like about as clear a case as any of taking people's property without consent. So the government is a thief.[11]

5. [Preferring Asian women as romantic partners] is not wrong . . . People have many preferences when it comes to marriage, dating, and sex. Consider heterosexual men's preferences for women who are thin, feminine, normal height, symmetrical, and so on. The preference to marry, date, or have sex with Asian women is morally similar to these preferences.[12]

6. Some people, upon finding out that a person they have been interested in is transgender, decide suddenly that they are no longer interested in dating that person. In some cases, their reason is that they're only sexually attracted to particular body types and genitals, not because they hate or fear transgender people. There's nothing morally wrong with someone refusing to date trans people for this kind of reason, since it's morally no different than a gay man refusing to "try out women" at the request of their homophobic relatives. Just as there's nothing wrong with a gay man choosing to date only other men, there's nothing wrong with refusing to date a trans person if you're not attracted to their body type.

7. Some people, upon finding out that a person they have been interested in is transgender, decide suddenly that they are no longer interested in dating that person. Clearly, a person of good character would not do this. You can see this by noting that it is similar, morally speaking, to a White person choosing, whenever possible, to work only with other White people on the job. Even if the person does this not because they consciously hate or fear people of color but because they grew up without much experience working in diverse groups, this tendency would not be admirable or virtuous. For the same reasons, neither is refusing to date a person because you've found out they don't have the genitals you expected.

8. People are right to be morally outraged by female genital mutilation (FGM). This practice comes in many varieties. One is known as clitoridectomy, which is when a woman or young girl's clitoris is surgically removed. (There are a

[11]Quoted from "Is Taxation Theft?" a blog post by Michael Huemer. https://www.libertarianism.org/columns/is-taxation-theft

[12]Quoted from the abstract of Stephen Kershnar, "In Defense of Asian Romantic Preference," *International Journal of Applied Philosophy*, 32, no. 2 (2018):243–256.

variety of reasons people give for this procedure, but often it is viewed as a rite of passage that reduces a woman's ability to feel sexual pleasure and so ensures both her fidelity to her husband and her focus on prescribed household duties.) It is clearly wrong to perform a clitoridectomy on a young girl, because it is a medically unnecessary surgical procedure that the child can't consent to.

What's surprising is that, in contrast to attitudes about FGM, many people seem unconcerned about male circumcision of young boys. This procedure is morally no different from FGM, because it is also medically unnecessary and the child is unable to consent to it. So, we should admit that male circumcision is actually male genital mutilation and treat it with the same justifiable scorn we treat FGM.[13]

9. One unfortunate fact about our country is that your skin color to some extent determines how people treat you: in America, the darker your skin is the more likely you'll be treated as the object of suspicion, hostility, or dismissal. Now, suppose a mixed-race couple, knowing society's tendency to treat darker skinned people worse, wanted to use genetic screening to determine their fetus's skin color. If the fetus has dark skin, they will abort and try again. If the fetus has light skin, the will continue the pregnancy. It seems to me that even if they are motivated only by a desire to benefit their future child, it is still wrong of them to use genetic screening in this way.

How is this any different from using genetic screening to avoid having a child with a disability? In both cases, the screened-for characteristic (skin color, physical impairment) doesn't itself make the baby inherently worse off. Instead, it is society's prejudiced reaction to the condition that threatens to make the baby worse off. Aborting fetuses with dark skin and aborting fetuses with disabilities only serves to perpetuate the social prejudices that make life more difficult for people with dark skin and people with disabilities. Just as it would be wrong to screen for skin color, it is wrong to screen for disabilities.[14]

10. Suppose someone made a film whose sole purpose was to display the suffering of a group of inmates in a Nazi concentration camp. We are to imagine that the filmmakers are not interested in expressing any kind of judgment on Nazi atrocities. Their aim is simply to display the atrocities as vividly and realistically as possible, giving the audience various powerful emotions in response to the events shown in the film (the prisoners' journey in sealed train cars, their arrival at the camp and the trauma of being separated from their families, their physical and emotional suffering at the hands of sadistic guards, the ghastly consequences of medical experiments conducted by Nazi doctors, etc.) The purpose of this hypothetical film—which we will refer to as a "Nazi cruelty film"—is simply to give the audience a thrill ride, sending it out of the theater

---

[13]Adapted from an argument suggested in Arif Akhtar, "Female Genital Mutilation Is Bad, So Why Is Male Circumcision for Non-Medical Reasons OK?" *Medium*, May 9, 2017. https://medium.com/@arifakhtar/female-genital-mutilation-is-bad-so-why-is-male-circumcision-for-non-medical-reasons-ok-3d453ee7f1c9)

[14]Adapted from an argument in Harriet McBryde Johnson, "Unspeakable Conversations," *New York Times* Magazine 16 (2003).

with the feeling of having witnessed a spectacle of extreme violence and unparalleled emotional intensity.

I want to make a simple argument: (1) For reasons that are not easy to specify . . . it seems correct to say that it would be morally wrong to produce, distribute, and view a Nazi cruelty . . . film; (2) in terms of their content, of the filmmakers' intent, and of the effects on the audience, gorefest films such as The Texas Chain Saw Massacre and the many similar products it inspired do not significantly differ from a Nazi cruelty . . . film; so, (3) one should subject gorefest films to the same kind of moral condemnation to which one would subject Nazi cruelty . . . films.[15]

11. Fans of horror films have occasionally faced moral condemnation from their broader communities. In England during the 1980s, and in the United States during the 1990s, conservatives singled out horror movies as a kind of cultural pollution. They believed that the depictions of suffering and death displayed in horror films are so dangerous, so morally corrupting, that access to these films should be restricted. Their fundamental worry was that watching scenes of suffering and death, as depicted in horror movies, would corrupt the moral character of horror fans by making them callous to suffering and death in the real world.

I don't think this objection to the moral permissibility of horror movies makes sense. There are many unobjectionable movies in other genres that depict scenes of suffering and death. Think of Schindler's List, Titanic, Saving Private Ryan, and Fargo, among others. It isn't morally wrong to watch these movies, even though they depict suffering and death for purposes of entertainment. Is there any moral difference between watching characters die in these movies and watching characters die in horror movies? I can't see one. If there is no moral problem with watching non-horror depictions of suffering and death, then there probably isn't a problem with watching horror depictions either.[16]

12. Consider the following scenario. Marvin is in desperate need of food. Perhaps someone has stolen his food, or perhaps a natural disaster destroyed his crops; whatever the reason, Marvin is in danger of starvation. Fortunately, he has a plan to remedy the problem: he will walk to the local marketplace, where he will buy bread. Assume that in the absence of outside interference, this plan would succeed: the marketplace is open, and there are people there who are willing to trade food to Marvin in exchange for something he has. Another individual, Sam, is aware of all this and is watching Marvin. For some reason, Sam decides to detain Marvin on his way to the marketplace, forcibly preventing him from reaching it. As a result, Marvin returns home empty-handed, where he dies of starvation . . .

How does all this relate to US immigration policy? The role of Marvin is played by those potential immigrants who seek escape from oppression or economic hardship. The marketplace is the United States: were they allowed in,

[15]Quoted from Gianluca Di Muzio, "The Immorality of Horror Films," International Journal of Applied Philosophy 20, no. 2 (2006): 277–294.

[16]Adapted from an argument in Ian Stoner, "Barbarous Spectacle and General Massacre: A Defence of Gory Fictions," Journal of Applied Philosophy 37, no.4 (2019): 511–527.

most immigrants would succeed in meeting their needs (to a greater extent, at least, than they will if they are not allowed in). The role of Sam is played by the government of the United States, which has adopted severe restrictions on entry . . . In view of this, the actions of the US government . . . constitute serious violations of the rights of potential immigrants.[17]

13. The most attractive neighborhood in Blandland was overseen by a homeowner association covering about 100 homes, belonging to a wide variety of singles and families. The neighborhood included the best park and the best elementary school in the region; it had little crime and immaculate lawns.

The homeowner association convened a meeting to discuss a new issue: whether or not to allow homeowners to convert their garages into rentable rooms. Several homeowners had fielded requests from people in Greater Blandland who would like to move into the neighborhood, but had no chance of buying a house there. (There weren't any homes for sale, and most would-be renters lacked the money for a down-payment anyway.) One case in particular forced the issue. Sam, a homeowner, planned to modify his garage in order to rent it to Marvin, who would move in with his 6-year-old daughter so that she could attend the desirable elementary school.

The association discussed the issue and voted decisively to ban converted garages as rental rooms. The residents who voted to ban renters voted, as voters always do, for a variety of reasons, some good and some bad. Some residents had an irrational prejudice against renters. Others were concerned that people without an ownership stake in the neighborhood wouldn't invest in it the same way property owners do. Others worried about overcrowding in the park and school if too many renters moved in. Regardless: the vote to ban converted garages came out 87 to 13 against.

Did the neighborhood association do anything morally wrong? Of course not; they did exactly what such associations are developed to do: implement the neighborhood's best understanding of what's best for it. But that homeowner association was doing, on a small scale, exactly what American democracy does on a larger scale. If there's nothing wrong with the homeowner association excluding potential renters, there's nothing wrong with the United States excluding potential immigrants, either.

14. Suppose Great Granny has twenty great-grandchildren, and she has sliced up an apple pie to serve them. The kids are all eager for the pie but, to their surprise, they find out that Great Granny has divided the pie unevenly: two of the great-grandchildren get 80 percent of the pie, and the other eighteen have received the remaining 20 percent. Even after much searching and asking around, the children can find no good reason why Great Granny has doled out the dessert the way she did. It isn't even clear that she has a reason; the uneven slices might be an accident. And that is no comfort to the 18 children staring forlornly at their tiny slivers of pie.

[17]Quoted from Michael Huemer, "Is There a Right to Immigrate?" *Social Theory and Practice*, Vol. 36. No. 3, 2010.

How should the two children with the enormous slices respond to this situation? Obviously, they should even things out by giving more pie to the other children.

This hypothetical situation is similar in important ways to the current distribution of wealth across the globe. A few countries—about 10 percent—have 80 percent of the global wealth, while the rest make do with the crumbs. Just as the beneficiaries of Great Granny's arbitrary slicing should redistribute their pie more evenly, countries that have acquired massively disproportionate shares of global wealth have a moral reason to redistribute their wealth to poorer countries.[18]

15. Consider a couple who, right now, lives a lifestyle that has as much environmental impact as an average American. They generate an average amount of garbage, emit an average amount of carbon dioxide, use an average amount of water, and so on. Suppose they feel their life is not entirely fulfilled, and they discuss changes they could make that would make them happier. Together, they decide to change their lifestyle to one of massive over-consumption. They deliberately triple their output of garbage and carbon dioxide, triple their use of water and other resources. And it works: when they survey their new lives of overconsumption, they feel more fulfilled than they did when their environmental impact was average.

I expect you'll agree that choosing this lifestyle of over-consumption is morally wrong. But it is not meaningfully different from choosing to have children. Couples who choose to have two children effectively choose to triple their environmental impact. (And that doesn't even count further environmental costs if their children also choose to have children.) If it is wrong to seek personal fulfillment by choosing a lifestyle of massive over-consumption, then it is wrong to seek personal fulfillment by choosing to have children, too.[19]

16. In 1939 Otto Schmidt was working as a laboratory assistant at a distinguished medical research institute in Germany. He learned, through chance remarks and his own observation, that another unit of the institute was receiving mentally retarded patients from a nearby asylum, and using them as research subjects. The patients were exposed to various poisonous gases, including nerve gas, and then forced to continue walking up and down an inclined ramp. They frequently vomited, and showed other symptoms of illness; but if they stopped, they were beaten with sticks. After a few days, most patients died from the poison gases they had inhaled; the remainder were put to death.

Schmidt was horrified by his discovery. At first he assumed that the scientists carrying out this research were doing so without authority, and that if the authorities were informed, it would be stopped. But his initial attempts to act on this assumption failed when the director of the institute made it clear that

[18]Adapted from an argument discussed in Jason Brennan, "Global Justice and Misleading Metaphors," http://bleedingheartlibertarians.com/2018/09/global-justice-and-misleading-metaphors/ Accessed Jan. 2, 2019.

[19]Adapted from an argument in Thomas Young, "Overconsumption and Procreation: Are They Morally Equivalent?" *Journal of Applied Philosophy*, 18, no. 2 (2001).

he had special permission from the highest levels to carry out this research "in the interests of the German soldier, who may again be exposed to chemical warfare." Schmidt attempted to contact these higher authorities, but he received no response. He also tried to alert the relatives of the patients, but his inquiries revealed that only patients who had no contact with relatives were selected for the experiments.

There was little more, legally, that Schmidt could do, but the experiments were continuing, and he could not simply forget about them. Therefore he decided on the only course of action he could think of that stood a chance of stopping the experiments. The unit conducting the experiments was housed in a separate and specially equipped building. One night, when neither staff nor experimental subjects were in the building, Otto obtained a supply of petrol and set fire to the building. His plan was entirely successful; the building was destroyed, and because of shortages of resources at the time, never rebuilt. No further experiments with poison gases were conducted at that research institute.

What attitude should we take to what Otto Schmidt did? In criticism of his actions, it might be argued that he broke the law of his own country. Although he had certainly attempted to use legal channels to stop the research, it could not be said that he had exhausted all legal channels, since he had not received a definite and final response to his letters to higher authorities. It may also be said that Schmidt caused the destruction of a costly scientific research facility, and stopped a scientific research project that was adding to our knowledge about the capacities of human beings to continue working after exposure to harmful chemicals. Schmidt was not qualified, it might plausibly be asserted, to assess the scientific value of this work, nor its importance to the German Army.

Yet I do not think many of us will find these criticisms convincing. Schmidt was witnessing an atrocity. While the subjects of the experiments were suffering every day, he could not be expected to wait indefinitely for an official response—especially since this response might well be that the project should continue. As for the claim that Schmidt was not qualified to judge the value of the project, in this particular situation it seems clear that the project was unjustifiable. Schmidt did indeed use his own moral judgment on this matter, but his judgment was sound. For this—and also, of course, for his personal courage—he deserves not criticism, but the highest praise.

Now consider a more recent incident:

At a prestigious research institute in the United States, monkeys were trained to run in a cylindrical treadmill. The monkeys received electric shocks unless they kept the treadmill moving. Once the monkeys had completed initial training at keeping the treadmill in motion, they were subjected to varying doses of radiation. Monkeys receiving the higher doses vomited repeatedly. They were then put back into the treadmill to measure the effect of the radiation on their ability to keep it moving. During this period, if a monkey did not move the treadmill for one minute, shock intensity was increased to 10 mA. (This is an intense electric shock, causing severe pain.)

Some monkeys continued to vomit while in the treadmill. The irradiated monkeys took up to five days to die.

Animal liberationists learned that the institute was conducting these experiments. For several years they protested against them through a variety of legal channels, without success. Then an animal activist—let us call her Olivia Smith—succeeded in entering the laboratory in which these experiments were carried out and caused such damage to the laboratory and its equipment that the experiments stopped and were not resumed.

What attitude should we take to what Olivia Smith did? If we think that Schmidt was a hero, should we also think of Smith in the same way?[20]

17. Imagine the Louvre decided to raise funds by auctioning off the rights to destroy Mona Lisa, one of the world's most famous works of art. Many rich people have expressed interest in this auction, and the Louvre stands to raise a ton of money. Many art lovers are, of course, upset at the prospect of this masterwork being destroyed. But the Louvre has a response: "Don't worry," they say. "We have commissioned a replica of the painting. After the original is destroyed we will display the replica, which is just as good."

In this story, the Louvre is doubly wrong. They are wrong that a replica is just as good as the original, and they are wrong that displaying a replica mitigates the wrong of destroying the original work.

What the Louvre has suggested in this imaginary story is not meaningfully different from what people do when they try to "restore" logged forests by planting new trees, or "reclaim" destroyed wilderness by re-seeding native plants. A replica of nature is not just as good as nature, and it doesn't mitigate the tragedy of a logged forest if the logging company promises to plant new trees.[21]

18. Suppose someone claimed to be "aracial"—they claimed not to have a race. When asked to check a box for the census about their race, they chafe and respond that "I'm just human." When people call them White, based upon their appearance, they feel insulted and argue that they don't identify as White, because they feel no affinity towards White culture or the expectations that come with it. "Racial categories," they say, "are part of the problem that has led to racism and injustice, and they are arbitrary social constructions we have chosen simply because they help sustain racial oppression." For these reasons, they identify as aracial.

Clearly, it would be morally objectionable for this person to claim they are aracial. Even if race is a social construction, it is still a real force in the world and pretending it is not there just perpetuates oppression. Recognizing this leads to a startling conclusion about another identity people have recently tried to claim: being agender. Although the use of the term "agender" is constantly evolving, some use it to mean that they are not any gender at all—they are not a man, a woman, or any other "non-binary" gender either. For that

---

[20]Quoted from Peter Singer, "To Do or Not to Do?," *The Hastings Center Report*, 19, no. 6 (1989): 42–44.

[21]Adapted from Elliot, Robert. "Faking Nature." *Environmental Ethics,* 16 (1995): 76–88.

reason, some also reject being referred to with gendered pronouns (like he/him or she/her), because they say that they do not identify with any gender regardless of how they are categorized by society. They may dress and behave in ways that read as masculine to others, and indeed may have done so for most of their lives, but they insist that they are nevertheless agender. But here's the problem. If it's morally objectionable to claim to be aracial, then it's morally objectionable for someone to claim to be agender (if that's supposed to mean you don't have a gender). Why? Well, the same thing that makes claiming to be aracial problematic applies to claiming to be agender. Just as claiming to be aracial ignores the reality of racial oppression, claiming to be agender ignores the reality of gender oppression. These points entail a startling but unavoidable conclusion: it is morally objectionable for someone society categorizes as a man to claim to be agender.

To be clear, this doesn't mean that people who claim to be agender should be treated badly. Nor does it say anything about other, different claims about gender—it doesn't imply that it's morally objectionable for a trans woman to claim to be a woman, for instance. What the argument does show is that claiming to be without gender at all—to be agender—is a serious moral mistake.

CHAPTER 10

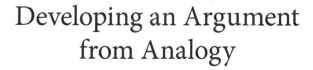

Developing an Argument
from Analogy

CHAPTER GOALS

In this chapter, you will learn how to:

- Develop an original Argument from Analogy.
- Prepare your argument for presentation to others.

DEVELOPING AN ARGUMENT FROM ANALOGY

In the previous chapter we practiced evaluating Arguments from Analogy. If you can critically evaluate analogies written by others, then you already understand the key features of a good Argument from Analogy; you thus already know what goal you seek in writing your own.

This chapter discusses strategies for constructing original Arguments from Analogy that are worthy of the kind of critical engagement you practiced in the previous chapter.

REVIEW: FEATURES OF A GOOD ANALOGY

All Arguments from Analogy are grounded in a particular described case. That described case can be drawn from the real world (as in the Jewish refugees argument) or it can be invented (as in Thomson's burglar argument). In order to ground an effective Argument from Analogy, any described case, whether realistic or fanciful, must have two features.

First, nearly everyone who hears the case forms the same moral judgment about it. In the Jewish refugees argument, almost everyone agrees that the United States did something morally wrong in excluding Jewish refugees fleeing Hitler's Holocaust. In Thomson's burglar analogy, almost everyone who hears the case agrees that voluntarily opening your window does not grant a burglar the right to ransack your home.

Second, the described case must share enough important parallels with the controversial case at hand so that most people in the audience recognize that there's good reason, at least at first blush, to transfer their judgment about the described case to the controversial case at hand. There are, for example, many important parallels between Jewish refugees during World War II, and Syrian refugees today: both fled a lethally dangerous environment; both fled under such urgent circumstances that they have none, or nearly none, of their own property in tow and so will need some public support to get on their feet; both come from cultural and religious backgrounds that make some American traditionalists uncomfortable; both present a possible but unlikely vector by which enemy agents could infiltrate the country. The reason this argument is powerful is because there are so many morally relevant parallels between the cases that most people immediately recognize there is good reason to evaluate the morality of exclusion similarly.

Writing a described case for use in an Argument from Analogy is a creative act. Whether you scour history or literature for an existing story, or write your own scenario from scratch, you are unavoidably engaged in the creative task of developing a described case that satisfies the two criteria of a good Argument from Analogy. Although developing an Argument from Analogy is a creative process, there are steps that can help structure the process.

DEVELOPING AN ANALOGOUS CASE

Let us take as our topic for discussion a specific controversy surrounding Androgen Deprivation Therapy. Androgen Deprivation Therapy (ADT), colloquially known as chemical castration, is an oral medication typically taken for two to six years, which reduces sexual fantasies and sexual motivation by sharply reducing testosterone levels. ADT has a number of potential side-effects, including risk of reduced bone mineral density, increased body fat, sperm reduction, hot flashes, and mood disturbances. However, by some estimates ADT administered to high-risk sex offenders reduces re-offense by up to 45 percent. Because of its effectiveness in high-risk cases, some lawmakers and advocates for victims of sexual abuse have argued that courts should have the ability to order violent sex offenders to undergo ADT as a part of their sentence.

The moral question we will investigate using Argument from Analogy is this: Is it morally permissible for states to order the involuntary chemical castration of violent sex offenders?

The search for a good analogy involves three steps. First, identify what you believe to be the morally salient features of the case in question. Second, brainstorm candidate analogies that strike you as sharing those morally salient features. Third, evaluate each candidate analogy according to whether it (a) elicits a clear and uncontroversial moral judgment from nearly everyone in the intended audience and (b) is relevantly similar, at least at first blush, to the controversial case at hand.

In the case of involuntary chemical castration, three features stand out to us as morally salient: it matters that the medical procedure is involuntary, that it carries the risk of harm to the person it is imposed upon, and that it is aimed at promoting the public good. What other cases share those three salient features? It is time to brainstorm and evaluate some candidates.

Vaccine mandates for school children might have occurred to you as a candidate analogy.

Vaccine Mandate: Many public schools require children to be vaccinated for measles, mumps, and rubella; without these vaccines, students are not allowed to enroll. These mandates are aimed at protecting the community from dangerous diseases, and because they are so effective they enjoy relatively broad public support. However, vaccines do carry a very small risk of adverse reaction to the vaccinated child, which leads some parents to object to them.

Vaccine Mandate shares the three morally salient features we identified in the case of involuntary chemical castration: vaccines are involuntary, they carry some risk to the child they are imposed upon, and they aim at promoting the public good. But to be worth pursuing, a candidate analogy should (a) elicit the same moral judgment from nearly everyone in the intended audience and (b) be relevantly similar, at least at first blush, to involuntary chemical castration.

Vaccine Mandate is not a promising candidate because it fails to satisfy the first criterion. People vigorously disagree about the moral status of exceptionless vaccine mandates, and so this case can't ground a useful Argument from Analogy. A general rule of thumb: real-world controversies are rarely a good source of cases on which to ground an Argument from Analogy, because they will almost always fail to satisfy the first criterion.

We next try inventing an uncontroversial candidate analogy, inspired by science fiction.

Kidney Harvest: Imagine that in response to a shortage of transplantable organs, a future government implements a program of kidney harvesting. Government agents select people at random, kidnap them, harvest a single kidney, and give it to a patient who would die without it. Those who have their kidneys harvested receive good medical care and usually live just fine afterwards, but sometimes the kidney removal has unwanted side-effects, including risk of pain and increased blood pressure.

Kidney Harvest shares the three morally salient features we identified in the case of involuntary chemical castration. Is it worth developing into an Argument from Analogy?

We expect nearly everyone will agree that a program involuntary kidney harvesting is morally impermissible. Kidney Harvest thus satisfies the first criterion for a good analogy: it is uncontroversial.

There is, however, a glaring difference between the two cases: chemical castration forces treatment on people in order to make them less of a threat to others; the kidney harvest forces treatment on people selected at random. This is such a central moral feature of the chemical castration case that it is hard to believe, even at first blush, that it isn't morally relevant. We can confirm this suspicion with a relevance test.

> **Relevance test:** Suppose that in the future, a new and baffling variety of spree killer emerges. These people remove their own right kidney, then go on a killing spree, bludgeoning as many victims as they can with their own kidney. Imagine that the government has developed a reliable way to identify these spree killers before they kill. One way to prevent the killings is to harvest their right kidney and donate it to a patient in need, leaving the would-be-killer unable to carry out their killings. Nearly all of these would-be kidney killers recover fully, and about 45 percent never commit any crimes at all after the harvesting of their right kidney.

In the original Kidney Harvest case, the harvest was uncontroversially impermissible. Does the re-imaged harvest case have the same moral status? We are not confident that it does. When used as a protective measure against violent crime, as chemical castration is, we're no longer confident in attributing clear moral status to kidney harvesting. This confirms our suspicion that the glaring difference between Kidney Harvest and chemical castration—the randomness of the selection in Kidney Harvest—is indeed morally relevant. Kidney Harvest fails to satisfy the second criterion.

The failures of the previous cases might lead us to think about the following realistic case:

> **Involuntary Quarantine:** Imagine an American nurse who has flown overseas to provide care during an Ebola outbreak. On his return flight to the United States, he begins to show symptoms of Ebola infection, and flight attendants notify medical personnel on the ground. The medical personnel recommend that the nurse be quarantined at the hospital, in order to avoid infecting others and triggering an outbreak. The nurse refuses to believe he is infected, and thus refuses to be quarantined. Citing the serious threat to others in the community, the medical personnel, assisted by law enforcement, quarantine the nurse against his will.

Involuntary Quarantine shares the three morally salient features we originally identified in the case of chemical castration: it is a case in which medical treatment, with possible unwanted consequences, is forced on a person for the good of the community. Is it worth developing into an Argument from Analogy?

Involuntary Quarantine satisfies the first criterion; nearly everyone judges that it is morally permissible for officials to involuntarily quarantine the nurse in this situation. It also, we believe, satisfies the second criterion; it does not have glaring differences that seem obviously morally relevant. It might, of course, contain morally relevant differences, but if so they are subtler and should be uncovered and discussed in the course of critically evaluating the argument. This is a candidate analogy worth pursuing.

USING THE CASE IN AN ARGUMENT

Once you've settled on a plausible analogy, develop it into an argument that fits the *General Form of Arguments from Analogy*:

1. Case *x* has moral status *S*.
2. Case *y* is relevantly similar to case *x*.

Therefore, case *y* has moral status *S*.

In the case of involuntary chemical castration, a complete standard-form representation of an argument based on the analogy to involuntary quarantine looks like this:

The Involuntary Quarantine Analogy

1. Authorities should be allowed to order the involuntary quarantine of the infected nurse.
2. Involuntary chemical castration of sex offenders is relevantly similar to involuntary quarantine of the nurse.

Therefore, authorities should be allowed to order the involuntary chemical castration of sex offenders.

Is this a good argument? There is work yet to be done before we decide: we must evaluate both premises. Note that while premise 2 does not assert a glaringly obvious disanalogy, careful thought suggests differences that might be morally relevant. For example, involuntary quarantine is of much shorter duration than chemical castration. Also, unlike involuntary quarantine, there may be comparably effective and less invasive alternatives to chemical castration. Further discussion, including relevance tests, will help determine if either of these differences constitutes a disanalogy that undermines the argument.

Is involuntary chemical castration morally permissible? There is even more work to do before we settle on an answer to that question. We have so far developed a single argument. Before we settle on a view about this controversial case, we should generate and vigorously evaluate the best arguments on both sides of the question, and then decide which arguments are the most persuasive. Developing this Argument from Analogy is only the first step in that process.

PREPARING YOUR ARGUMENT FOR PRESENTATION

With an Argument from Analogy, as with any argument, drafting in standard form is only the first step in presenting your argument. You must also include any supplementary information your audience needs in order to understand the question you're addressing, what your argument is saying (and what it's not saying), and why they should think the premises of the argument are true.

As with any other argument, one important type of supplementary information to provide is an explanation of what each premise is saying and why we should think it is true. In an Argument from Analogy, each premise requires a specific kind of explanatory information.

Premise 1 of an Argument from Analogy points to a described case and states that it has a particular moral status. So, at a minimum, to explain this premise you should give a clear and complete explanation of the case you're concerned with, and you should give some explanation about why that case has the moral status premise 1 says it does. For the Involuntary Quarantine Argument, the explanation might look something like this:

> **Explanation of premise 1:** Imagine the following case. An American nurse who has been caring for Ebola patients overseas begins to show symptoms on the flight home. By the time he lands, he shows clear signs of infection. Customs agents call medical personnel. Because Ebola is highly contagious when a person is symptomatic, and because the disease is difficult to treat and often fatal, the medical personnel recommend that the nurse be quarantined until he has recovered. The nurse resists, and declares that he does not want to be quarantined. Because they are confident that, outside of quarantine, the nurse poses a significant risk to others, medical personnel, assisted by law enforcement, force the nurse into quarantine against his will. In this case, the authorities did the right thing; they should be allowed to quarantine the nurse whether he wants it or not, because doing so significantly reduces the risk of serious harm to others.

Notice that premise 1 of our standard-form representation of this argument only asserts the judgment we expect audiences to form about the moral status of the Involuntary Quarantine case. It is that judgment that is crucial to the argument, but the judgment can only make sense when the case that generates it is clearly described and presented as supporting information.

The main task, in supporting premise 2, is to highlight the morally similar features of the two cases. For example:

> **Explanation of premise 2:** Cases of involuntary quarantine and chemical castration both involve a medical treatment that is forced on someone against their will. And in both cases, the justification is the same: both actions reduce the risk of serious harm to others. Forcibly quarantining the nurse prevents him from transmitting of a deadly disease; chemically castrating violent sex offenders prevents them from committing further acts of sexual violence. (Some studies suggest that chemical castration can reduce re-offense by as much as 45 percent in high-risk cases.) Involuntary chemical castration thus shares the morally salient features that make involuntary quarantine something that authorities should be allowed to order.

The explanations we've supplied give general audiences a basic understanding of the Involuntary Quarantine Argument. (For certain audiences, we might need to tailor, supplement, or expand these explanations.) They also illustrate the types of supplementary information that are crucial for presenting an Argument from Analogy clearly and persuasively. Supporting premise 1 requires explaining the described case that grounds your analogy and why it has the moral status premise 1 asserts. Supporting premise 2 requires highlighting the points of moral similarity between the two cases.

COMMON PITFALLS IN DEVELOPING ARGUMENTS FROM ANALOGY

In our experience, students asked to write an original Argument from Analogy for the first time most commonly stumble in one of two specific ways. As you begin to develop your argument-writing skills, be especially on the lookout for these two problems in your early drafts.

Pitfall 1: The described case is under-described

You must craft a described case that elicits the same judgment from all your readers. This requires you to include enough detail so that your readers understand what's at stake, morally, in your described case, and that they are able to form a judgment about it. Sometimes, minimal information is sufficient—some good described cases are just one sentence long. Other cases require more information to achieve their purpose. Brevity, when effective, is a virtue, but the omission of morally important details is a mistake.

Keep your audience in mind when you write. The case as you have imagined it might make perfect sense in your head, but confuse people who do not share your experiences or background knowledge. The best way to determine if you've included enough detail is to show your described case to friends or classmates and ask them to report to you their judgment about it. If they don't form the judgment you intended to elicit (or if they're confused about what is going on in your case), talk to them about why, and then write another draft.

Pitfall 2: The described case has obvious morally relevant differences from the controversial case

The central creative challenge is to construct an uncontroversial described case that is similar enough to the controversial case that we are justified in transferring our judgment from the uncontroversial case to the controversial case. The process we have described requires you to check each candidate you brainstorm for glaringly obvious morally relevant differences. But this can be difficult to do when you are developing an argument for a conclusion you already believe to be true.

This is the fundamental problem with the "Poisoned Skittles" argument we've discussed in previous chapters. There are *many* obvious morally relevant differences between Skittles and people. The only explanation for how these differences could be overlooked is that the author of the argument was unable to take a step back to critically examine the comparison. We can do better.

The best way to avoid overlooking an obvious morally relevant difference is to show your described case to friends or classmates who disagree with your argument's conclusion. Those are the peers who will be best attuned to morally relevant differences between your described case and the controversial case at hand. If you have no such peers, you will have to imagine that perspective and read your argument from it.

REVIEW: ARGUMENT FROM ANALOGY STEP BY STEP

We've recommended the following steps for developing Arguments from Analogy worth taking seriously:

1. Think carefully about the target case and identify the features that strike you as morally salient.
2. Identify or invent a different case that seems to share those morally salient features.
3. Test your case: is it one that (a) clearly and uncontroversially has a particular moral status and (b) is similar in the relevant ways to the target case? If not, go back to step (2).
4. Draft your Argument from Analogy in standard form.
5. Brainstorm objections to both premises of your argument, on your own and with the input of others who might disagree with you. Revise your argument as needed to address important objections.
6. Prepare your argument for presentation by including the supplementary information that will best help others understand the persuasive force of your argument.

As with other types of arguments, developing your own Arguments from Analogy requires practice and reflection. Along the way to an argument worth taking seriously, you may leave behind many less promising ones. You may even find yourself changing your mind about the topic under consideration. This, we have stressed, is to be expected and welcomed, because it is the way we refine our understanding of what matters and what doesn't.

CHAPTER 11

Analyzing Inference to the Best Explanation

CHAPTER GOALS

By reading this chapter and completing the exercises, you will learn how to:

- Represent a moral Inference to the Best Explanation (IBE) in standard form using the General Form of IBE
- Represent a Principle Justification sub-argument
- Represent a Principle Application sub-argument

ANALYZING MORAL INFERENCE TO THE BEST EXPLANATION

A moral Inference to the Best Explanation (IBE) is a special form of Argument from Principle. Instead of simply asserting a plausible principle, as is characteristic of Arguments from Principle, IBEs include two sub-arguments: one that argues in support of a moral principle, and another that applies that principle to a case.

This chapter demonstrates how to understand moral Inferences to the Best Explanation by analyzing their structure. The following chapters demonstrate how to evaluate them and develop your own.

INFERENCE TO THE BEST EXPLANATION IN FAMILIAR DOMAINS

IBE is a form of reasoning, sometimes called abductive reasoning, that is useful in a wide variety of contexts. An IBE starts by identifying a set of apparent facts. It then suggests an idea or theory that best explains those facts. The ability of an idea or theory to explain the facts better than the alternatives is evidence that the idea or theory is likely to be true.

If you have trouble-shot a technical problem, you probably used a form of IBE. Suppose that, in your house, your laptop has lost its wireless internet access, but your roommate's desktop, which is plugged into the internet with a wire, is still online. What explains the fact that your roommate has access but you don't? The best explanation is that there is a problem with your wireless access point, so you infer that you should focus your trouble-shooting efforts there.

IBE is the form of reasoning most closely associated with scientific investigation. For example, in 1847 an Austrian physician named Ignaz Semmelweis used IBE to solve a deadly puzzle. Of the two maternity wards at his hospital, one had an extremely high rate of infection and the other did not. Semmelweis noted that physicians in the ward with the high infection rate would often examine patients immediately after performing autopsies. Although scientists had not yet discovered that microorganisms cause infections, Semmelweis hypothesized that the best explanation of the available evidence was that doctors were transmitting a dangerous substance from the cadavers to the patients. He required physicians to wash their hands before examining living patients, and the infection rate plummeted.

Doctors typically use IBE when they diagnose sickness. Suppose a doctor sees a child with a low fever who complains of tiredness. The child has a rash on his back, and chicken pox has recently broken out at the child's school. The doctor judges that the best explanation of these facts is that the child has chicken pox and infers that the child probably has chicken pox.

Detectives in mystery stories characteristically use IBE. Sherlock Holmes gathers a large set of clues, and then identifies the criminal by identifying the best explanation of the available evidence.

In all these cases, reasoners identify a set of observations and then search for the best explanation of those observations. IBE reasoning doesn't give us absolute certainty. The child at the pediatrician might have chicken-pox-like symptoms that are caused instead by a rare disease. Your laptop might be offline because your nemesis has hired a hacker to harass you. These are *possible* explanations of what you observe, but that does not mean they are *probable*. The insight behind IBE is that the explanation that accounts for all of the available evidence in the simplest and most straightforward manner is the most likely to be true.

When scientists, detectives, and trouble-shooters use IBE, what they seek to explain are empirical observations of the world. When philosophers use a *moral* IBE, what they seek to explain is the moral status of *paradigm cases*— specific cases that have a clear and uncontroversial moral status. Paradigm cases provide the basis for a two-step reasoning process. First, philosophers articulate and defend a moral principle that best explains why those paradigm cases have the moral status that they do. Second, they apply that moral principle to the controversial topic at issue. To demonstrate this process, consider the following fictional scenario.

MORAL INFERENCE TO THE BEST EXPLANATION: AN INTRODUCTORY SCENARIO

Janus and Precarity are college students and friends. Precarity is enrolled in an English class that Janus aced the previous semester. Precarity is not doing well. A combination of unfortunate family circumstances and uncharacteristically low motivation have left her on the brink of failing. Her only hope of passing is to get an "A" on the final paper, but she has not learned the skills the paper requires and has no hope of writing an "A" paper herself.

Precarity has asked Janus to write the paper for her. Janus could produce an "A" paper, which would save Precarity from consequences Precarity insists are dire. ("I'd have to take another semester. I can't afford to pay those student fees again.") Janus recognizes that she is being asked to help Precarity cheat, and Janus is generally uncomfortable cheating. But she also wants to help her friend and wonders if this might be the sort of situation in which helping her friend is more important than being honest.

Janus visits her philosophy professor, Dr. Bookish, to ask for advice. Dr. Bookish offers the following two-stage argument, a moral Inference to the Best Explanation.

Dr. Bookish's IBE. After listening to Janus's story, Dr. Bookish agrees that this is a morally ambiguous situation. She suggests they begin by brainstorming other situations in which one person helps another person cheat and search those for cases that are *not* morally ambiguous. If they can find a group of aid-in-cheating cases that have a clear and uncontroversial moral status, they can begin their reasoning from there.

After a brainstorming session, Janus and Dr. Bookish settle on three cases of aid-in-cheating that they agree are *not* morally ambiguous.

Dope-dealing doctor: a physician helps a football player avoid getting caught for using performance-enhancing drugs by prescribing additional drugs that mask the banned drugs. Janus and Bookish agree that the doctor has done something wrong.

Election hacker: at the request of an unpopular politician, a computer hacker modifies voting machines to guarantee that he wins the election for governor. The hacker genuinely believes that it will be better for the state if the politician wins the election, and there is no way he could win without cheating. Janus and Bookish agree that the hacker has done something wrong.

Unjust draft: a dystopian society uses a computer to draft random people for roles in the military. Because of widespread social prejudices, members of a particular ethnic minority, when drafted, are typically subjected to abuse and unnecessarily dangerous work. A concerned citizen helps a resistance group to hack the computer that runs the draft. They alter the random number generator in a way that significantly reduces the chances that members of the oppressed minority will be drafted. Janus and Bookish agree that this is a morally permissible instance of aid-in-cheating.

Dr. Bookish poses a question: is there a moral principle that explains their shared judgments about these three cases of aid-in-cheating?

Janus recalls a simple principle taught by her elementary school teacher: it's always wrong to help someone cheat. This principle explains the first two cases, but it gets the third one wrong; helping people dodge an unjust draft is morally permissible.

Dr. Bookish recalls a principle advocated by her friend, a self-identified utilitarian: there is nothing wrong with helping someone cheat if you reasonably believe that will do the most good for society. This principle gets *Election hacker* wrong. It doesn't matter that the hacker believes the consequences for the state will be better. Secretly altering the outcome of an election is wrong.

Dr. Bookish suggests a third candidate principle: helping someone cheat is only morally permissible if it's necessary to counteract serious injustice. This principle explains why helping others cheat in the first two cases is wrong, and it allows that the cheating in the last case is permissible. Dr. Bookish has completed the first step of her argument: she has identified a moral principle that is plausible *because* it does a better job than the alternatives of explaining the cases.

In the next step of her argument, Dr. Bookish applies this principle to Janus's situation. Janus concedes that Precarity's position on the brink of failure is not the result of injustice. It is the result of bad luck and low motivation. If Janus were to provide the help Precarity wants, that would do nothing to counteract injustice. Thus, the principle implies that it would be morally wrong for Janus to write Precarity's paper for her.

Commentary. Dr. Bookish has offered an IBE for the conclusion that it would be morally wrong for Janus to help Precarity cheat. We represent her argument in standard form as two sub-arguments, corresponding to the two steps of her reasoning process.

The first sub-argument *justifies* a moral principle by offering it as the best explanation of a set of paradigm cases:

1. The aid-in-cheating in *Dope-dealing doctor* and *Election hacker* is wrong, while the aid-in-cheating in *Unjust draft* is morally permissible.
2. The best explanation of the cases in premise 1 is that helping others cheat is permissible only if it's necessary to counteract serious injustice.

So, helping others cheat is permissible only if it's the only way to counteract serious injustice.

The second sub-argument *applies* that principle to Janus's particular case:

1. Helping others cheat is permissible only if it's necessary to counteract serious injustice.
2. Helping Precarity cheat is not necessary to counteract serious injustice.

Therefore, helping Precarity cheat is not permissible.

Is Dr. Bookish's argument a good one? To establish that, we need to evaluate the premises of both sub-arguments using the techniques introduced in the next chapter.

THE GENERAL FORM OF MORAL IBE

Dr. Bookish's argument, like all instances of IBE, has the following general form:

General Form of Moral IBE:

Principle Justification Sub-argument:

1. Cases *v, w,* etc. have moral status *S* [and cases *y, z,* etc. have moral status *T*]. (PARADIGM CASES)

2. The best explanation of the cases in premise 1 is that cases of type *A* have moral status *S*. (EXPLANATION)

So, cases of type *A* probably have moral status *S*. (PRINCIPLE)

Principle Application Sub-Argument:

1. Cases of type *A* probably have moral status *S*. (PRINCIPLE)
2. Case *x* is of type *A*. (CASE)

Therefore, case *x* probably has moral status *S*. (CONCLUSION)

The second sub-argument should look familiar: it is nearly identical to the General Form of Argument from Principle. What IBE adds is the principle justification sub-argument.

REPRESENTING IBE IN STANDARD FORM

As with the other forms of moral argument covered in this book, understanding the General Form of IBE makes it easier to represent these arguments in standard form. As you read the following passages, first, identify the conclusion the author is arguing for. Then find the components the author uses to support that conclusion: paradigm cases, the moral principle that best explains those paradigm cases, and the claim that the controversial case at hand is an instance of the type covered by that moral principle. Finally, review the original passage and your representation of it, and ask if the author would approve of your work.

Example: Marquis against Abortion

There are many cases where it's clearly wrong to kill.[1] Outside of extreme circumstances, it's wrong to kill adult humans like you and me. It's wrong to kill adult humans even when they are asleep. It is wrong to kill infants. It's wrong to kill depressed teenagers, even if they don't wish to go on living. Killing hermits is wrong, even if they have no friends or family to grieve them. If peaceful and friendly extraterrestrials with psychological capacities similar to ours visited Earth in a spaceship, it would be wrong to kill them, too.

Why is it wrong to kill in these clear and uncontroversial cases? The answer can't be that killing is wrong only if the one killed wants to continue living; that wouldn't explain why it's wrong to kill the depressed teenager. It can't be that killing is wrong because it harms the friends and family of the one who dies; that wouldn't explain why it's wrong to kill hermits. Nor can it be that killing is wrong because it ends a human life, because that wouldn't explain why it's wrong to kill the peaceable extraterrestrials. The best answer is that

---

[1]Adapted from D. Marquis, "Why Abortion Is Immoral," *Journal of Philosophy*, 86, no. 4 (1989): 183–202.

these acts of killing are *pro tanto* wrong (that is, wrong barring presumably rare overriding considerations) because they deprive a being of the value of their own future—a future of projects, experiences, relationships, and activities that they would have (at some point) valued. In every one of these uncontroversial cases of wrongful killing, the killing is wrong *because* it deprives a being of a future of value.

This principle shows that abortion is, in all but the rarest cases, morally wrong. Abortion is typically a case of killing that deprives a being (the fetus) of a future of projects, experiences, relationships, and activities that it would, at some point, have valued. Thus, reflection on what makes other forms of killing wrong shows that, outside of extreme circumstances, abortion is morally wrong.

The first two paragraphs of this passage offer the principle justification sub-argument. The final paragraph offers the principle application sub-argument. Here's how we'd represent the justification sub-argument:

Principle Justification Sub-argument

1. It's wrong to kill adults (whether asleep or awake), human infants, hermits, E.T.s, and depressed teenagers. (PARADIGM CASES)
2. The best explanation of the cases in premise 1 is that killing is *pro tanto* wrong if it deprives a being of a future of value. (EXPLANATION)

   So, killing is *pro tanto* wrong if it deprives a being of a future of value. (PRINCIPLE)

Note that we have used the phrase "future of value" in premise 2. Although this is a term of art, not every-day English, the term is clearly defined in the original passage. Maintaining it in the standard form representation of the argument is concise and charitable. But when evaluating this argument, we must keep in mind that Marquis means something specific by "a future of value." He means a future with projects, experiences, relationships, and activities that will at some point be valued by the being whose future it is.

Turn now to the principle application sub-argument. This sub-argument is structurally identical to Argument from Principle, and you can use the same techniques to represent it in standard form.

Principle Application Sub-argument

1. Killing is *pro tanto* wrong if it deprives a being of a future of value. (PRINCIPLE)
2. Most abortions are killings that deprive a being of a future of value. (CASE)

   Therefore, most abortions are *pro tanto* wrong. (CONCLUSION)

We have analyzed the structure of Marquis's argument by representing both sub-arguments in standard form. The essential steps in his reasoning are clearly identified and ready to be individually evaluated.

Example: Stoner against the colonization of Mars

Consider three cases of people misbehaving in wilderness.[2] First, imagine a small group of people canoeing in the Boundary Waters Canoe Area Wilderness, a protected area in northern Minnesota that bans motor vehicles and requires visitors to leave nothing behind. Imagine that a member of this group finishes drinking from a water bottle, and, instead of carrying it out with him, he fills it with pebbles and carefully sinks it in the middle of a deep lake. Second, imagine a group of hikers in Goblin Valley State Park. This park in Utah features many ancient weathered rock formations, including boulders naturally perched on pedestals. Imagine the hikers, just for fun, topple a few of the balancing rocks. Third, imagine a group of elite spelunkers who discover a crystalline cave so deep and inaccessible that it is unlikely that any other explorers will ever find it. After admiring the crystal formations, which were millions of years in the making, the spelunkers have a competition to see who can destroy the most the fastest.

These are all examples of wrongful behavior in wilderness—but what makes them wrong? Some popular theories of environmental ethics cannot explain them. Human-centered conservationists argue that actions are wrong when they harm other people who would like to visit the wilderness. But no one will be able to access the crystalline cave, and no one will ever know about the sunken water bottle. Biocentrists argue that actions are wrong when they harm living things. But toppling a balancing rock doesn't harm any living things. I propose a less ambitious principle that more straightforwardly explains these cases: when we visit wilderness, we have an obligation to behave in such a way that evidence of our presence is soon erased by natural processes. This is exactly what naturalists mean when they teach young hikers to "leave no trace."

Mars is currently pristine wilderness. Like any pristine wilderness, we should only visit it in a careful and responsible way—a way that leaves no trace. Unfortunately, it is impossible to send humans to the surface of Mars in a way that would leave no trace. We already know that some of the bacteria and fungi we carry around with us can survive on Mars, and it is entirely possible that we would introduce invasive microorganisms that would fundamentally change its environment forever. Since it is impossible for humans to walk on Mars responsibly, we shouldn't walk on it at all. Colonization of Mars is morally wrong.

This passage groups its paradigm cases in paragraph 1, its suggestion of the principle that best explains those paradigm cases in paragraph two, and its

---

[2]Adapted from I. Stoner, "Humans Should Not Colonize Mars," *Journal of the American Philosophical Association*, 3, 3 (2017): 334–353.

application of the principle to the case of Mars colonization in paragraph three. In standard form for IBE:

Principle Justification Sub-argument

1. It is morally wrong to leave litter in the Boundary Waters, topple balanced rocks in Goblin Valley, and destroy the crystals in the crystalline cave. (PARADIGM CASES)
2. The best explanation of the moral judgments expressed in premise 1 is that it is morally wrong, when visiting wilderness, to change it in such a way that the traces we leave aren't soon erased by natural processes. (EXPLANATION)

So, it is probably morally wrong, when visiting wilderness, to change it in such a way that the traces we leave aren't soon erased by natural processes. (PRINCIPLE)

Principle Application Sub-argument

1. It is probably morally wrong, when visiting wilderness, to change it in such a way that the traces we leave aren't soon erased by natural processes. (PRINCIPLE)
2. Colonizing Mars would change the Martian wilderness in such a way that the evidence of our presence would never be erased. (CASE)

Therefore, colonizing Mars is probably morally wrong. (CONCLUSION)

The essential steps in this argument are now clearly identified and ready to be individually evaluated.

WHY USE IBE?

Some controversies about practical ethics invite broad consensus concerning the principles relevant to the controversy. These debates typically earn their status as controversies because people disagree about what those consensus principles require.

But there are many controversies in which participants disagree about which principles are, or ought to be, at the center of the debate. When a controversy is very new, and there has been little time to explore the values at stake in it, consensus about principles is rare. The debate about the ethics of Mars colonization is an example of this kind of controversy. At the other end of the spectrum, participants in very old, deeply entrenched debates usually disagree about which principles are plausible and relevant. The abortion debate is an example of this kind of controversy.

In controversies like these, simply asserting a principle probably won't help advance the discussion. But an argument in favor of a principle probably will. Inference to the Best Explanation is a powerful method of arguing for the truth of a moral principle, and of applying that principle to an especially difficult case.

REVIEW

A moral IBE is a special form of Argument from Principle, containing two sub-arguments. The first sub-argument offers a moral principle as the best explanation of a set of paradigm cases. The second sub-argument applies that principle to the controversial target case at hand. Familiarity with the General Form of IBE will make it easier to represent these arguments in standard form.

Paradigm case: a concrete and uncontroversial case that shares the morally salient features of a target case

The General Form of IBE.

Principle Justification Sub-argument:

1. Cases w, x, etc. have moral status S [and Cases y, z, etc. have moral status T]. (PARADIGM CASES)
2. The best explanation of the cases in premise 1 is that cases of type A have moral status S. (EXPLANATION)

   So, cases of type A probably have moral status S. (PRINCIPLE)

Principle Application Sub-argument:

1. Cases of type A probably have moral status S. (PRINCIPLE)
2. Case v is of type A. (CASE)

   Therefore, case v probably has moral status S. (CONCLUSION)

To test your understanding of the material introduced in this chapter, complete the Demonstration Exercises and then check your answers against the solutions that follow.

Demonstration Exercises

Demonstration Exercises are designed to give you immediate feedback on your grasp of the skills introduced in this chapter. To use them effectively, you should attempt answers to all of them, then check your work against our suggested answers, which follow. For a detailed explanation of how best to use Demonstration Exercises, read the book's Introduction.

Demonstration Exercises 11A: Identifying Premises and Conclusions

Exercise Instructions: supply the missing premise or conclusion to make the argument fit the pattern in the Principle Justification Sub-Argument of the General Form of IBE.

1.
   1. Adult humans and human infants matter for their own sake.
   2. The best explanation of the cases in premise 1 is that only human beings matter for their own sake.

   So, . . .

(continued)

2.

> **1.** Drinking while driving and texting while driving are wrong.
>
> **2.** ...
>
> So, it's wrong to do things behind the wheel that put yourself and others at unnecessary risk.

Exercises 11B: Representing arguments in standard form

Exercise Instructions: *represent each of the following arguments in standard form using both sub-arguments in the General Form of IBE.*

1. Illegal downloading

Sometimes people illegally download movies and music. This practice, while illegal, is not morally wrong. To see why, consider a few clear-cut cases:

- It is *not* wrong to repeat for a friend a joke that you heard at a stand-up show.
- It *is* wrong to steal a stand-up comedian's laptop.
- It is *not* wrong to recreate at home your favorite dish from a local restaurant.
- It *is* wrong to take the silverware from that same restaurant.

These cases establish that the story cannot be so simple as "taking something without permission is always morally wrong." It is not wrong to "take" a comedian's joke or recreate a favorite recipe because those activities do not actually deprive the comedian or the chef of anything—even after you retell the joke, the comedian has no more and no less than what they had before you retold it. The best explanation of these cases is thus a more nuanced principle: taking the fruits of others' labor without their permission is wrong if and *only* if it *deprives* them of something they already have.

Downloading music and movies doesn't deprive anyone of anything they already have. It may be illegal, but it isn't morally wrong.

2. Parental licenses[3]

We appropriately require people to be licensed to do things like drive cars or fly planes or to be doctors, lawyers, or teachers. But it would be wrong to require people to be licensed to play golf with their friends, or to cook food in their own houses. Why? Why should we require licenses for the first set of activities, but not for the second?

The best explanation is that we should require a license for people to perform activities that are potentially seriously harmful to others when they are performed by unskilled people. If I am an unskilled golfer, I pose no threat to other people. If I am an unskilled pilot, I shouldn't be allowed anywhere near the cockpit, because I could seriously harm the passengers on the plane.

What people don't notice is what this principle implies about parenting. Parents who lack certain specific skills (such as emotional regulation, effective and kind discipline, etc.) can do serious harm to kids. Some parents have seriously injured or even killed their own children because they are unable to control

---

[3]Adapted from Hugh LaFollette, "Licensing Parents," *Philosophy and Public Affairs*, 9, no. 2 (1980): 182–197.

their own anger. Some parents have seriously malnourished their own babies, because they did not know the basics of nutrition and feeding.

Parents who have not developed basic parenting skills can seriously harm vulnerable others. Parenting is exactly the kind of activity for which we should require a license.

3. Racist patients

American hospitals today often advertise how hard they work to accommodate patients' preferences. But some preferences raise difficult moral questions. For example, suppose a White patient requests to be treated exclusively by White doctors and nurses. If it is possible for the hospital to accommodate this racist preference, *should* it?

Surprisingly, even if we're committed to racial equality, the best answer to this question is "yes." Consider some of the many cases in which we clearly should accommodate patient preferences when possible:

- A female patient at an obstetrics and gynecology clinic requests only female doctors and nurses because she is uncomfortable around male doctors.

- A Hmong patient requests a family care physician who is Hmong, because it would make it easier to explain how their medical choices are informed by their cultural and spiritual views.

- A male client at a counseling center requests a male psychologist. The client doesn't explain why they want a male psychologist, but they appear to be uncomfortable with the idea of a female provider.

American hospitals should accommodate preferences like these when they can. Why? Here's one plausible answer: whenever it is possible to accommodate patient preferences in a way that would increase a patient's receptiveness to the quality health care provided, we should do so. This principle implies that we should also accommodate patients' preferences for the race of their health care providers, even if those preferences are racist.

Solutions to Demonstration Exercises

Demonstration Exercises are most useful if you make your best attempt to complete them before you look at the answers. If you haven't yet attempted answers to all the Demonstration Exercises, go back and do that now.

Solutions to Demonstration Exercises 11A: Identifying Premises and Conclusions

1.
   1. Adult humans and human infants matter for their own sake.
   2. That best explanation of the cases in premise 1 is that only members of the human species matter for their own sake.

   So, *only members of the human species matter for their own sake.*

2.
   1. Drinking while driving and texting while driving are wrong.

(continued)

2. *The best explanation of the cases in premise 1 is that it's wrong to do things behind the wheel that put yourself and others at unnecessary risk.*

So, it's probably wrong to do things behind the wheel that put yourself and others at unnecessary risk.

Solutions to Demonstration Exercises 11B: Representing Arguments in Standard Form

1. Illegal downloading

Principle Justification Sub-argument:

1. It's wrong to steal a comedian's laptop and to take silverware from a restaurant, but it's not wrong to repeat for a friend a comedian's joke or cook at home a dish you had at a restaurant. (PARADIGM CASES)

2. The best explanation of the cases in premise 1 is that taking the fruits of others' labor without their permission is wrong if, and only if, it deprives them of something they already have. (EXPLANATION)

So, taking the fruits of others' labor without their permission is probably wrong if, and only if, it deprives them of something they already have. (PRINCIPLE)

Principle Application Sub-argument:

1. Taking the fruits of others' labor without their permission is probably wrong if, and only if, it deprives them of something they already have. (PRINCIPLE)

2. Downloading music and movies (even when illegal) does not deprive anyone of something they already had. (CASE)

Therefore, downloading music and movies (even when illegal) is probably not wrong. (CONCLUSION)

2. Parental licenses

Principle Justification Sub-argument

1. We should require licensing for drivers, pilots, doctors, lawyers, and teachers; we should not require licensing to play golf, or cook at home. (PARADIGM CASES)

2. The best explanation of the cases in premise 1 is that we should require licensing for an activity if the activity is potentially seriously harmful to others when performed by unskilled people. (EXPLANATION)

So, we should probably require licensing for an activity if the activity is potentially seriously harmful to others when performed by unskilled people. (PRINCIPLE)

Principle Application Sub-argument

1. We should probably require licensing for an activity if the activity is potentially seriously harmful to others when performed by unskilled people. (PRINCIPLE)

2. Parenting is an activity that is potentially seriously harmful to children when performed by unskilled people. (CASE)

Therefore, we should probably require licenses for parenting. (CONCLUSION)

3. Racist patients

Principle Justification Sub-argument

1. Hospitals should accommodate the female patient's request for a female Ob/Gyn, a Hmong patient's request for a Hmong doctor, and a male client's request for a male psychologist. (PARADIGM CASES)

2. The best explanation of the cases in premise 1 is that hospitals should accommodate any patient requests that would increase that patient's receptiveness to the care provided. (EXPLANATION)

So, we should probably accommodate any patient requests that would increase that patient's receptiveness to the care provided. (PRINCIPLE)

Principle Application Sub-argument

1. We should probably accommodate any patient requests that would increase that patient's receptiveness to the care provided. (PRINCIPLE)

2. Accommodating patient requests for care providers of a specific race would increase their receptiveness to the care provided. (CASE)

Therefore, American hospitals should probably accommodate patient requests for care providers of a specific race. (CONCLUSION)

CHAPTER 11 PRACTICE EXERCISES:

ANALYZING MORAL INFERENCE TO THE BEST EXPLANATION

Exercises 11A: Identifying Premises and Conclusions

Exercise Instructions: *supply the missing premise or conclusion to make the argument fit the pattern of the Principle Justification Sub-Argument of the General Form of IBE.*

1. Paradigm cases:[4]

Firefighter: a firefighter opposed to abortion refuses to help put out a fire at an abortion clinic.

Vegan Burger-Slinger: a line cook at Doublemeat Palace, who has recently converted to veganism, refuses to prepare or serve meat, although that was what they were hired to do.

1. . . .

2. The best explanation of the cases in premise 1 is that an employee does not have a right to be protected from punishment by their employer if they refuse to do a task that is part of their job description.

---

[4]Cases adapted from Eva LaFollette and Hugh LaFollette, "Private Conscience, Public Acts," *Journal of Medical Ethics*, 33, no. 5 (2007): 249–254.

So, an employee does not have a right to be protected from punishment by their employer if they refuse to do a task that is part of their job description.

2. Paradigm cases:

Tragic prognosis: a physician discovers that a patient has a serious and debilitating illness for which there is no treatment. The patient is competent to understand the prognosis and has said that they want to know the truth, no matter how disheartening it is. The doctor worries that the truth is too painful and wonders if they should hide the results from the patient.

Business Trouble: A and B are business partners, and A has found out that their business is about to be sued. B cannot do anything about the lawsuit—the lawyers will take charge of that. Even though A and B have agreed to discuss any matters impacting their business, A worries that telling B the bad news will be stressful for B and won't benefit the business.

1. The doctor in Tragic Prognosis and person A in Business Trouble should not hide the truth.
2. The best explanation of the cases in premise 1 is that it's wrong to hide the hurtful truth from someone if they're competent to understand the truth and it concerns a project that's important to them.

So, . . .

3. Paradigm cases:

Grandparental Misdeeds: Seamus's grandfather stole a bike from Yi's grandmother. The bike was lost ages ago; Seamus has never seen it himself, and Yi was not disadvantaged by her grandmother's loss of the bike.

Bike Thief: Megan stole Javier's bike, which he had worked hard to buy. She sold the bike for a tidy sum.

1. Seamus is *not* morally obligated to pay reparations to Yi for his grandfather's misdeeds; Megan *is* morally obligated to pay reparations to Javier.
2. The best explanation of the cases in premise 1 is that person X owes person Y reparations only if X is the person who wronged Y.

So, . . .

4. Paradigm cases:

Classroom Abuse: college student A spends ten minutes before class openly berating classmate B, explaining why A thinks B is a terrible, horrible, no good, very bad person. As a result, B feels unwelcome in the classroom and leaves; the other students are upset by what they have seen, and struggle to pay attention in the class session.

Lunchroom Offense: during lunch at the college cafeteria, a few friends are discussing their views about religion. They agree that organized religions are harmful, and they offer to each other many examples from history and current events to support their view. Another student, who is devoutly religious, overhears their conversation and is offended. The offended student could easily move to another part of the lunchroom so they don't have to hear the other students' discussion, but they chose not to.

1. The college should prohibit student A's speech in Classroom Abuse, but it should not prohibit the friends' speech in Lunchroom Offense.
2. . . . .

So, schools should prohibit student speech if, but only if, doing so is necessary to promote equal opportunity for a safe learning environment.

5. Paradigm cases:

Unwanted Treatment: a hospitalized patient diagnosed with cancer decides to refuse chemotherapy. The patient has been given all the relevant information about the treatment options, and has come to a decision after careful reflection on their options. The doctor begins the chemotherapy against the patient's wishes because they think the patient has made the wrong decision.

Emergency C-section: a patient comes into the emergency room unconscious and seriously injured. The patient is 8 months pregnant, and doctors determine that an emergency C-section is in the best interests of both the patient and the baby. Since the patient is unconscious, and no family or friends can be found, the doctors perform an emergency C-section without the patient's consent.

1. . . . .
2. The best explanation of the cases in premise 1 is that a physician should always get informed consent for a treatment unless the patient is incapable of giving consent.

So, a physician should always get informed consent for a treatment unless the patient is incapable of giving their consent.

6. Paradigm cases:

Donor Match: Mr. Y, who has end-stage kidney failure, will die within 3 months unless he receives a donated kidney. Through a fortuitous turn of events, doctors discover that a healthy former patient, Mrs. X, is an ideal match for Mr. Y. Mrs. X and Mr. Y do not know each other, but doctors contact Mrs. X and ask if she would donate a kidney to Mr. Y. The surgery would have minimal long-term consequences for Mrs. X, since she's healthy and complications are very rare in cases like hers. Mrs. X wonders if she should agree to donate her kidney to Mr. Y.

Hypoglycemia Help: Yasmeen is hiking on a long wilderness trail and comes upon another hiker, Wesley, who is in serious trouble. Wesley is diabetic and accidentally injected too much insulin; he is beginning to feel the effects of dangerously low blood sugar. If he does not eat some carbohydrates soon, he could die. Wesley has no food, but Yasmeen has a pocket full of energy bars.

Yasmeen believes it is unlikely that anyone else will find Wesley before he dies, but she knows that the jurisdiction she lives in does not *legally* require her to help him.

Bibliophile Woes: Reggie explains to his friend that he is sad because he lost his only copy of his favorite book. Harper, who happens to own two copies of that very book, overhears this conversion. She likes having two copies so that she can have one at home and one at work. She wonders: should she give one copy to Reggie?

1. Mrs. X is *not* morally obligated to donate her kidney to Mr. Y and Harper is *not* morally obligated to give her book to Reggie, but Yasmeen *is* morally obligated to give an energy bar to Wesley.
2. . . . .

So, you are morally obligated to give to someone else only if doing so would prevent imminent injury or death and no one else could give to prevent those things.

Exercises 11B: Representing Arguments in Standard Form
Exercise Instructions: *represent each of the following arguments in standard form using both sub-arguments in the General Form of IBE.*

1. There are rare cases in which taking someone else's property without their permission can be morally justified by appealing to some other, weightier value. For example, when Jean Valjean steals a loaf of bread to feed his starving nieces and nephews in *Les Miserable*, he takes someone's property with good moral justification. We think he did the right thing in that case because it was the only way to save those children's lives. In almost every other case, though, it is wrong to take someone else's property without their permission. It is wrong to steal a phone from a store, and it is wrong to pick someone's tomatoes from their garden without asking first. It is wrong to take a bike from someone's yard, and wrong to steal beer from the back of a delivery truck. These examples suggest that stealing is rarely morally permissible, and then only when the stakes are very high. I would frame this thought as a general principle, with a built-in exception: taking someone else's property without their permission is wrong *unless it's necessary to avoid disaster.*

   Although intellectual property is a special kind of property, with a complicated relationship to the people who own it, it is undoubtedly a form of property. When people illegally download movies and music from the Internet, they are taking another person's property without their permission. And downloaders are not downloading movies and music in order to prevent disaster—they are doing it because they want to consume entertainment for free. This is the argument that has persuaded me that illegally downloading music and movies is *morally* wrong.

2. Aggression against the property or person of another is always wrong. This follows from practical commitments that all reasonable people share.

- If I want money, it is wrong for me to mug you. Why? Because mugging is a form of aggression.
- If I want my fields planted, it is wrong for me to enslave you and force you to do it. Why? Because slavery is a form of aggression.
- If I've had a bad day at work, and need to blow off some steam, it is wrong for me to smash the windows out of your car. Why? Because destroying your property is a form of aggression.
- If I don't like you, it is wrong for me to punch you in the nose. Why? Because punching you is a form of aggression.

Aggression is always wrong. But sometimes, the form aggression takes is subtle. Paying your taxes, for example, might not feel, in the moment, as if you are the victim of aggression. But you are. Imagine what would happen if you did not pay your taxes. Eventually, the government would show up with their guns and throw you in prison. That, obviously, is a form of aggression.

Since taxation is a form of aggression, and aggression is always wrong, taxation is always wrong.[5]

3. People have a *prima facie* right to own guns. We can see this by examining some cases everyone on the political spectrum could agree on.

Suppose you were attacked in a dark alley and had a choice: you could urinate on yourself, expecting that your attacker will be so disgusted he will leave you alone. Or you could fight back, punching him in the nose so that he runs away in pain. Surely you have a right to choose the latter, more dignified, option even if the pants-peeing option were equally effective. Or, suppose you are fleeing an attacker, fumbling to find the can of pepper spray you keep in your backpack. Just as you grab your pepper spray, you notice an open sewer grate. You could squirm inside and cower neck-deep in a pool of human waste; your pursuer would not find you. Or you could stand your ground and use the pepper spray to defend yourself. Surely you have a right to choose the pepper spray option.

These cases show us something important: people have a *prima facie* right to defend themselves in a dignified rather than undignified way. In some cases, guns will provide the only dignified means of self-defense. People therefore have the right to defend themselves with guns.[6]

4. There are many cases where it would be wrong for the government to prohibit people from engaging in hobbies and activities that have personal or cultural significance for them. It would be wrong, for instance, for the government to prohibit people from playing role-playing board games, going to black metal

---

[5]Adapted from an argument critiqued in the blog post "Six Reasons Libertarians Should Reject the Non-Aggression Principle," by Matt Zwolinski, Apr. 8, 2013. https://www.libertarianism.org/blog/six-reasons-libertarians-should-reject-non-aggression-principle Accessed Nov. 11, 2019.

[6]Adapted from an argument made by Dan Demetriou: https://honorethics.org/2015/04/30/defense-with-dignity-is-violent-resistance-more-dignified-and-if-so-what-follows-for-gun-rights/#more-671

concerts, or practicing sword-swallowing, even if most other people see no value in such things.

Still, there are cases where it *is* justifiable for the government to limit or regulate activities even if those activities have personal or cultural value. For instance, there is no problem with the government regulating the sale of dynamite, even though some people would enjoy detonating it for fun. There is no problem with the government prohibiting the marriage of young girls to older men. Regardless of the personal or cultural value some people might attach to these things, governments are justified in regulating or banning them.

Reflection on these cases reveals there are limits to people's rights to engage in practices with personal or cultural significance: governments are justified in regulating activities that risk significant harm to those who haven't consented to take part in them. This lesson has implications for gun-control laws. Governments are justified in regulating gun use and ownership, even for gun owners who attach significant personal or cultural value to their guns.

5. People sometimes disagree about what counts as the wrongful sexual use of another person. Like that news story about Mr. Bigshot, the CEO of his own private movie company who offered an actress a role in a movie in exchange for sexual favors. Some people seem to think this was no big deal, while others are out for his blood.

But this disagreement is hard to square when we reflect on other cases. Suppose a successful businessman, Danny, is attracted to an intern, Eva, at one of his companies. Dan has made a point of explaining to Eva how powerful he is and how well-respected he is, and he's always touting his influence at the company. Knowing she'll be hesitant to resist, Danny gropes Eva in the copy room one day, even though she clearly looks uncomfortable when he comes close. Feeling scared about the interaction but hesitant to resist for fear of reprisal, Eva lets the groping happen but leaves at the first opportunity. Danny, I think we can all agree, has wrongfully used Eva.

What makes Danny's conduct wrongful use of another is that he uses his position of power to get what he wants from someone with less power. This also explains other cases. Suppose Belinda, a teacher, seduces her high-school student into a sexual relationship, or that a police officer threatens to ignore criminal threats against someone unless they cough up money for a bribe. As in Danny's case, Belinda and the officer are wrongfully using others because they're using their power over others for their own benefit.

This provides clarity on cases like Mr. Bigshot's. If using your power over others to get what you want counts as wrongfully using them, then Mr. Bigshot is clearly wrongfully using the actress.[7]

6. Mr. Bigshot, the CEO of his own private movie company, was just revealed to have done something shocking: he offered an actress a role in one of his movies

---

[7]This passage and the next are adapted from cases discussed in Thomas Mappes, "Sexual Morality and the Concept of Using Another Person," in *The Philosophy of Sex,* ed. Raja Halwani et al., 7th ed. (London, England: Rowman & Littlefield, 2017), 273–292.

in exchange for sexual favors. Many have charged that he wrongfully used the actress for sex. This charge is unwarranted.

Consider some clear cases of wrongful sexual use. Sean knows Gertrude will not have sex with him unless they use birth control, so he lies to her and tells her that his doctor has certified he is sterile. Grant gets Shanice extremely drunk so that she can no longer resist his advances, as she always has before. Max threatens to accuse Lola of cheating on an exam unless she has sex with him.

Consider also a case where wrongful sexual use is clearly absent. Mark and Dominick are in a long-term, loving relationship. Sometimes, when Dominick is not in the mood, Mark persists in trying to persuade him by giving him a long back rub, which eventually leads to their both desiring and having sex.

These cases show that threats, force, or deception are necessary conditions of wrongful use. Sean, Grant, and Max are wrongfully sexually using others because they hope to obtain sex through force, threat, or deception. Mark is not sexually using Dominick because he's not using force, threat, or deception to win him over.

What of Mr. Bigshot? He offered an actress a role in exchange for sex. This is not an instance of force, threat, or deception. Since he did not meet the necessary conditions of wrongful sexual use, Mr. Bigshot did not wrongfully sexually use the actress.

7. A number of public libraries across the country have recently hosted a controversial event: drag queen story hour. Although organizers and participants emphasize the ways they could help combat invidious bias against LGBT people, some library patrons find these events morally problematic. Some have gone so far as to suggest that drag queen story hour should be banned on the grounds that these events use taxpayer money to promote morally questionable behavior to children.

But even those of us who agree with the moral criticisms of drag queen story hour should not seek to have them banned. Virtually no one would advocate that hunting clubs, horror movie clubs, or evangelical Christian churches should be prohibited from using public library space to host their meetings. Many people are morally opposed to hunting, horror movies, and evangelical churches, but nearly everyone believes these groups should be allowed to meet in the library.

Cases like these are what motivate many people to endorse a principle of viewpoint neutrality: it is unjust to limit an individual or group's access to public facilities on the basis of their worldview or values.

The principle of viewpoint neutrality entails that banning drag queen story hour would be unjust.[8]

8. In 1999, the Animal Liberation Front (ALF), a group of animal rights activists, carried out a massive direct action campaign against the University of Minnesota.

---

[8]Adapted from an argument in David French, "Viewpoint Neutrality Protects Both Drag Queens and Millions of American Christians," *National Review Online*, Sept. 9, 2019. https://www.nationalreview.com/corner/viewpoint-neutrality-protects-drag-queens-and-millions-american-christians (Accessed Nov. 11, 2019).

Activists broke into twelve labs, destroying and vandalizing equipment and freeing more than one hundred animals (including pigeons, mice, rats, and salamanders). The raids caused $1 million in damage and, according to officials at the University, have seriously impeded important medical research on conditions such as cancer and Parkinson's disease. After taking credit for the raid, the ALF announced that the animals had already been placed in homes.[9]

Despite their admirable concern for the welfare of animals, however, this raid violates basic standards of moral decency. Suppose someone who opposed the negative environmental impacts of cars went around destroying people's personal vehicles. Clearly that would be wrong. The same would be true of well-meaning activists who destroyed soda machines (in ways that scared children) to help prevent childhood obesity, or an opponent of a local tax referendum who used personal threats to silence opponents. These cases suggest it is morally wrong to use methods intended to spread fear as a means to achieving a controversial social or political objective.[10] It is therefore obvious that the ALF's Minneapolis raid was morally reprehensible.

9. If we look outside our own culture, it is easy to recognize instances in which removing statues and other honorific monuments was clearly the right thing to do. After World War II, it was appropriate for Germans to remove statues of Hitler. It would have been wrong to leave them up. Similarly with cities, parks, and schools named after Stalin. It would have been wrong for the Soviet government not to change the names of those places after the end of his reign. Similarly with statues of Saddam Hussein. After the fall of his regime, it was appropriate for Iraqis to remove his statues, and it would have been wrong to leave them up.

When we look at these uncontroversial historical examples, two points in particular are salient. First, these are all three men who carried out grave injustices. Second, leaving those statues and monuments in place would continue to confer honor and esteem on them. (That is, after all, why these monuments were established in the first place.) Once we've recognized these salient points, it is easier to explain exactly why these statues needed to come down: it is morally wrong to confer honor and esteem on people who have carried out grave injustices. That is why it would be morally wrong to maintain monuments that confer honor upon Hitler, Stalin, and Hussein.

Now, let us turn our attention closer to home, to the issue of monuments to Confederate generals and soldiers who fought against America during the US Civil War. There is no doubt that these men carried out grave injustices—they fought a war in defense of racial slavery. And there is no doubt that monuments

---

[9] For these and other details on the raid, see Martin Kettle, "Animal Activists Vandalise US Labs," *The Guardian*, Apr. 6, 1999. https://www.theguardian.com/world/1999/apr/07/martinkettle2 (Accessed 11 Nov 2019).

[10] This principle is adapted from one applied in a briefing for a US Senate hearing on "Eco-Terrorism Specifically Examining the Earth Liberation Front and the Animal Liberation Front," May 18, 2005. https://www.govinfo.gov/content/pkg/CHRG-109shrg32209/html/CHRG-109shrg32209.htm

to these men, like all monuments, confer honor and esteem upon them. We should apply to monuments of our own the same moral principle that we correctly apply to monuments to Hitler, Stalin, and Hussein. It is morally wrong to maintain statues of Confederate soldiers.[11]

10. Many more people need liver transplants than can get them—the supply of transplantable livers is far, far smaller than the demand for them. This makes the ordering of transplant wait-lists literally a matter of life and death; people at the top of the list are more likely to get a liver, and people at the bottom are more likely to die waiting for one.

Some have argued that the order of the list should take into account the kind of liver failure a patient is experiencing. The most common cause of liver failure is chronic alcohol abuse, but that is not the only cause. Some people who believe that alcoholics are responsible for bringing their liver failure on themselves believe that alcoholics should be de-prioritized on the transplant wait lists, and people whose livers are failing for reasons unrelated to alcohol should be moved ahead of them in line. I believe de-prioritizing recovering alcoholics for liver transplant is obviously morally wrong.

The wrongness becomes clear as soon as we start imagining other cases of doctors de-prioritizing patients for treatment based on the judgment that they are responsible for their own condition. Imagine a religious doctor who declines to treat an atheist patient, because he believes the sickness is a punishment for sin. Imagine a socially conservative doctor who refuses to treat a patient for an STD, based on the judgment that she brought it on herself with a promiscuous lifestyle. Imagine a team of doctors who wait to treat a person injured in a car crash until they can establish that they were not driving drunk.

As soon as we turn our attention to cases like these, it becomes obvious that it is always morally wrong for medical professionals to withhold care from patients based on their moral evaluation of those patients. Doctors should provide the best possible care to patients even if they believe those patients are sinners, or jerks, or dirtbags, or deadbeats. No doctor should ever ask, "is this person someone who morally deserves medical care?"

Too many doctors forget this general principle when faced with recovering alcoholic patients suffering from alcohol-related liver failure. The question should not be "does this patient morally deserve care?" because that is never the appropriate question. The question, as always, should be "what is the best possible course of treatment for this patient under the circumstances?" In some cases—as when a patient has been unable to stop drinking—a liver transplant is not the best course of action, because it has little chance of success. In other cases, when an alcoholic patient is in recovery and has demonstrated a commitment to sobriety, a liver transplant might be the best course of treatment. The fact that some doctors believe the patient brought their liver failure on themselves is irrelevant. It doesn't matter whether or not alcoholics are to

---

[11]Adapted from Burch-Brown, Joanna, "Is it wrong to topple statues and rename schools?" *Journal of Political Theory and Philosophy*, 1, no. 1 (2017): 59–88.

blame for "bringing it on themselves." To de-prioritize recovering alcoholics for transplant is morally wrong.

11. Imagine that there are two homeowners, and that each has his or her home destroyed. In one case, the homeowner sets his own house on fire and watches it burn down. In the other, the homeowner watches her house be destroyed by a tornado. If we only had enough relief to provide for one of the homeowners, whom should we choose? Intuitively, we would fund the second homeowner, since her house was destroyed through no fault of her own. This intuition might drive some more general moral principle which says that we must hold individuals accountable for what they do and prioritize those who are blameless over those who are blameworthy. If we accept this principle—and I expect most all of us would—then we might have a reason to deprioritize alcoholics [who are waiting for liver transplants] on the grounds that they are to blame for their condition.[12]

12. Many cases can be marshaled in support of the ethical principle that scarce health care resources should be allocated in such a way that they do the most good. Consider just these few:

- Two people have dangerous bacterial infections, but the hospital has only a single course of a single antibiotic: penicillin. Patient A is not allergic to penicillin, and patient B is.
- Two patients face imminent death from blood loss. There is only enough whole blood available to treat one of them. Patient A will likely recover fully after the transfusion. Patient B will almost certainly die within hours from multiple organ damage, whether or not he gets the transfusion.
- An EMT is called to the site of an accident. There are two casualties, both gravely injured: patient A is a 19-year-old woman and patient B is a 97-year-old woman. The EMT must pick one to treat first and the other is likely to die.

In all these cases, it is Patient A who should receive the treatment. Why? It isn't because Patient A is the first in line, or has the best insurance, or is the youngest, or is the sickest. In all these cases, Patient A should receive the treatment *because* scarce resources should be allocated in such a way that they do the most good.

Donated livers are every bit as scarce as the resources in the fanciful examples. Livers, then, should be allocated in such a way that they do the most good. Recovering alcoholics, obviously, are at greater risk than non-alcoholics of relapsing into alcoholism. They are thus at greater risk of destroying scarce livers. Transplanting those livers to non-alcoholics would thus do more good. That's why non-alcoholics should be moved ahead of recovering alcoholics on wait-lists for liver transplants.[13]

---

[12]Quoted from Fritz Allhoff, "Should Alcoholics Be Deprioritized for Liver Transplantation?" *Virtual Mentor*, 7, no. 9 (2005). Available online: http://journalofethics.ama-assn.org/2005/09/oped1-0509.html

[13]Adapted from A. H. Moss and M. Siegler, "Should Alcoholics Compete Equally for Liver Transplantation?" *Journal of the American Medical Association*, 265, no. 10 (1991): 1295–1298.

CHAPTER 12

Evaluating Inferences to the Best Explanation

CHAPTER GOALS

By reading this chapter and completing the exercises, you will learn how to:

- Evaluate a moral Inference to the Best Explanation.
- Raise objections to premise 1 of a Principle Justification sub-argument by challenging paradigm cases.
- Raise objections to premise 2 of a Principle Justification sub-argument by identifying and testing opposing explanations.

EVALUATING INFERENCE TO THE BEST EXPLANATION

The previous chapter demonstrated how to understand the structure of moral Inference to the Best Explanation (IBE) arguments by representing them in standard form. IBE arguments include two sub-arguments. The first sub-argument *justifies* a principle by suggesting it as the best explanation of a group of paradigm cases; the second sub-argument *applies* that principle to the controversial case at issue.

This chapter demonstrates strategies for evaluating IBE arguments, focusing especially on the technique of identifying alternative explanations.

WAYS IBE ARGUMENTS CAN GO WRONG

Recall the General Form of IBE:

Principle Justification Sub-argument:

1. Cases *v, w,* etc. have moral status *S* [and cases *y, z,* etc. have moral status *T*]. (PARADIGM CASES)
2. The best explanation of the cases in premise 1 is that cases of type *A* have moral status *S*. (EXPLANATION)

So, probably, cases of type *A* have moral status *S*. (PRINCIPLE)

Principle Application Sub-argument:

1. Cases of type *A* probably have moral status *S*. (PRINCIPLE)
2. Case *x* is of type *A*. (CASE)

Therefore, probably, case *x* has moral status *S*. (CONCLUSION)

An IBE's premises do not *guarantee* the truth of its conclusion. Even if we've made the correct judgments about the paradigm cases and the principle we've identified explains those judgments better than the alternatives, it is still *possible* that the principle is false or flawed. What an IBE gives us is good evidence that its conclusion is *probably* true.

In practice, evaluating an IBE involves the same general process as every other form of argument. We ask, of each premise: is this premise true? An IBE that includes an implausible or false premise gives little or no evidence that its conclusion is probably true.

The Principle Application portion of an IBE has the General Form of Argument from Principle and should be evaluated using the same critical techniques you practiced in Chapter 6.

This chapter focuses on evaluating the Principle Justification portion of an IBE. Because it has two premises, there are two main ways a Principle Justification sub-argument can go wrong.

Failure 1: Poor selection of paradigm cases

Authors of Inferences to the Best Explanation begin by selecting a group of paradigm cases. To work effectively, this group of cases must elicit similar moral judgments from nearly everyone who reads them. A Principle Justification sub-argument is weak if the author asserts judgments about the paradigm cases that are (or should be) controversial.

For example, consider the following weak argument that seeks to justify a principle relevant to the debate about the morality of physician-assisted suicide.

Paradigm cases:

Willing Slave: in order to pay off family debts, a competent adult offers to sell himself to Walter as a slave. The would-be slave agrees to give up all rights to control over his life and body. Walter buys him.

Dinner's On: a competent adult volunteers to be killed and eaten by Armin, who has expressed an interest in experimenting with cannibalism. Armin kills and eats the volunteer.

Skydiver: a competent adult chooses to go skydiving, knowing that parachutes sometimes fail and, when they do, skydivers die. She hires Amelia, a skydiving expert, to teach her this potentially deadly hobby. Amelia takes her on as a student.

Principle Justification Sub-argument:

1. Walter's, Armin's, and Amelia's actions are all morally permissible. (PARA-DIGM CASES)
2. The best explanation of the cases in premise 1 is that harming or killing a person is morally permissible in cases in which they have competently asked for it. (EXPLANATION)

Therefore, harming or killing a person is probably morally permissible in cases in which they have competently asked for it. (PRINCIPLE)

Principle Application Sub-argument:

1. Harming or killing a person is probably morally permissible in cases in which they have competently asked for it. (PRINCIPLE)
2. Physician-assisted suicide is a case of killing a person after they have competently asked for it. (CASE)

Therefore, physician-assisted suicide is probably morally permissible. (CONCLUSION)

This argument has several problems, but the problem with premise 1 of the Principle Justification sub-argument is glaring: the claim that Walter and Armin have done nothing wrong is, at best, highly controversial. Many readers are likely to accept the common view that rights to life and liberty are *inalienable*—they cannot be given away, even by a competent and informed adult. If life and liberty are inalienable rights, then Walter and Armin act immorally, regardless of their victims' requests. Since two of the three judgments asserted in premise 1 are controversial or implausible, this premise is weak. The author has done a poor job of assembling paradigm cases.

Failure 2: The proposed principle does not best explain the paradigm cases

The second premise of a Principle Justification sub-argument is weak if the author's proposed explanation is *not* the best explanation of the paradigm cases. Later in this chapter, we'll discuss several of the many subtle factors that can make one explanation better or worse than another. For this introductory section, let us focus on an unambiguous form of this failure: a principle that purports to explain a set of paradigm cases cannot be the *best* explanation of those cases if an opposing principle *obviously* explains those same cases at least as well. For example, consider the following revision of the requested-harm argument. Here, the author has jettisoned the controversial cases, and replaced them with much better paradigm cases.

Paradigm cases:

Voluntary Chemotherapy: a competent patient with advanced cancer requests chemotherapy from Dr. Grey. The patient understands that all treatment plans, including chemotherapy, are unlikely to work, and that the side-effects of chemotherapy are likely to be painful and exhausting. Dr. Grey administers chemotherapy.

War Correspondent: a student graduating from journalism school would like to apply for a job as a war correspondent, fully understanding that many war correspondents have died on the job. She asks Professor Higgins for a letter of recommendation, which Prof. Higgins writes.

Skydiver: a competent adult chooses to go skydiving, knowing that parachutes sometimes fail, and when they do skydivers die. She hires Amelia, a skydiving expert, to teach her this potentially deadly hobby. Amelia takes her on as a student.

Principle Justification Sub-argument:

1. Dr. Grey's, Prof. Higgins's, and Amelia's actions are morally permissible. (PARADIGM CASES)
2. The best explanation of the cases in premise 1 is that harming or killing a person is morally permissible in cases in which they have competently asked for it. (EXPLANATION)

Therefore, harming or killing a person is probably morally permissible in cases in which they have competently asked for it. (PRINCIPLE)

(The Principle Application sub-argument remains unchanged.)

Premise 1 of this revised argument is plausible, but premise 2 now has a problem. Although premise 2 suggests an explanation of the cases, it is unlikely that it is the *best* explanation of them.

The paradigm cases all involve one person helping another person pursue a risky goal. The author's proposed principle, which focuses on harming and killing people, has little or nothing to do with these cases. It is thus easy to brainstorm alternatives that do a better job of explaining them. For example: helping a person pursue a goal that includes some risk of unwanted death or harm is morally permissible, provided that they have competently evaluated the risks and voluntarily asked for help. This alternative better explains our judgments about the paradigm cases, and it doesn't support the author's conclusion about assisted suicide.

In more thoughtfully crafted IBEs, authors will have taken care to develop a principle that plausibly explains the paradigm cases, so raising an objection to the second premise of a Principle Justification sub-argument is typically a more challenging task. The remainder of this chapter explains in more detail how to critically engage a Principle Justification sub-argument by identifying and evaluating alternative explanations.

MINIMUM CRITERIA OF A CRITICAL ALTERNATIVE EXPLANATION

Don Marquis's anti-abortion argument, introduced in the previous chapter, is a moral IBE. He begins by justifying a principle about the wrongness of killing:

1. It's wrong to kill adults (whether asleep or awake), human infants, hermits, E.T.s, and depressed teenagers. (PARADIGM CASES)

2. The best explanation of the cases in premise 1 is that killing is *pro tanto* wrong if it deprives a being of a future of value. (EXPLANATION)

So, probably, killing is *pro tanto* wrong if it deprives a being of a future of value. (PRINCIPLE)

He then applies this principle to the case of abortion:

1. Killing is *pro tanto* wrong if it deprives a being of a future of value. (PRINCIPLE)
2. Except in rare cases, abortion deprives a fetus of a future of value. (CASE)

Therefore, probably, except in rare cases abortion is *pro tanto* wrong. (CONCLUSION)

Is the Future of Value Principle the *best* explanation of the paradigm cases Marquis has assembled? This chapter introduces several alternative explanations and demonstrates techniques that can help determine whether Marquis, or one of his critics, best explains paradigm cases of wrongful killing.

To even count as a criticism of Marquis's argument, an alternative explanation must meet two minimum criteria. First, the critic's alternative explanation must yield an opposing principle. Second, the critic's alternative explanation must be consistent with Marquis's set of paradigm cases.

Minimum criterion: The alternative explanation must yield an opposing principle

To show that Marquis's principle does not provide the best explanation of the paradigm cases, a critic may try to offer an alternative explanation that is at least as good. At a minimum, this alternative explanation must yield an *opposing* principle; that is, it must yield a principle that, when applied to the controversial target case, does not imply an identical conclusion. To count as an opposing principle, an alternative principle need not imply the polar opposite conclusion. An opposing principle might imply the opposite conclusion, or it might imply a *different* conclusion, or it might remain silent on the controversial issue at hand. But an alternative explanation does not constitute a criticism of an argument if it leaves the argument's conclusion untouched.

For example, in other debates about cases of wrongful killing, some authors have focused on humans' apparently distinctive capacity for making decisions based on moral considerations. This is typically offered as a necessary and sufficient condition of the wrongness of killing.

The Moral Capacities Principle: Killing a creature is wrong if and only if that creature will at some point have the capacity for moral decision making.

This alternative explanation does explain our judgments in all of Marquis's paradigm cases, since in every case those creatures either currently have, or eventually will have, the capacity for moral decision making.

But this alternative explanation does not yield an *opposing* principle, and so does not constitute a criticism of Marquis's argument. If we were to adopt the

Moral Capacities Principle, we would complete the argument with the following Principle Application sub-argument:

1. Killing a creature is probably wrong if and only if that creature will at some point have the capacity for moral decision making. (PRINCIPLE)
2. Most abortions kill a creature that will at some point have the capacity for moral decision making. (CASE)

Therefore, most abortions are probably wrong. (CONCLUSION)

Even if the Moral Capacities Principle were the better explanation of Marquis's paradigm cases, the conclusion of the argument would remain unchanged. To function as a *criticism* of Marquis's argument, an alternative explanation must yield an *opposing* principle—a principle that does *not* imply that most abortions are probably wrong.

Minimum criterion: The alternative explanation must give guidance consistent with paradigm cases

In addition to yielding an opposing principle, an alternative explanation offered as a criticism of an IBE must meet a second minimum condition: the alternative explanation must imply guidance consistent with our judgments about the paradigm cases. Any decent IBE will offer a principle that does not contradict our judgments about those cases—it will allow that the clearly right cases are right, the clearly wrong cases are wrong, and so on. Marquis's principle about killing is consistent with our judgments about his paradigm cases. So, an alternative principle will only be at least as good as his if it is also consistent with those judgments.

For example, Marquis expects some critics who hope to defend a pro-choice conclusion will be inclined to suggest a different explanation of the wrongness of killing.

The Desire Principle: killing a being is only wrong if that being desires to continue living.[1]

Since early term fetuses have no desires, and thus no desire to continue living, this principle implies that killing them is not wrong. But this explanation is not a serious contender for an explanation that is better than Marquis's Future of Value Principle, because the Desire Principle gets some of the paradigm cases completely wrong. It is obviously wrong to kill sleeping people, even though they have no desires while asleep. It is obviously wrong to kill suicidal depressed teenagers, even though they do not want to live. Since the Desire Principle implies guidance that is inconsistent with our judgments about these paradigm cases, it is not a viable candidate for a better explanation of those cases.

There are other candidate explanations that do clear this minimum threshold. Consider two opposing principles that do imply guidance consistent with our judgments about Marquis's collection of paradigm cases.

---

[1]See Don Marquis, "Why Abortion Is Immoral," *The Journal of Philosophy* 86, no. 4 (1989): 195–197.

Nearly everyone has projects, plans, and relationships that have been developing continuously throughout their lives. Killing a person imposes an abrupt end to all of the elements that make up their story. That we lament as tragic the abrupt discontinuation of a victim's story suggests an alternative explanation of the wrongness of killing.

> The Discontinuity Principle: killing a creature is wrong if it discontinues the projects, plans, and relationships of the creature who is killed.

This alternative explanation yields an opposing principle. Since fetuses do not yet have projects, plans, or relationships, this principle does not entail that killing them is wrong. It also explains all of Marquis's paradigm cases, including those that revealed a problem with the Desire Principle. Sleeping people and depressed teenagers do not currently *desire* to live, but they do have projects, plans, and relationships that their deaths would discontinue. Just like Marquis's principle, the Discontinuity Principle gives guidance that is consistent with our judgments about those cases.

Another alternative explanation comes from David Boonin, who offers an upgraded version of the Desire Principle:

> The Dispositional Idealized Desire Principle: if a being has a future of value and has a dispositional, idealized desire to preserve that future, then killing that being is wrong.[2]

This principle uses some terms of art. A *dispositional desire* is a tendency to desire things under certain conditions. This is different from an *occurrent desire*, which is the active desiring of something at a particular time. For example, you probably hope that your friends speak well of you, even when you are not with them. Most of the time, you are not actively thinking about what your distant friends are talking about, and so have no occurrent desires about their distant conversations. But even when you are thinking about something else entirely, you still have the *dispositional* desire that your friends speak well of you. If a friend reports that you were, earlier, a topic of conversation, then you will experience an *occurrent* desire that their comments were positive.

Boonin also distinguishes *actual desires* from *idealized desires*. Idealized desires are the things a person *would* desire if they were fully informed and able to reason well about their choices. For example, imagine a vegetarian at a restaurant searching the menu for vegetarian options. Of the options that do not mention meat, they find the chopped salad most appealing. They thus have an *actual* desire to order the chopped salad. Unbeknownst to them, the chopped salad includes chicken, and the only vegetarian item on the menu is the baked potato. If they were fully informed about the dishes' ingredients, they would want the baked potato, not the chopped salad. They thus have an *idealized* desire to order the baked potato, despite their *actual* desire to order the chopped salad.

---

[2]Paraphrased from David Boonin, *A Defense of Abortion* (Cambridge, UK: Cambridge University Press, 2003), 62–85. We have restated Boonin's principle more simply for pedagogical purposes.

Boonin's alternative explanation yields an opposing principle. Since fetuses do not have any desires that we could idealize, this principle does not entail that killing them is wrong. The principle thus does not generate the same conclusion about abortion as Marquis's Future of Value principle does.

The Dispositional Idealized Desire Principle also explains Marquis's original set of paradigm cases, including the cases that caused problems for the simpler version of the Desire Principle. A sleeping person has no occurrent desire to continue to live, but they do have a *dispositional* desire to live: if you woke them up and asked them if they wanted to continue living, they would say "yes!" A depressed teenager may have an actual desire to die, but if they were better able to understand the transient nature of their depression and the range of available options for coping, they *would* want to live. The depressed teenager has an *idealized* desire to live. Boonin's principle thus gives guidance consistent with our judgments about all the paradigm cases, just as Marquis's does.

We have two principles that meet the minimum criteria of critical alternative explanations: Discontinuity and Dispositional Idealized Desire. We now turn to evaluating these explanations, to determine if either of them is at least as good as Marquis's Future of Value principle.

EVALUATING ALTERNATIVE EXPLANATIONS BY ADDING A DECISIVE PARADIGM CASE

When more than one explanation is consistent with the original set of paradigm cases, one standard technique is to expand the pool of paradigm cases with at least one additional case that highlights differences between the candidate explanations. In some cases, it is possible to locate an additional paradigm case that decisively reveals a problem with one or more of the candidate explanations. A decisive paradigm case is, in effect, an additional case that functions as a counterexample to some candidate explanations but not to others.

Marquis uses this method to argue that the Future of Value Principle is better than the Discontinuity Principle. Consider the following additional paradigm case, adapted from Marquis's discussion:[3]

> *Mercy killing*: a soldier on a battlefield suffers a terrible wound that will un-questionably kill them in a matter of hours. It is immediately clear to the soldier and their friend that treatment is impossible. The soldier begs their friend to kill them quickly and painlessly with an overdose of morphine from the medical kit; otherwise they will suffer unbearable agony for hours before dying.

If killing in *Mercy killing* is not morally wrong, then we have a new paradigm case that highlights a difference between the Future of Value Principle and the Discontinuity Principle. Since the mortally wounded soldier does *not* have a

---

[3]We have developed this case from Marquis's suggestion that it is not wrong to "kill a patient who begs for death and who is in severe pain that cannot be relieved short of killing." See Don Marquis, "Why Abortion Is Immoral," *Journal of Philosophy*, 86, no. 4 (1989): 195–197.

future of value, the Future of Value Principle does *not* imply that killing them is wrong. However, since the killing in *Mercy killing* discontinues the soldier's projects, experiences, and relationships, the Discontinuity Principle implies this killing *is* morally wrong.

The Future of Value Principle is consistent with our judgments about the newly expanded set of paradigm cases; the Discontinuity Principle is not consistent with our judgment that killing is permissible in *Mercy killing*. This is good evidence that Future of Value is a better explanation than Discontinuity.

Note that Boonin's Dispositional Idealized Desire principle handles *Mercy killing* just as well as Future of Value does. The soldier does not have a future to value, and full information about their situation would not change their desire to escape a few hours of pointless agony. Since the soldier does not have a dispositional, idealized desire to experience the value of their own future, the Dispositional Idealized Desire Principle does not imply that killing them is wrong. *Mercy killing* highlights a serious problem with the Discontinuity Principle, but it does not illuminate any difference between Boonin's and Marquis's proposed principles.

EVALUATING THE EXPLANATORY VIRTUES OF ALTERNATIVE EXPLANATIONS

Two competing explanations remain: Marquis's Future of Value Principle, and Boonin's Dispositional Idealized Desire Principle. It may not be possible to identify an additional paradigm case that will decisively settle which of these explanations is better. Nevertheless, there may be good reasons to prefer one of these principles, if one of the principles displays more explanatory virtues than the other.

Explanatory virtues are qualitative features common to good explanations in a wide variety of domains. While a full discussion of explanatory virtues is a book-length project of its own, we can highlight several examples of explanatory virtues that are often relevant to discussions evaluating moral IBEs.

Explanatory virtue: Simplicity

Explanations that account for the paradigm cases without unnecessary complexity are usually better than explanations that rely on that complexity.

Boonin's explanation requires two additional concepts—dispositional desires and idealized desires—that complicate his explanation. On the other hand, Boonin believes that his explanation is simpler because it need only appeal to present desires, while Marquis's explanation (Boonin argues) implicitly depends on concepts of present *and future* desires. If we were confident that one explanation is simpler than the other, we would have some reason to prefer the simpler explanation.

Explanatory virtue: Salience

Explanations that focus on the features that most directly contribute to the paradigm cases having the moral status they do are usually better than explanations that focus on their peripheral features.

The Future of Value principle explains the wrongness of killing in terms of the loss it imposes on the victim. The Dispositional Idealized Desire principle explains the wrongness of killing in terms of the violation of the victim's (idealized) desire to live. Both of these principles have a plausible initial claim to salience. (They do not, for example, explain the wrongness of killing by appealing to peripheral considerations such as the loss of the victim's future tax revenue, or the environmental damage their funeral will cause.) Both Boonin and Marquis have at points argued that their explanation is superior on grounds of salience. If we were confident that one of the explanations captures more plausibly the wrong-making features of the paradigm cases, that would give us some reason to prefer that explanation.

Explanatory virtue: Comprehensiveness

Explanations that imply our judgments about a larger set of paradigm cases are usually better than explanations that imply our judgments only about a smaller set.

Boonin believes that Dispositional Idealized Desire is a more comprehensive principle than Future of Value. He offers an additional (non-decisive) paradigm case in support of this belief:

> _Franz_: Franz is so depressed that he is completely unable to value his future. Indeed, he has a permanent chemical imbalance that will leave him forever unable to value the projects, experiences, and activities that make up his life.[4]

It would be wrong to kill Franz. Both of our competing explanations are _consistent_ with this judgment. However, the two competing principles say different things about Franz's case.

Although Franz may never have an actual desire to live, he does have an idealized desire to live, because that is what he _would_ want if his chemical imbalance were removed. The Dispositional Idealized Desire principle thus implies that killing Franz is morally wrong.

On the other hand, since Franz will _never_ value any aspect of his own future, the Future of Value principle _doesn't_ imply that killing him is wrong. Nor does it imply that killing him is permissible. The Future of Value principle is silent about Franz's case.

Boonin argues that Dispositional Idealized Desire displays the virtue of comprehensiveness because it implies our judgments about all of Marquis's paradigm cases, _plus_ the additional case of Franz, while Future of Value remains silent about Franz. If Boonin is right that Dispositional Idealized Desire is more comprehensive than Future of Value, then we have some reason to prefer Boonin's alternative principle.

---

[4]Paraphrased from David Boonin, _A Defense of Abortion_ (Cambridge, UK: Cambridge University Press, 2003), 76.

THE DISCUSSION CONTINUES

Suppose you have written an Inference to the Best Explanation, and a critic responds with an alternative opposing principle. This is not necessarily the end of the discussion. It could be that they have put their finger on a serious flaw in your thinking. But there are at least two other possibilities that would require the discussion to continue.

First, it could be that their alternative explanation does not, in fact, better explain the paradigm cases. Perhaps their judgment about a newly-offered paradigm case is contentious. Or perhaps they have misjudged the guidance their principle gives. Marquis, for example, argues that Boonin's Dispositional Idealized Desire principle, just like the Future of Value Principle, is silent about Franz's case, because Franz probably does *not* have an idealized desire to continue living with his permanent chemical imbalance.[5] To determine if Marquis is right, the discussion should continue.

Second, there may be other paradigm cases not yet discussed that would more clearly favor one of the candidate explanations. Can we give decisive evidence for preferring one explanation by identifying additional cases of clearly wrongful or permissible killing that one of the principles can explain but the other cannot? Is there another case that could give us suggestive evidence that one of the principles is better because it is simpler, more salient, or more comprehensive? The discussion should continue.

REVIEW

A moral IBE contains two sub-arguments: one justifies a principle by showing it best explains paradigm cases, and another applies that principle to a controversial target case.

A Principle Justification sub-argument has two premises: premise 1 asserts judgments about paradigm cases, and premise 2 offers a principle that is supposed to give the best explanation of those cases.

> **Best explanation:** an explanation is the best when it gives guidance that is consistent with our judgments about all the paradigm cases, and other principles are either inconsistent with those judgments or comparatively lack the virtues of good explanations (such as simplicity, comprehensiveness, salience, etc.).

To evaluate a Principle Justification sub-argument, we must evaluate both premises.

Raising an objection to premise 1 requires showing that the judgments it asserts about the paradigm cases are not as clear and uncontroversial as the author believes them to be.

Raising an objection to premise 2 requires that we show the author's proposed principle is *not* the best explanation of the paradigm cases. Objections to

---

[5]Don Marquis, "Abortion Revisited," in *The Oxford Handbook of Bioethics* (Oxford, UK: Oxford University Press, 2007), 412.

premise 2 typically take the form of an alternative opposing principle. If we are able to identify an opposing principle that explains the paradigm cases as well as the author's proposed principle, we call into question whether the author's proposed principle is indeed the *best* explanation of those cases.

> **Opposing principle:** a moral principle that does not imply the same conclusion about the controversial target case as the author's proposed principle.

When two competing principles are both consistent with our judgment about a set of paradigm cases, two techniques can help determine which explanation is better.

If possible, identify an additional paradigm case that functions as a counterexample to one principle, but not to the other. This technique can decisively settle the dispute between competing principles.

In cases in which you are unable to identify an additional, decisive paradigm case, evaluate the competing principles by determining which of them displays explanatory virtues to a greater degree.

> **Explanatory virtues:** qualitative features, such as simplicity, comprehensiveness, and salience, that are broadly shared features of good explanations in a variety of domains.

To test your understanding of the material introduced in this chapter, complete the Demonstration Exercises and then check your answers against the solutions that follow.

Demonstration Exercises

Demonstration Exercises are designed to give you immediate feedback on your grasp of the skills introduced in this chapter. To use them effectively, you should attempt answers to all of them, then check your work against our suggested answers, which follow. For a detailed explanation of how best to use Demonstration Exercises, read the book's Introduction.

Demonstration Exercises 12A: Brainstorming Alternative Explanations

Exercise Instructions: the following exercises offer a set of judgments about paradigm cases and supply a moral principle intended to explain those judgments. For each, suggest an alternative principle that explains the judgments as well or better than the supplied principle.

1. **Judgments**: All adult humans and human infants matter for their own sake, and not merely for the benefits they bring to other people.

   Principle: Only beings with human DNA matter for their own sake.

2. **Judgments**:
   - We shouldn't allow children under 18 to do recreational drugs.
   - We shouldn't allow children under 18 to participate in humiliating or dangerous hazing rituals in order to become part of a sports team.

Principle: We shouldn't allow children under 18 to engage in any activity that could harm them.

3. Judgments:

- Suppose you know that your family is planning a surprise party, tomorrow, for your uncle. Your uncle asks you what you're doing tomorrow, and you tell him that you're going out with friends. This is a lie, but it is a morally permissible lie.

- Suppose you and your partner have been trying and failing to get pregnant. On a visit to your doctor you learn that you are infertile, and will never be biologically able to produce a child. When you come home, your partner asks you what the doctor said. You know your partner would feel sad for a while if they knew the truth, but you also suspect that if you could talk about adoption, your partner would warm to the idea. In the end, you worry so much about their temporary sadness that you decide to lie: "the doctor says there are no problems at all." It is morally wrong to tell this lie.

Principle: It's permissible to lie to a close friend or family member if doing so would make them happier over the long-term.

Demonstration Exercises 12B: Evaluating Explanations in IBE

Exercise Instructions: for each of the following arguments, do the following things.

- *First, represent the argument in standard form using the General Form of IBE.*
- *Second, evaluate premise 2 of the Principle Justification Sub-argument by suggesting an opposing alternative principle that explains the paradigm cases.*

1. Illegal downloading

Sometimes people illegally download movies and music. This practice, while illegal, is not morally wrong. To see why, consider a few clear-cut cases:

- It is *not* wrong to repeat for a friend a joke that you heard at a stand-up show.
- It *is* wrong to steal a stand-up comedian's laptop.
- It is *not* wrong to recreate at home your favorite dish from a local restaurant.
- It *is* wrong to take the silverware from that same restaurant.

    These cases establish that the story cannot be so simple as "taking something without permission is always morally wrong." It is not wrong to "take" a comedian's joke or recreate a favorite recipe because those activities do not actually deprive the comedian or the chef of anything—even after you retell the joke, the comedian has no more and no less than what they had before you retold it. The best explanation of these cases is thus a more nuanced principle: taking the fruits of others' labor without their permission is wrong if and *only* if it *deprives* them of something they already have. Downloading music and movies

(continued)

doesn't deprive anyone of anything they already have. It may be illegal, but it isn't morally wrong.

2. Parental licenses[6]

We appropriately require people to be licensed to do things like drive cars or fly planes or to be doctors, lawyers, or teachers. But it would be wrong to require people to be licensed to play golf with their friends, or to cook food in their own houses. Why? Why should we require licenses for the first set of activities, but not for the second?

The best explanation is that we should require a license for people to perform activities that are potentially seriously harmful to others when they are performed by unskilled people. If I am an unskilled golfer, I pose no threat to other people. If I am an unskilled pilot, I shouldn't be allowed anywhere near the cockpit, because I could seriously harm the passengers on the plane.

What people don't notice is what this principle implies about parenting. Parents who lack certain specific skills (such as emotional regulation, effective and kind discipline, etc.) can do serious harm to kids. Some parents have seriously injured or even killed their own children because they are unable to control their own anger. Some parents have seriously malnourished their own babies, because they did not know the basics of nutrition and feeding.

Parents who have not developed basic parenting skills can seriously harm vulnerable others. Parenting is exactly the kind of activity for which we should require a license.

3. Racist patients

American hospitals today often advertise how hard they work to ac- commodate patients' preferences. But some preferences raise difficult moral questions. For example, suppose a White patient requests to be treated exclusively by White doctors and nurses. If it is possible for the hospital to accommodate this racist preference, *should* it?

Surprisingly, even if we're committed to racial equality, the best answer to this question is "yes." Consider some of the many cases in which we clearly should accommodate patient preferences when possible:

- A female patient at an obstetrics and gynecology clinic requests only female doctors and nurses because she is uncomfortable around male doctors.

- A Hmong patient requests a family care physician who is Hmong, be- cause it would make it easier to explain how their medical choices are informed by their cultural and spiritual views.

- A male client at a counseling center requests a male psychologist. The client doesn't explain why they want a male psychologist, but they appear to be uncomfortable with the idea of a female provider.

American hospitals should accommodate preferences like these when they can. Why? Here's one plausible answer: whenever it is possible to accommodate patient preferences in a way that would increase a pa- tient's receptiveness to the quality health care provided, we should do

---

[6]Adapted from Hugh LaFollette, "Licensing Parents," *Philosophy and Public Affairs* 9, no. 2 (1980): 182–197.

so. This principle implies that we should also accommodate patients' preferences for the race of their health care providers, even if those preferences are racist.

Demonstration Exercises 12C: Complete Argument Evaluation

Exercise Instructions: for the following passage:

- *First, represent the argument in standard form using the General Form of IBE.*
- *Second, offer what you believe to be the best objection to the argument. This objection could be to any premise of the Principle Justification or Principle Application portion of the argument. Clearly identify which premise you are engaging: "Premise 1 of the Principle Justification Sub-argument is false because ..." or "Premise 2 of the Principle Application Sub-argument is false because ..."*
- *Third, briefly explain how you believe the discussion should continue. What do you think is the author's best reply to the objection you have just raised?*

1. Gamete donor privacy

In many jurisdictions, fertility service providers pay people to donate their gametes. Paying people to undergo the potentially embarrassing or invasive process of sperm or egg donation undoubtedly helps provide a stable supply of sperm and eggs that can be used to help people have children when they would otherwise be unable to do so. But paying for gametes raises several tough questions. One, in particular, has remained controversial for decades: should children who are born from donated gametes have a legal right to know the identity of the donor(s)? Or should donors be allowed to keep their identities private?

There are many cases in which people should not have a legal right to others' personal information even if they might be interested in having it. A public school student may *want* to know their teacher's religious affiliation but they should not have a legal right to compel the teacher to tell them. A couple interested in adopting a child should not have a right to know the identity of the child's biological parents, even if they'd like to know it.

On the other hand, there are cases when a person clearly should have a legal right to certain personal information from others. An owner of a daycare facility should have the right to know if a job applicant has a legal record of violent behavior. A patient should have a legal right to know if their doctor has been convicted of malpractice by the state medical board. A blood donation facility should have the legal right to verify that a would-be donor does not have blood-borne pathogens.

What explains these cases? A plausible answer is that a person has a right to another's personal information when that information is essential for protecting the well-being of the information-seeker or those they are responsible for.

This principle suggests that people have no right to know the identity of donors whose gametes created them, because there is no sense in which

(continued)

that information is essential for a person's well-being. A person may *want* to know, but it is no more essential to their living a good life than is the student who wants to know their teacher's religious affiliation. Children born from sperm or egg donations thus have no right to know whose donations brought them into this world.

2. **Pandemic mask mandate**[7]

During the COVID-19 pandemic, many countries, states, and communities debated whether to require people to wear cloth face masks in public. In some localities, small groups vocally objected to this idea, claiming that such a requirement would violate their right to liberty.

This is an obviously false claim. While it is true that defending individual liberty is important, there are a number of cases where it is clearly and uncontroversially justifiable for the government to limit it. Now that the harms of second-hand smoke are clear, there is broad support for banning smoking in public places such as restaurants, malls, airplanes, and hospitals. It may be your prerogative to drink till you destroy your liver, but it is clearly within the government's rights to prohibit you from driving while intoxicated. The explanation for these cases is simple: the government has a right to restrict your individual liberty if doing so is necessary to minimize or prevent serious harm to others. Since there is clear evidence that wearing cloth masks in public would significantly reduce the transmission of coronavirus and thus prevent needless deaths, mandating masks does not violate anyone's rights.

---

[7]Adapted from ideas in Jeff Grabmeier, "Why Governments Have the Right to Require Masks in Public," *Medical Xpress*, July 16, 2020. https://medicalxpress.com/news/2020-07-require-masks.html

---

Solutions to Demonstration Exercises

Demonstration Exercises are most useful if you make your best attempt to complete them before you look at the answers. If you haven't yet attempted answers to all the Demonstration Exercises, go back and do that now.

Solutions to Demonstration Exercises 12A: Brainstorming Alternative Explanations

1. **Alternative explanation**: a being matters for its own sake if it is capable of feeling pleasure or pain.

2. **Alternative explanation**: we shouldn't allow minors to engage in an activity if it would be likely to have significant, long-term negative effects on their health or development.

3. **Alternative principle**: It's permissible to lie to a close friend or family member only if they would likely prefer not to know the truth.

Solutions to Demonstration Exercises 12B: Evaluating Explanations in IBE

1. Illegal downloading

The argument in standard form:

Principle Justification Sub-argument:

1. It's wrong to steal a comedian's laptop and to take silverware from a restaurant, but it's not wrong to repeat for a friend a comedian's joke or cook at home a dish you had at a restaurant. (PARADIGM CASES)

2. The best explanation of the cases in premise 1 is that taking the fruits of others' labor without their permission is wrong if and *only* if it *deprives* them of something they already have. (EXPLANATION)

   So, taking the fruits of others' labor without their permission is probably wrong if and *only* if it *deprives* them of something they already have. (PRINCIPLE)

Principle Application Sub-argument:

1. Taking the fruits of others' labor without their permission is probably wrong if and *only* if it *deprives* them of something they already have. (PRINCIPLE)

2. Downloading music and movies (even when illegal) does not deprive anyone of something they already had. (CASE)

   Therefore, downloading music and movies (even when illegal) is probably not wrong. (CONCLUSION)

Alternative opposing explanation:

An alternative opposing explanation will be a principle that *does* explain the paradigm cases, but does *not* imply that downloading music and movies (even when illegal) is not wrong.

For example: Premise 2 of the Principle Justification sub-argument is false because there is an alternative explanation: it's wrong to take the products of someone's labor in ways they would not consent to. This alternative principle explains why it's permissible to retell the comedian's joke to your friend and to try to cook the dish you had at a restaurant: there's no reason to think the comedian and restaurant owners/chef would object. This alternative principle also explains why it's wrong to take the laptop and the silverware: the comedian and restaurant owners would not consent to that! In addition to explaining the paradigm cases, this alternative principle implies that downloading music and movies is (at least sometimes) wrong—it is wrong in cases in which the artist would not consent if you asked permission.

2. Parental licenses

The argument in standard form:

Principle Justification Sub-argument

1. We should require licensing for drivers, pilots, doctors, lawyers, and teachers; we should not require licensing to play golf or cook at home. (PARADIGM CASES)

(continued)

2. The best explanation of the cases in premise 1 is that we should require licensing for an activity if the activity is potentially seriously harmful to others when performed by unskilled people. (EXPLANATION)

So, we should probably require licensing for an activity if the activity is potentially seriously harmful to others when performed by unskilled people. (PRINCIPLE)

Principle Application Sub-argument

1. We should probably require licensing for an activity if the activity is potentially seriously harmful to others when performed by unskilled people. (PRINCIPLE)
2. Parenting is an activity that is potentially seriously harmful to children when performed by unskilled people. (CASE)

Therefore, we should probably require licenses for parenting. (CONCLUSION)

Alternative opposing explanation:

An alternative opposing explanation will be a principle that *does* explain the paradigm cases but does *not* imply that we should require licenses for parenting.

For example: Premise 2 of the Principle Justification argument is false because there is an alternative explanation: We should require a person to get a license for an activity only if that activity provides services to people other than their family or friends. Driving, flying planes, practicing medicine, practicing law, and teaching are all activities that are typically not performed exclusively for the benefit of a person's friends and family. Playing golf and cooking at home are things we do with friends and family. This alternative principle thus explains all the paradigm cases. But because parenting is a service one provides to one's family, the principle does not imply we should license parents.

3. Racist patients

The argument in standard form:

Principle Justification Sub-argument

1. Hospitals should accommodate the female patient's request for a female Ob/Gyn, a Hmong patient's request for a Hmong doctor, and a male client's request for a male psychologist. (PARADIGM CASES)
2. The best explanation of the cases in premise 1 is that hospitals should accommodate any patient requests that would increase that patient's receptiveness to the care provided. (EXPLANATION)

So, we should probably accommodate any patient requests that would increase that patient's receptiveness to the care provided. (PRINCIPLE)

Principle Application Sub-argument

1. We should probably accommodate any patient requests that would increase that patient's receptiveness to the care provided. (PRINCIPLE)

2. Accommodating patient requests for care providers of a specific race would increase their receptiveness to the care provided. (CASE)

Therefore, American hospitals should accommodate patient requests for care providers of a specific race. (CONCLUSION)

Alternative opposing explanation:

An alternative opposing explanation will be a principle that *does* explain the paradigm cases but does *not* imply that we should accommodate patient preferences about the race of their care providers.

For example: premise 2 of the Principle Justification sub-argument is false because there is an alternative explanation: hospitals should accommodate a patient request only if accommodating that request does not harm members of the hospital staff. Accommodating a request for a female Ob/Gyn doctor, a Hmong doctor, or a male psychologist does not harm anyone. This alternative principle gets the paradigm cases right. But non-White doctors and nurses are already under-represented in hospitals, where they have fewer opportunities for advancement, and more or less constantly face subtle and not-so-subtle forms of stigma and implicit bias. If hospitals were to accommodate explicitly racist requests and remove non-White providers from care teams, that would harm them by making it clear that the hospital does not have their back. Because accommodating explicitly racist requests would harm health care professionals of color, this principle does *not* imply that hospitals should accommodate those requests.

Solution to Demonstration Exercise 12C: Complete Argument Evaluation

1. Gamete donor privacy

Part 1: in standard form for IBE:

Principle Justification Sub-argument:

1. A public school student doesn't have a right to know their teacher's religious affiliation, and a couple adopting a child doesn't have a right to know the identity of the child's parents; however, a daycare employer has a right to know about abusive behavior of a potential employee, a patient has a right to know about a doctor's history of ethics violations, and a blood-donation center has a right to know if a donor has blood-borne pathogens.

2. The best explanation of the cases in premise 1 is that a person has a right to another's personal information when that information is essential for protecting the well-being of the information-seeker or those they are responsible for.

So, a person probably has a right to another's personal information when that information is essential for protecting the well-being of the information-seeker or those they are responsible for.

Principle Application Sub-argument:

1. A person probably has a right to another's personal information when that information is essential for protecting the well-being of the information-seeker or those they are responsible for.

(continued)

2. A child knowing their gamete donor's identity is not essential for protecting the well-being of the child or those they are responsible for.

Therefore, a child probably does not have a right to know their gamete donor's identity.

Part 2: The best objection to this argument:

One of the paradigm cases is a bit controversial: it isn't *obviously* true that a couple doesn't have a right to know the identity of their adopted child's biological parents. This claim is probably about as controversial as the target case of gamete donor privacy. But the argument would not be any worse if you left that case out, so I'll focus on a different objection.

The more serious problem with this argument is that premise 2 of the Principle Application sub-argument is false. There are at least two ways that knowing a gamete donor's identity can be essential for protecting a person's well-being. First, many diseases are genetically linked. Knowing your biological parents' health history is thus an important part of maintaining your own health, and the health of any children you might have. Second, for some people, the desire to know the identity of their biological parents is much more than simple curiosity. For some people, not knowing who made their existence possible can be a source of psychological stress and suffering.

Part 3: Discussion continues/Author's reply:

The author of the argument should probably respond to this objection by arguing that it does not succeed in showing that knowing your gamete donor's identity is essential to your well-being. Doctors can test directly for heritable diseases; knowing your biological parents' health history is thus not necessary to discover genetic risk factors. In addition, while it may be true that some people want to know who their gamete donors are, it is not clear how widespread this desire is or that it is intractably painful not to have this information. It is possible that supportive counseling would be an acceptable alternative for those who are bothered by not knowing their gamete donor's identity. We need more information to determine with confidence whether premise 2 of the Principle Application sub-argument is true.

2. Pandemic mask mandate

Part 1: in standard form for IBE:

Principle Justification Sub-argument:

1. It's justifiable for the government to enforce smoking bans in public places and to prohibit drunk driving.
2. The best explanation of the cases in (1) is that the government has a right to restrict your individual liberty if doing so is necessary to minimize or prevent serious harm to others.

So, the government probably has a right to restrict your individual liberty if doing so is necessary to minimize or prevent serious harm to others.

Principle Application Sub-argument:

1. The government probably has a right to restrict your individual liberty if doing so is necessary to minimize or prevent serious harm to others.

2. A mask mandate during the Covid-19 pandemic is necessary to minimize or prevent serious harm to others.

Therefore, the government probably has a right to enforce a mask mandate during the Covid-19 pandemic.

Part 2: The best objection to this argument:

Premise 2 of the Principle Justification sub-argument is probably the best candidate for criticism. If we can locate an opposing principle that explains the paradigm cases just as well as the proposed principle, we can show that the argument is weak.

One candidate for an alternative opposing principle is this: the government has a right to restrict your individual liberty only if it prevents you from doing an *inherently unhealthy* activity that could harm others. This principle is consistent with our judgments about the paradigm cases, since it can allow that smoking bans and prohibitions against drunk driving are justified on the grounds that they are inherently unhealthy activities that are also dangerous to others. However, since going out without a mask is not inherently unhealthy, this principle does not imply that the government has a right to enforce mask mandates.

Part 3: Discussion continues/Author's reply:

The author's best reply is to defend their original proposal. They can do that effectively by using the method of adding a decisive paradigm case: driver's licenses. It is legitimate for the government to require people to have a driver's license before driving on public roads. The author's original principle explains why: ensuring that a person is capable of driving safely minimizes the potential harm to others. The objector's opposing principle cannot explain why driver's licenses are legitimate, because driving a car is *not* inherently unhealthy. The objector's opposing principle implies that the government has no right to require driver's licenses. That is implausible.

Since the author's original principle gets the driver's license case right, while the critic's "inherently unhealthy" principle gets the driver's license case wrong, this is very good evidence that the author's original proposal is the better of the two explanations.

CHAPTER 12 PRACTICE EXERCISES:

EVALUATING MORAL INFERENCE TO THE BEST EXPLANATION

Exercises 12A: Brainstorming Alternative Principles

Exercise Instructions: *the following exercises offer a set of judgments about paradigm cases and supply a moral principle intended to explain those judgments. For each, suggest an alternative principle that explains the judgments as well or better than the supplied principle.*

1. **Judgments:**
   - Inga and Leonard are a man and a woman who are in love and want to get married. They eventually want to have kids. They are also atheists who do not believe in any gods. They should be allowed to get a civil marriage license.
   - Peter and Brenda have each been married and divorced three times. They have recently fallen in love and want to get married. They do not plan to have children. All of their friends and relatives think a marriage would be a bad idea, because they haven't known each other very long. Still, Peter and Brenda should be allowed to get a civil marriage license.

     Principle: Civil marriage should be allowed only for adult heterosexual couples.

2. **Judgments:**
   - A patient with cancer decides to refuse chemotherapy. They have been given all the relevant information about the treatment options, and made their decision after careful reflection on those options. Their doctor begins chemotherapy against their wishes because the doctor believes the patient made the wrong decision. This is morally wrong.
   - A patient comes into the emergency room unconscious and seriously injured. The patient is 8 months pregnant, and doctors determine that an emergency C-section is in the best interests of both the patient and the baby. The patient is unconscious and no family members can be found. The doctors do the emergency C-section. This is morally permissible.

     Principle: a physician should always get informed consent before performing a treatment unless the patient is incapable of giving their consent.

3. **Judgments:**
   - Sam goes out on weekends to hunt critically endangered birds. He knows they are at risk of extinction, and that killing them harms the local ecosystem. But he does it anyway, because shooting rare birds is fun. What Sam is doing is wrong.
   - Tia captures stray dogs to sell to local dog fighters for use as "bait dogs." Trainers exercise champion dogs by allowing them to maul or kill bait dogs. What Tia is doing is wrong.

     Principle: It's always wrong to use animals for human benefit.

4. **Judgments:**
   - It is not racist and wrong for Lena, a movie producer, to refuse to cast a White actor to play the Black civil rights leader Kwame Ture.[8]
   - It is racist and wrong for Trent, a White American man, to yell racial slurs at an Asian-American family playing at a local park.

---

[8] Adapted from an example in Daniel M. Hausman, "Affirmative Action: Bad Arguments and Some Good Ones," in *The Ethical Life*, 3rd Ed., ed. Russ Shafer-Landau (New York: Oxford University Press, 2015).

- Michelle is part of a property management company considering whether to rent a high-end apartment to a Black couple. The would-be renters have a solid financial and rental history, and Michelle harbors no hatred or animosity towards Black people. Still, she believes that Black people are prone to irresponsible decisions and so are not a good fit for the building, and recommends that their application be rejected. She feels compassion for the Black couple and hopes they find a place that is a good fit for them, viewing them with the same goodwill she has towards well-meaning young people who attempt to take on adult responsibilities they're not equipped for. Michelle's action is racist and wrong.

    Principle: an action is racist and wrong if it is based upon the false or unjustifiable belief that someone is inferior because of their race.

5. **Judgments**:
    - Suppose a group wants to protest wage inequality, and they do so by blocking the entrance to the local emergency room so that ambulances can't get in. As a result of the protest, doctors and medical staff have to wait to see patients seeking attention for critical conditions. There are other ways they could raise awareness about wage inequality, but they choose this method because it forces people to pay attention. Protesting in this way is unjustified and wrong.
    - On February 1, 1960, four African-American men protested segregation at a Woolworth store. When they sat down at the "whites only" counter, staff refused to serve them. The "Greensboro Four" (David Richmond, Franklin McCain, Ezell Blair, Jr., and Joseph McNeil) refused to leave and remained sitting at the counter. They repeated this sit-in for days, eventually attracting the support of hundreds of other protesters. As a result of this sit-in, the Greensboro Woolworth store was desegregated the following July. The Greensboro Four's protest was morally justified.

    Principle: A protest is morally justified only if it produces more good than harm.

6. **Judgments**:
    - A firefighter opposed to abortion refuses to help put out a fire at an abortion clinic. The firefighter has no right to be protected from firing or reprimand by their employer for their refusal.
    - A line cook at Doublemeat Palace, who has recently converted to veganism, refuses to prepare or serve meat, though that was what they were hired to do. The cook has no right to be protected from firing or reprimand by their employer for their refusal.
    - A psychologist who works for the CIA is asked to assist with "advanced interrogation techniques" that are to be used on terrorism suspects. This is not specifically part of their formal job description, though assisting with agency operations is. The psychologist believes these techniques are forms of torture, and therefore morally wrong. Although it is unclear if the

techniques are legal, they appear to be inconsistent with the psychologist's professional code of ethics. If the psychologist refuses to participate in the enhanced interrogation, they should be protected from being punished for their refusal.

> **Principle:** an employee does not have a right to be protected from punishment by their employer if they refuse to do a task that is clearly part of their job description.

Exercises 12B: Evaluating Explanations in IBE

Exercise Instructions: *in this section you will revisit the arguments you analyzed in the* Chapter 11 *Practice Exercises 11B. For each of the arguments in Practice Exercises 11B, do the following things. (Number your answers with the corresponding numbers from Practice Exercises 11B. For example, label your answer 12B3 when examining the argument from 11B3.)*

- *First, represent the argument in standard form using the General Form of IBE.*
- *Second, evaluate premise 2 of the Principle Justification Sub-argument by suggesting an opposing alternative principle that explains the paradigm cases.*

Exercises 12C: Complete Argument Evaluation

Exercise Instructions: *for each of the following passages:*

- *First, represent the argument in standard form using the General Form of IBE.*
- *Second, offer what you believe to be the best objection to the argument. This objection could be to any premise of the Principle Justification or Principle Application portion of the argument. Clearly identify which premise you are engaging: "Premise 1 of the Principle Justification Sub-argument is false because . . ." or "Premise 2 of the Principle Application Sub-argument is false because . . . "*
- *Third, briefly explain how you believe the discussion should continue. What do you think is the author's best reply to the objection you have just raised?*

1. There are many places where people make money from using their bodies. Workers in meat-packing plants stand for hours and prepare frozen chickens. DJs dance, mix, and chant to entertain people. In-home care workers lift, clean, and feed their clients. Childcare workers hug, clean, and play with their charges. Models use their bodies to showcase the newest fashions. Workers on fishing boats brave unpredictable weather to acquire their quarry. Professional mixed martial arts fighters endure and deal bodily punishment for money. Some of these jobs are not well-paid. Some can be emotionally or physically harmful. Still, people should clearly be allowed to perform these jobs. This shows us something important: people should be allowed to make money performing bodily services as long as the practice is regulated to minimize the potential risks and to ensure participation is not coerced.

This has an important—and, to some, startling—implication: sex work should be legalized and regulated.[9]

2. [T]he government can't force Jehovah's Witnesses to salute the flag. It can't force newspapers to carry columns by politicians criticized in their pages. It can't force drivers to carry license plates with a state-imposed (though utterly banal) slogan ("Live Free or Die"). It can't force companies to include third-party messages in their billing envelopes. Political majorities are entitled to enact their beliefs into law, but not to force dissenting minorities to affirm those or anyone else's beliefs in word or deed.[10]

   [The Supreme Court has established a principle that explains why.] [I]t's unconstitutional for the government to force you to say, do, or create something expressive (whether verbal or not) that carries a message you reject—unless coercing you in this way serves a compelling public interest. [This has implications for the case of Jack Phillips, the Christian bakery owner who refused to sell any wedding cakes to same-sex couples.] Forcing Phillips to custom-design and create same-sex wedding cakes is compelled speech: it forces him to create an expressive (artistic) product carrying a message he rejects. It forces certain content onto his artistic work, in a kind of political censorship of art. And it does so without serving the type of interest that our constitutional law would consider a legitimate (much less a compelling) justification for interfering with anyone's free speech. So Colorado's decision violates Phillips's First Amendment rights.

3. Business owners generally have wide discretion over what they do and do not sell: A vegan bakery needn't sell real buttercream cakes. A kosher bakery needn't sell cakes topped with candied bacon, or in the shape of crosses. By contrast, business owners generally do not have discretion over how their products are later used: A kosher bakery may not refuse to sell bread to non-Jews, who might use it for ham-and-cheese sandwiches. . . . Imagine a fabric shop owner who makes artistic silk-screened fabrics. It would be one thing if she declined to create a particular pattern, perhaps because she found it obscene. It would be quite another if she offered that pattern to some customers, but wouldn't sell it to Muslims who intend it for hijabs.[11]

---

[9]Adapted from Martha C. Nussbaum, "'Whether from Reason or Prejudice': Taking Money for Bodily Services," *Journal of Legal Studies*, 27, no. 2 (1998): 693–723.

[10]Quoted from Sherif Girgis, "The Christian Baker's Unanswered Legal Argument: Why the Strongest Objections Fail," *Public Discourse*, Nov. 29, 2017. https://www.thepublicdiscourse.com/2017/11/20581/ Accessed Nov. 12, 2019. The bracketed portions of the passage are simplified adaptations of Girgis's argument. Girgis's argument may be intended to be an Argument from Principle with examples that illustrate the principle, but we have adapted it here to be an Inference to the Best Explanation.

[11]Quoted from John Corvino, "Drawing a Line in the 'Gay Wedding Cake' Case," *The New York Times*, Nov. 27, 2017. https://www.nytimes.com/2017/11/27/opinion/gay-wedding-cake.html (Accessed Nov. 11, 2019.) The bracketed portion of the passage is a simplified paraphrase of Corvino's argument.

[These cases suggest a principle: business owners have a right to refuse to sell products or services without being punished by the state if their refusal is based *what* they sell, but not *to whom* they sell. This principle provides clear guidance about the Masterpiece Cakeshop case. In that case, Jack Phillips, the cake shop's owner, refused to sell any wedding cake, regardless of the design, to a gay couple, because he personally objected to same-sex marriage. Phillips's refusal was based on an objection to the customer, not to the product. He has no right to be protected from punishment for such a clearly person-based refusal.]

4. The resurrection of dinosaurs, as portrayed in *Jurassic Park*, is a fantasy. But we are in the early stages of developing the technology that would allow us to resurrect more recently extinct species, whose tissues or DNA we have well-preserved samples of. Extinct species that are candidates for resurrection include the woolly mammoth (whose tissues have been found preserved in permafrost) and the passenger pigeon (whose tissues have been preserved in museums). Many less famous species, from frogs to goats, are candidates for future de-extinction.

The ethics of de-extinction has split the environmentalist community. Should those who believe that humans have a duty to protect and preserve the environment support or oppose de-extinction projects? I am convinced that environmentalists should support de-extinction projects—or, rather, support at least some of them.

To begin, let us consider some interventions that environmentalists broadly accept as morally good.

First, consider the re-introduction of the gray wolf to Yellowstone National Park. Yellowstone's wolf population was hunted to (local) extinction in the 1920s. In 1995, conservationists introduced a breeding population of gray wolves transported from Jasper National Park in Alberta, Canada. The effect on Yellowstone Park has been incredible. The wolves control the elk population, which has allowed a huge increase in biodiversity, to the extent that the return of erosion-resisting native plants has altered the flow of rivers. Not everyone is happy— many ranchers and others who live near the park display the same fear and loathing of wolves that prompted their eradication in the 1920s. Despite these complaints, environmentalists broadly consider the reintroduction of wolves to Yellowstone among the movement's noblest triumphs.

Second, consider the captive breeding programs that saved the California condor from extinction. In the early 1980s, only 23 California condors were known to exist. They were all placed in a captive breeding program, with the goal of stabilizing their numbers and eventually re-introducing wild populations. The program continues, but has been successful thus far. Though the California condor is still critically endangered, hundreds have been introduced to the wild and are breeding there. This program required confining birds, and breeding them in captivity in a way that is starkly different from their natural breeding practices. But environmentalists broadly agree that pulling the bird back from the brink of extinction was the right thing to do.

Finally, consider the protections extended to the Arctic National Wildlife Refuge. This tract of land is critical habitat for many species, including polar bears, Porcupine caribou, and Dall sheep. Environmentalists have fought for years to protect this refuge from oil companies who would drill there. Environmentalists certainly accept that companies could make a tidy profit extracting oil from the refuge. They believe that protecting the refuge is the right thing to do, even if it costs an oil company an opportunity for additional profit.

What do these three causes have in common that makes them all paradigm cases of morally worthy conservation efforts? It isn't that everyone wants them—ranchers didn't want the wolves. It isn't that they are about stepping back and letting nature have the space to take its course—the captive breeding program for the condors was quite invasive. It isn't that they foster profit—protecting the Arctic National Wildlife Refuge from drilling does not.

Triumphs of environmentalism aren't always profitable, or politically popular, or convenient for humans, or even lovely to humans. What makes something a triumph of environmentalism—an environmental goal *morally* worth pursuing—is that it secures or promotes biodiversity. That is the feature these paradigm cases have in common. They are all good *because* they secured or promoted biodiversity.

Whatever else might be said about the technologies that allow us to pursue de-extinction, this much is clear: to de-extinct a species (and subsequently to restore a breeding population to the wild) promotes biodiversity. Environmentalists should embrace de-extinction efforts for that reason.[12]

5. The capacity for suffering and enjoyment is a prerequisite for having interests at all, a condition that must be satisfied before we can speak of interests in a meaningful way. It would be nonsense to say that it was not in the interests of a stone to be kicked along the road by a schoolboy. A stone does not have interests because it cannot suffer. Nothing that we can do to it could possibly make any difference to its welfare. The capacity for suffering and enjoyment is, however, not only necessary, but also sufficient for us to say that a being has interests - at an absolute minimum, an interest in not suffering. A mouse, for example, does have an interest in not being kicked along the road, because it will suffer if it is.[13] [Therefore, a being has interests that deserve consideration if, but only if, it has the capacity for suffering and enjoyment. Since many non-human animals have this capacity, they have interests that deserve consideration.]

---

[12]Adapted from D. I. Campbell, and P. M. Whittle, *Resurrecting Extinct Species: Ethics and Authenticity* (Springer, 2017). See especially chapter 4, section 2, "The Biodiversity Restoration Argument for De-Extinction."

[13]Quoted from Peter Singer, *Animal Liberation*. 2002 Ed. (New York, NY: Harper Collins, 2002): 6–7.

CHAPTER 13

Developing an Original Inference to the Best Explanation

CHAPTER GOALS

In this chapter, you will learn how to:

- Develop an original moral Inference to the Best Explanation.
- Prepare your argument for presentation to others.

WHEN TO USE INFERENCE TO THE BEST EXPLANATION

Like Arguments from Principle, a moral Inference to the Best Explanation (IBE) applies a moral principle to a particular case to generate moral guidance. The key difference between the two argument forms is that IBE offers a sub-argument in support of its principle. This feature of IBE makes it well-suited to controversies in which the relevant moral principles are not obvious, or are themselves controversial.

Consider this controversy, which we'll use to focus the discussion in this chapter. In 2018, Keziah, a high school senior from Utah, wore a cheongsam—a traditional Chinese style of gown—to her prom. The pictures she posted to Twitter prompted a massive response. The cheongsam traces its origins to sixteenth Century China, it was popularized in 1920s Shanghai, it is internationally recognizable as a symbol of Chinese fashion, and it is the standard formal attire of Chinese female diplomats. Keziah is not Chinese. Many Twitter users accused her of wrongful cultural appropriation—they believe she should not have borrowed a fashion style so closely associated with a culture that is not her own. Other Twitter users endorsed Keziah's own position: that she had selected a gown she found to be beautiful and modest, and it should not matter that it happened to be a cheongsam.

The question debated on Twitter was a *moral* question: was it a *wrongful* act of cultural appropriation for Keziah to wear a distinctively Chinese gown? Argument from Principle is not well-suited to this controversy. Public debates about cultural appropriation are relatively new, with controversy surrounding not just how to characterize the wrongness of cultural appropriation, but about what does and does not count as an instance of wrongful cultural appropriation. It is unlikely that any principle, simply asserted, could be sufficiently broadly accepted to support a useful Argument from Principle.

Indeed, many of the principles offered in the Twitter storm that followed Keziah's post are open to obvious counterexamples. We noticed at least these three principles asserted (usually implicitly) as self-evidently true:

- If a majority of members of a culture have not consented to your use of an idea, artifact, or practice from their culture, then it's wrongful cultural appropriation for you to use it.

But this can't be right. There are no Ancient Romans alive to consent, but it is not wrong for a child to dress up as a centurion or gladiator for Halloween.

- Wrongful cultural appropriation occurs when a person uses an idea, artifact, or practice from another culture in ignorance of its history or importance to that culture.

This can't be right. It is not wrong for a Korean college student studying in the United States to cook and serve their take on kimchi tacos, even if they are ignorant of the fact that tacos originated in Mexican cuisine.

- Using an idea, artifact, or practice from another culture is permissible so long as the user has no intent to demean or insult that culture.

This can't be right. It would be wrong for a White pop star to wear blackface and dress as a slave, even if their performance of Antebellum spirituals was motivated by genuine reverence for the genre and the culture that generated it.

In controversies like Keziah's cheongsam, it is unlikely that any simple assertion of a general principle will strike most people as the right principle for the occasion. What we need, if we are to make progress via principled thinking, is *an argument in support of a principle*. A moral Inference to the Best Explanation fits that bill. This chapter demonstrates how to construct a moral IBE that stands a better chance of advancing the discussion about Keziah's case. The process, strategies, and tips we suggest along the way will be useful to you as you write your own moral IBEs on the controversies that are especially interesting or important to you.

DEVELOPING AN INFERENCE TO THE BEST EXPLANATION

Developing an IBE involves three main steps. First, identify the morally salient features of the controversial target case you plan to write about. Second, create or identify paradigm cases that share those salient features. Third, brainstorm principles until you generate one that best explains the paradigm cases while also generating guidance on the target case.

Clarifying the target

Our target case is Keziah's decision to wear a cheongsam to prom. To develop a moral IBE relevant to this case, we begin by clarifying the morally salient features of her case. What, specifically, are the features of the case that made it so controversial?

Keziah's critics focused on the fact that she adopted a style of dress from a culture that was not her own, a culture she never claimed to understand. Some of her defenders focused on the fact that her use of the dress was entirely personal, unlike corporations that have taken practices or artifacts from oppressed cultures and used them for financial gain. Other defenders focused on the fact that Keziah liked the dress because it was beautiful; she was not motivated by a desire to mock, or demean, or insult Chinese culture.

These clarifications help narrow the question we hope to answer with a principle: when, if ever, is it morally permissible for a person to appropriate a practice or artifact from another culture, without demeaning intent, and for personal use (as opposed to financial gain)?

If we had a clear answer to that question, it would provide guidance in Keziah's controversial case. The next step in the process of answering that question is to identify paradigm cases of this type.

Identifying paradigm cases

A good paradigm case will be a concrete, morally uncontroversial case that displays the three features we identified in the "Clarifying the Target" section: 1) a person appropriates a practice or artifact from another culture 2) for their own personal use and 3) with no demeaning intent.

Identifying paradigm cases usually takes thought, creativity and research. Brainstorming with friends or colleagues can often help start the ideas flowing. It is generally a good idea to brainstorm more cases than you need, and afterwards select the best paradigm cases from the list.

Here is an initial brainstorm of candidate paradigm cases in which adopting a practice or artifact from another culture is morally permissible.

> **Alan:** Alan, a White man, discovered Arabian string music while in high school, bought an oud, and taught himself how to play it. Now an adult, he spends much of his free time studying the history and theory of music from the Arabian Peninsula, mastering traditional songs, and composing his own songs that draw upon them.

> **Ji-hoon:** Ji-hoon, a Korean-American woman, enjoys making kimchi tacos for her friends on Saturday nights.

> **Mary:** Mary, a hearing woman, is an avid boater who has adopted American Sign Language (ASL) as a means of communicating with other hearing boaters when distance or ambient noise make verbal communication impossible.

> **Wesley:** A Cherokee actor, Wesley, wears a war bonnet while playing the role of a Sioux leader in a play about the Dakota War of 1862. (Sioux war bonnets

are feathered headdresses that historically recognized bravery in battle, and currently serve ceremonial roles for the Sioux.)

Are these *good* paradigm cases? These are all relatively uncontroversial cases; they satisfy that criterion. They are all cases in which a person borrows from a culture that is not their own; they satisfy that criterion. In no case does the character intend to mock or demean another culture; they satisfy that criterion. Alan, Ji-hoon, and Mary's case are all three clear cases of personal use of an artifact. It is not as clear that Wesley's case meets that criterion. If Wesley is paid for his work, or if the theater sells tickets to its productions, it is unclear whether this should count as personal use. We will proceed with Alan, Ji-hoon, and Mary's cases, and discard Wesley's as a case that is less well-suited to this specific controversy.

Here is an initial brainstorm of candidate paradigm cases in which adopting a practice or artifact from another culture is morally wrong:

Jared: Jared, a young White man, wears a re-creation of a Sioux war bonnet to a music festival. He thinks he looks great in it, and posts dozens of selfies to his social media accounts.

Vanessa: Vanessa is a huge fan of her town's college baseball team, as are her parents and grandparents. The team's nickname is the Scalpers, their logo is a cartoon of a Native American waving a bloody tomahawk, and fans perform a war dance during the seventh inning stretch. Vanessa participates enthusiastically, believing the name, logo, and team practices all honor Native American tribes as formidable warriors.

Cheong: Cheong is a rapper in a Korean hip hop crew, which is heavily inspired in its fashion, dance, and music by American hip hop. Cheong himself has never been interested in American hip hop, and is only vaguely aware that his crew has adopted many of the practices, artifacts, and styles of a specifically American cultural group.

Are these *good* paradigm cases? Jared and Vanessa are relatively uncontroversial cases of morally impermissible behavior. They are clearly cases of personal use that is done without the *intent* to demean another culture. (Although they may in fact be demeaning other cultures, that is not their *intent*.) Cheong's case is less useful. Korean hip hop has a strong claim to being a distinct and authentic strain of hip hop descended from American hip hop. To claim that Cheong and his crew are doing something morally wrong is, at least, controversial. Because it is controversial, Cheong's case cannot function as a paradigm case. We will discard it, and proceed with Jared and Vanessa.

That leaves us with five paradigm cases to begin with: three cases most people agree are permissible appropriations, and two cases most people agree are wrongful appropriations. We are now ready to move on to the next phase of the process. What principle explains *why* the permissible cases are permissible and the wrongful cases wrong?

Before we move on, note two additional points about paradigm cases in IBE. First, some of our paradigm cases are imaginary but realistic, while others are adapted from news stories or our own experiences. We also could have added fanciful examples that would have functioned well as paradigm cases. What matters is not how realistic or historically informed a case is, but rather how well it satisfies the criteria of a paradigm case. Is it uncontroversial? Does it share the morally salient features of the target case?

Second, there is no fixed number of paradigm cases required for a good IBE. In general, as your number of good paradigm cases increases, it becomes more challenging to identify a principle that plausibly explains them all. But if you succeed in the more challenging task, your resulting principle will be more likely to avoid obvious counterexamples.

Brainstorming principles that explain the paradigm cases

We have three paradigm cases of morally permissible appropriation: Alan, Ji-hoon, and Mary. We have two paradigm cases of wrongful appropriation: Jared and Vanessa. What principle explains why the permissible cases are permissible and the wrongful cases wrongful? A good strategy is to search first for a principle that seems interesting and thought provoking to you. You can certainly brainstorm your own, starting from scratch. But if you talk to others, or read existing arguments about the topic, you may find another person who can help jump-start your thinking.

For example, we found thought-provoking a blog post by Josie Pickens, on a different controversy about cultural appropriation. Is it morally permissible for White people to wear dreadlocks, a hairstyle borrowed from Black culture? Pickens writes:

> When [White singer Justin Bieber] spoke about his brand new and bleached blonde dreadlocks being "just hair," I wondered if he observed that the Black people who made locs popular in the United States and throughout the African Diaspora were militants who hoped and worked to annihilate their White oppressors—men who looked just like The Biebs … Seeing that [Bieber and other White men with dreadlocks] are protected by a combination of privileges (class and education, status and fame, maleness, whiteness), I'm sure they get along just fine in the world whether they are wearing dreadlocks or not. The privilege of being able to wear locs sans scrutiny, while simultaneously not needing to know anything about their history, is what pisses Black folks off.[1]

Pickens's insight is that Black dreadlocks are associated with historical and present oppression that White people have not experienced. Her suggestion is that what makes it *wrong* for Bieber to choose this style is that he is adopting a fashion that has been socially costly for members of the Black culture that developed it, while paying none of those costs himself. Bieber's position as a rich, famous, White man allows him to reap the benefits of a borrowed hairstyle without paying the costs borne by members of the Black cultures he has borrowed it from.

---

[1]"Dear White People: Locs are Not 'Just Hair'," *Ebony*, 6 April 2016. https://www.ebony.com/style/justin-bieber-locs/

This suggests a principle of wrongful cultural appropriation:

The Benefitting from Privilege Principle: wrongful cultural appropriation occurs when a member of a privileged culture borrows a practice from another culture whose members face exclusion or stigmatization for their use of that practice.

Though we have found the Benefiting from Privilege principle helpful for thinking about the case of White dreadlocks, it does not appear to explain all the paradigm cases we have assembled to help us think about Keziah's case. It can certainly explain what is wrong with Jared and Vanessa's behavior: they are both appropriating practices that are a focus of past and present oppression. But the Benefiting from Privilege principle does not appear to explain the remaining cases. Mexican, Arab, and Deaf people have all faced—and continue to face—exclusion and stigmatization in the United States, but Alan, Ji-hoon, and Mary have adopted immediately recognizable practices from those cultures in a way that doesn't seem morally wrong.

Since it cannot explain all of our paradigm cases, the Benefitting from Privilege Principle will not help us develop an argument about Keziah's cheongsam. But Josie Pickens's discussion of White dreadlocks points us in a promising direction. Alongside the benefits of privilege, Pickens highlights the attitude Bieber displays toward the cultures he has borrowed his hairstyle from with his dismissive comment that "it's just hair." In all five of our paradigm cases, our characters express *some* attitude toward the cultures they borrow from. Can we articulate a principle that explains all five cases by focusing on the attitudes the characters express?

The Scalper's team name and rituals recite a false historical narrative that portrays Native Americans as violent savages; it portrays Native cultures as *inferior.* By participating in these practices, Vanessa expresses *an inferiorizing attitude.* Note that this has nothing to do with her intent; we can of course send inferiorizing messages even if we have no idea we're doing that.

Jared's case is different. By wearing a headdress he thinks makes him look great, he is not obviously expressing an inferiorizing attitude toward Native cultures. The trouble is closer to Pickens's charge against Bieber: Jared has taken a practice with a deep social meaning for the Sioux, and used it as a prop in a way that strips it of its social meaning. The trouble with his appropriation is that it expresses *a trivializing attitude* toward this aspect of Sioux culture.

If the inferiorizing and trivializing attitudes expressed by Vanessa and Jared explain what makes their appropriations wrong, that supports an attitudes-focused principle. For example:

The Oppressive Attitude Principle: an appropriation of a practice from another culture for personal use is wrongful if, but only if, it expresses an inferiorizing attitude toward the culture or a trivializing attitude toward the practice.

In addition to explaining what is wrong with Jared and Vanessa's appropriations, the Oppressive Attitude Principle also explains why Ji-hoon's, Alan's, and Mary's appropriations are permissible. One social meaning of tacos in Mexican culture is as a delicious and convenient food; that is how Ji-hoon treats the tacos she makes for her friends. One social meaning of the oud in Arabian cultures is as an instrument for making beautiful music; that is how Alan treats his oud. One social meaning of ASL in Deaf culture is as a language for communication in a visual mode; that is how Mary treats ASL. None of these three expresses a trivializing attitude toward the practices they adopt; nor do they express an inferiorizing attitude toward the cultures they borrow from.

We now have in hand a candidate principle that explains the moral status of all five of our paradigm cases. What does this principle say about the case of Keziah's cheongsam? Choosing the dress for prom because she thought it was beautiful does not appear to express an inferiorizing attitude toward Chinese culture. The real question is: does Keziah express a *trivializing* attitude toward Chinese culture by wearing a cheongsam to prom? Though there is certainly room for debate, the evidence suggests that her use of the cheongsam did not express a trivializing attitude. Although the dress was historically worn for daily activities, it is now usually reserved for special events, such as weddings, parties, and political meetings. One social meaning of the cheongsam, for contemporary Chinese culture, is as elegant formal wear; that is how Keziah treats her cheongsam. This suggests Keziah was not expressing a trivializing attitude by wearing the dress to prom.

REPRESENTING THE ARGUMENT IN STANDARD FORM

We have now assembled all of the components of our argument. The next step is to represent the full argument in standard form using the *General Form of IBE*:

Principle Justification Sub-argument:

1. Cases v, w, etc. have moral status S [and cases y, z, etc. have moral status T]. (PARADIGM CASES)
2. The best explanation of the cases in premise 1 is that cases of type A have moral status S. (EXPLANATION)

So, cases of type A probably have moral status S. (PRINCIPLE)

Principle Application Sub-argument:

1. Cases of type A probably have moral status S. (PRINCIPLE)
2. Case x is of type A. (CASE)

Therefore, case x probably has moral status S. (CONCLUSION)

Our paradigm cases, and the Oppressive Attitude Principle that explains them, generate the following argument about Keziah's case:

Principle Justification Sub-argument:

1. Alan, Ji-hoon, and Mary have borrowed from another culture in a morally permissible way; Jared and Vanessa have wrongfully appropriated from another culture. (PARADIGM CASES)

2. The best explanation of the cases in premise 1 is that an appropriation of a practice from another culture for personal use is wrongful if, but only if, it expresses an inferiorizing attitude toward the culture or a trivializing attitude toward the practice. (EXPLANATION)

So, an appropriation of a practice from another culture for personal use is probably wrongful if, but only if, it either expresses an inferiorizing attitude or a trivializing one. (PRINCIPLE)

Principle Application Sub-argument:

1. An appropriation of a practice from another culture for personal use is probably wrongful if, but only if, it expresses an inferiorizing attitude toward the culture or a trivializing attitude toward the practice. (PRINCIPLE)

2. Keziah's use of the cheongsam did not express an inferiorizing or trivializing attitude. (CASE)

Therefore, Keziah's use of the cheongsam was probably not wrongful appropriation. (CONCLUSION)

As always, offering an argument is the beginning of a discussion about this controversy, not the end of it. You should critically evaluate each premise. What is the best case against the claim that Keziah does *not* express a trivializing attitude? Are there alternative opposing principles that handle the paradigm cases as well as the Oppressive Attitude Principle? Are there additional paradigm cases that would reveal a problem with the Oppressive Attitude Principle?

One obvious worry about the Oppressive Attitude Argument is that it is grounded entirely in the attitudes expressed by appropriators; it makes no reference to harms done to the people they appropriate from. Would a principle grounded in harm, instead of expression, explain the paradigm cases as well or better than the oppressive attitude principle? If so, what would that principle imply about non-Chinese use of the cheongsam? The discussion should continue.

PREPARING YOUR ARGUMENT FOR PRESENTATION

Once you have represented your argument in standard form, it is time to prepare it for presentation to readers. As with the other argument forms, your goal should be to explain and support each premise as needed to allow your readers to understand what that premise means, and to give them reason to believe it is true. Although moral IBE is the most structurally complicated form of argument we have covered, the work you've done to develop your argument and represent it in standard form should make preparing it for presentation straightforward.

General background. As always, provide the background information readers require to understand your topic and why it is important. As always, explain any terms—such as "cheongsam"—that are important to your topic, but are probably not familiar to all readers. Highlight for your readers what you take to be the morally salient features of the case. You will have done most of this work already, in the "Clarifying the Target" phase of writing; the task now is to write up that work in a way that is accessible to your readers.

Principle Justification Sub-Argument, Premise 1. The clarity and persuasiveness of this premise depends almost entirely on the effectiveness of your paradigm cases. Make sure that your paradigm cases are sufficiently detailed and clear-cut that your readers will understand them, and form in response to them the judgments you expect them to form. The best way to double-check the effectiveness of your paradigm cases is to show them to friends or colleagues and ask for their feedback. You will probably have done this already, in the "Identifying Paradigm Case" phase of writing; your paradigm cases should be ready to go.

Principle Justification Sub-Argument, Premise 2. This premise is the heart of your argument, and you should take special care in presenting it clearly. Explain any technical terms or jargon you use in the simplest and most precise language possible. (For example, the Oppressive Attitude Principle uses the terms "trivializing attitude" and "inferiorizing attitude." Those terms should be defined or explained.) Explain in as much detail as needed to show that your proposed explanation fits each of your paradigm cases well.

Support for this premise should usually include comparison with alternative explanations. To make the case that your proposed explanation is the *best* explanation, you should identify the strongest opposing principles and explain why your principle explains the paradigm cases better than its competitors. This suggestion is something close to a requirement in cases in which your readers are likely to have an opposing alternative already in mind. To give them reason to accept premise 2, you must show that your proposal explains cases better than the principle they already have in mind. You will already have evaluated competing explanations in the process of brainstorming and developing your own explanation; the task now is to write up that work in a way that is accessible to your readers.

Principle Application Sub-Argument, Premise 1. The Principle Justification Sub-Argument is the support for this premise; this premise needs no separate explanation or support.

Principle Application Sub-Argument, Premise 2. Just as with the second premise in an Argument from Principle, supplementary information often helps. This premise might assert an empirical claim; if so, you should support that claim with evidence from reliable sources. This premise might assert a judgement—such as our claim that Keziah's cheongsam does *not* express an inferiorizing or trivializing attitude. If so, you should explain why you believe that claim is true.

Finally, when necessary, clarify your position by distinguishing your conclusion from different claims your readers might mistakenly read you as making.

COMMON PITFALLS IN DEVELOPING INFERENCE TO THE BEST EXPLANATION ARGUMENTS

In our experience, students asked to write an original IBE for the first time most commonly stumble in one of two specific ways. As you begin to develop your argument-writing skills, check for these two problems in your early drafts.

Pitfall 1: Poor selection of paradigm cases

First, descriptions of paradigm cases must be sufficiently detailed that readers can form a judgment about them. Vaguely described cases are not useful. For example:

> **Michelle:** Michelle, a comedian, wears a piece of clothing associated with another culture as a part of her stand-up routine. She just wants to get a laugh. This is wrongful appropriation.

This description of Michelle's case does not contain enough detail for the reader to understand the situation and make the judgment the author hopes to elicit. Without further details about what kind of clothing, what the other culture is, and how the clothing is being used, we cannot judge whether the author is right that this is a paradigm case of wrongful appropriation.

Second, controversial paradigm cases are also not useful. For example:

> **Wendy:** Wendy is a White woman who wears dreadlocks. She started wearing locs after seeing them worn by Black musicians in the reggae, ska, and punk bands she loved in her youth. Although she knows the hairstyle has cultural and spiritual significance for many Black people who wear it, she sees her dreadlocks as a way to express her punk-rock identity and her defiance of mainstream culture. Wendy's appropriation of dreadlocks is morally wrong.

Wendy's case is too controversial to serve as a paradigm case for an IBE argument about Keziah's cheongsam. There is at least as much controversy over whether it is wrongful cultural appropriation for Wendy to wear dreadlocks as there is over Keziah's cheongsam.

Third, too few paradigm cases can be misleading. Suppose that, in making an argument about Keziah's prom dress, we began developing our argument from a single paradigm case: Ji-hoon's kimchi tacos. This case is clear, relevant, and uncontroversial. But this single case cannot capture the full complexity of the disagreements about cultural appropriation. Although there is no hard-and-fast rule for how many paradigm cases are needed for a good IBE argument, it pays to ensure they are sufficient in number and variety to account for the moral complexities of the topic at hand.

Pitfall 2: Neglect of better explanations

Identifying a principle that best explains a set of paradigm cases is always challenging. The task itself is difficult—it requires intellectual rigor and creative thought to articulate what matters across varied circumstances. But we are all additionally impeded by our general tendency to overlook principles that conflict with our "default positions." It is tempting to stop after identifying a principle that addresses our paradigm cases in a way that gets us the conclusion we'd like to be true. As we've stressed throughout this book, neglecting opposing views in this way is bad philosophical and moral practice. To develop an IBE argument that can help us get at the truth, we should take pains to examine a variety of principles with different implications for our target case.

In this chapter, we've identified and demonstrated some strategies that can help make this process easier. First, choose sufficiently varied paradigm cases that capture the complexities of the moral phenomenon you're after. Second, use discussion, reflection, and research to identify a variety of principles that could explain the paradigm cases; be sure to consider and evaluate candidate principles that entail conclusions you currently oppose. For example, if you come to the cultural appropriation controversy already inclined to view Keziah's appropriation as permissible, be sure to consider and evaluate principles (such as the one suggested by Josie Pickens, above) that entail that Keziah's appropriation was morally wrong. Discuss the issue with friends or family, *especially* if they disagree with you. By considering and evaluating as many explanations as you can, you'll increase the chance that your resulting argument will withstand critical scrutiny, invite productive discussion, and support insightful reflection.

REVIEW: INFERENCE TO THE BEST EXPLANATION STEP-BY-STEP

We've recommended the following steps for developing a moral IBE worth taking seriously:

1. Clarify what type of case is at issue by identifying the morally salient features of that case.
2. Brainstorm paradigm cases that share those salient features, and select a small set of the best cases, as varied in their details as possible.
3. Brainstorm principles that explain the paradigm cases.
4. Identify the principle that best explains your judgments about the paradigm cases. If necessary, identify additional paradigm cases to help you do so.
5. Draft your moral IBE in standard form.
6. Brainstorm objections to the premises of your argument, on your own and with the input of others who might disagree with you. Revise your argument as needed to address important objections.
7. Prepare your argument for presentation by including the supplementary information that will best help others understand the persuasive force of your argument.

As with other types of arguments, developing your own moral IBE requires practice and reflection. Along the way to an argument worth taking seriously, you may leave behind several less promising drafts. The process of writing may lead you to refine your own position, or even to change your mind. This, we have stressed, is an outcome you should welcome. None of us was born with all and only true beliefs. Improving our set of beliefs, and moving slowly closer to the truth, sometimes requires changing our minds.

Glossary

Analyzing a moral argument The process of identifying an argument's component parts and understanding how they fit together. The presentation format called *standard form* is a tool for analyzing moral arguments.

Argument A chain of reasoning in which a set of claims (the *premises*) is offered in support of a further claim (the *conclusion*).

Argument from analogy An argument that generates guidance about a controversial case by drawing connections between it and a different, but morally analogous case.

Argument from principle An argument that generates guidance about a controversial case by applying a moral principle to it.

Best explanation An explanation is the best when it gives guidance that is consistent with our judgments about all the paradigm cases, and other principles are either inconsistent with those judgments or comparatively lack the virtues of good explanations (such as simplicity, comprehensiveness, salience, etc.).

Broadly accessible example An example that nearly everyone in the target audience is able to understand and evaluate.

Claim A declarative sentence that must be true or false, correct or incorrect.

Conclusion In an argument, the conclusion is the controversial claim the argument aims to support.

Counterexample A description of a specific case that shows a *universal claim* is false. Among other uses, the search for counterexamples is a standard part of critically evaluating the moral principle on which an Argument from Principle is based.

Described case A concrete case described in some detail. Described cases are often used as illustrative examples, counterexamples, analogous cases, and paradigm cases.

Descriptive claim A claim about the way the world actually is (or was or will be).

Developing a moral argument The process of generating and refining an original moral argument and preparing it for presentation to others.

Disanalogy A difference between two analogous cases. In the context of evaluating an Argument from Analogy, a disanalogy constitutes an objection to the argument when it identifies a *genuine* and *relevant* difference between the two cases the argument is built on.

Evaluating a moral argument The process of determining whether an argument actually establishes its conclusion. This process involves testing the plausibility of each premise in the argument.

Explanatory virtues Qualitative features, such as simplicity, comprehensiveness, and salience, that are broadly shared features of good explanations in a variety of domains.

Fanciful example A short, wholly fictional described case, which may be unrealistic or even wildly imaginative.

Generalization A claim that is not about an individual case but rather about a range of cases.

Genuine difference A characteristic of *disanalogies*; a difference is genuine when one case actually has a feature that the other lacks.

Illustrative example A clearly explained concrete case of the type identified by a generalization.

Implicit premise A premise that is essential to an argument but not explicitly stated by the argument's author.

(Moral) inference to the best explanation An argument that uses paradigm cases to infer a moral principle, which is then applied to give guidance about a particular target case.

Moral argument An argument whose conclusion is a moral claim.

Moral claim A claim that either prescribes (by saying what ought or ought not be) or evaluates (by saying what's right or wrong, good or bad). This usage is specific to this textbook; philosophers typically use the term *normative claim* where we use *moral claim*.

Moral principle A claim about the moral status of a range of cases, such as types of actions, types of traits, types of policies, etc.

Normative claim See *moral claim*.

Opposing principle In the context of Moral Inference to the Best Explanation arguments, an opposing principle is a moral principle that does not imply the same conclusion about the controversial target case as the author's proposed principle.

Paradigm case A concrete and uncontroversial case that shares the morally salient features of a target case. Among other uses, paradigm cases are components of moral Inference to the Best Explanation (IBE) arguments.

Premise A claim that is intended to serve as evidence or justification for the conclusion of an argument.

Prima facie Latin for "on the first look." Often used in moral principles or judgments that hold in most situations but not in others. "Lying is *prima facie* morally wrong" means that in most situations, lying is wrong, but in some situations, on closer inspection, lying is not wrong at all. (As, for example, when one lies to one's friend to lure them to a surprise party they will be delighted to experience.) Compare *pro tanto*.

Pro tanto Latin for "to the extent." Often used of moral principles or judgments that do hold in a situation, but may be overridden by more stringent moral duties. "Leaving litter in a public park is *pro tanto* morally wrong" means that you shouldn't leave litter in the park, but that it is possible for this duty to be overridden by a more important one. (As, for example, when you must leave your picnic litter to rush an injured friend to the hospital.) Compare *prima facie*.

Realistic example A described case drawn from real-world events, or from areas of broadly shared experience.

Relevance test An argument evaluation technique used to determine if a proposed disanalogy constitutes a morally relevant difference in the context of an Argument from Analogy.

Relevant difference In the context of an Argument from Analogy, a difference between two cases is relevant when it identifies a difference that plays a role in shaping our judgment about the uncontroversial case the argument is built on.

Standard form A style of argument presentation in which each essential premise is placed on its own numbered line, followed by the conclusion.

Supplementary information Information beyond the main premises and conclusion that is intended to help audiences better understand the argument.

Uncontroversial example An example that nearly everyone in the target audience evaluates in the same way.

Universal claim A generalization that purports to hold true of every possible case. Some are true: "all cats are mammals." Others are not: "all cats are gray."

Index